Divine
Interventions

Books by Dan Millman

The Peaceful Warrior Saga
Way of the Peaceful Warrior
Sacred Journey of the Peaceful Warrior

Guidebooks
Everyday Enlightenment
The Life You Were Born to Live
No Ordinary Moments
The Laws of Spirit
Body Mind Mastery

Children's Books
Secret of the Peaceful Warrior
Quest for the Crystal Castle

For further information: www.danmillman.com

By Doug Childers

The White-Haired Girl (with Jaia-Sun Childers)

For further information: www.dougchilders.com

Divine
Interventions

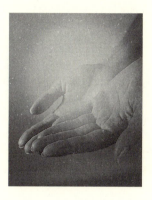

True Stories of Mystery and Miracles
That Change Lives

DAN MILLMAN
AND DOUG CHILDERS

Daybreak Books
An Imprint of Rodale Books
Emmaus, Pennsylvania

Daybreak is a registered trademark of Rodale Press, Inc.

Printed in the United States of America on acid-free ∞, recycled paper ♻

Cover and Interior Designer: Joanna Reinhart
Cover Photographer: Kurt Wilson/Rodale Images

The story "Mind Over Matter" is based upon excerpts from *The Spiritual Journey of Joseph L. Greenstein: The Mighty Atom* (© 1979, 1998; all rights reserved) by Ed Spielman, who has graciously granted permission to use this material.

The story "Bridge between Worlds" is from *Of Water and the Spirit* by Malidoma Some. © 1994 by Malidoma Patrice Some. Used by permission of Putnam Berkley, a division of Penguin Putnam, Inc.

Library of Congress Cataloging-in-Publication Data

Millman, Dan.
    Divine interventions : true stories of mystery and miracles that change lives / Dan Millman and Doug Childers.
        p.   cm.
    Includes bibliographical references and index.
    ISBN 1–57954–100–3   hardcover
    1. Miracles—Case studies.   2. Providence and government of God—Case Studies.   I. Childers, Douglas.   II. Title.
BL487.M55   1999
291.4'32—dc21   99–36496

Distributed to the book trade by St. Martin's Press

2   4   6   8   10   9   7   5   3   1   hardcover

Visit us on the Web at www.rodalebooks.com, or call us toll-free at (800) 848-4735.

─── OUR PURPOSE ───

*We publish books that empower
people's minds and spirits.*

I had an experience.
I can't prove it . . . I can't even explain it,
but everything that I know as a human being,
everything I am, tells me that it was real.
I was given something wonderful,
something that changed me forever . . .

~ "Dr. Ellie Arroway," played by Jodie Foster in the film
CONTACT, based on the book by Carl Sagan

To all those whose lives
have been touched by the Divine
this book is lovingly dedicated.

Contents

Contents

Contents

Contents

Contents

Contents

Contents

Introduction

There are three mysteries in this world:
air, to the birds;
water to the fish;
and humanity to itself.

~Hillel

This book owes its very existence to divine interventions in both the authors' lives: One night in the summer of 1966, a motorcycle crash shattered the leg and ended the Olympic dreams of a young gymnast named Dan Millman; 12 years later, on a dark San Francisco street, two thugs, one armed with a metal pipe, closed in to attack a young writer named Doug Childers. Both of the authors' lives were changed by these events.

Back then, Dan and Doug did not know of one another's existence or that, years later, their lives would intersect or that they would become the best of friends and collaborate on this book. Nor did they know that a divine thread connected their own turning points to the transformations of countless other individuals. All these stories—markedly different in detail, yet sharing the same mystery—convey the many facets and forms of divine intervention. No story you read will be quite like the one before it.

For the purposes of this book, we define divine intervention as a form of extraordinary guidance, revelation, or grace that transforms human lives by leading to a higher path, courageous choice, inspired creation, or call to service in the world.

The true evidence of divine interventions, no matter how spiritual they may appear, is found not in their drama but in their fruits. Whether they strike like lightning or take root over time, these divine wake-up calls open doorways to a higher reality; expand our awareness; promote wholeness, growth, and wisdom; heal wounds; bestow uncommon gifts; unleash extraordinary creative and spiritual powers; relieve the fear of death; and give new meaning to life.

They have even changed the course of history.

No matter what one believes about the phenomena themselves, their outcomes are as real as they are mysterious.

Bridging Faith, Religion, and Reason

Within each of us lives a skeptic inclined toward reason—and a believer drawn to faith. When asked to choose between these two apparent opposites, the wise embrace both, seeing in each a necessary part of the whole. Only with the two eyes of faith and reason can we see the transcendent truths that set us free. Therefore, this book invites believers and skeptics alike to witness in these stories the evidence of phenomena both timeless and universal. These stories portray the transformations of individuals infused with a variety of religious faiths. Yet even nonbelievers will encounter in these pages a nameless power that reveals the spiritual dimensions hidden within the natural world.

Whether you believe that these stories demonstrate the loving grace of God or the changing winds of fate, you will find both substance and spirit here. It is not our business or mission to prove the reality of divine interventions or to insist on a particular spiritual worldview. We let the stories speak for themselves.

Historical records, based on memory and perception, are ultimately unprovable—no testimony can claim absolute truth.

In our research and selection process, we declined obvious fiction or fantasy as well as events easily explained away as coincidence, suggestion, or wishful thinking. We often checked and cross-referenced a variety of sources to establish, as much as possible, the validity of the events and phenomena described.

Some of the most "unbelievable" stories in this book—from levitations, miraculous healings, and angelic visitations to spiritual apparitions witnessed by tens of thousands—are also the most well-documented.

Ultimately, doubts about the authenticity of specific phenomena are balanced by the compelling evidence of lives transformed as a result of the experiences. Must others share our experiences in order to validate them? Must an apparition appear in an outward, tangible form to be authentic? After all, how substantial is light? How tangible is love? Can those angels who appear in our visions be less than genuine if they transform our hearts and minds and change the course of our lives?

Our universe contains many realities, each operating according to hidden laws. The "supernatural" may be quite natural after all. Perhaps our bodies, minds, and psyches contain built-in mechanisms—divine abilities we don't yet fully understand—that account for spontaneous healings, visionary experiences, levitation, and enlightenment. Perhaps our full powers and divine destinies are still waiting to reveal themselves to us.

Life's Larger Questions

Those who doubt the reality of divine interventions may ask: Why does God seem to help some people, answer some prayers, and apparently ignore others? Why is one person saved or cured, and another lost? Why does evil sometimes seem to triumph over good? They may point out that for every person miraculously healed, thousands die of their diseases. For every pilgrim fed, millions go hungry. Is grace, or God, arbitrary and capricious? Or is there sense to our suffering and a spiritual purpose in our adversity?

Some view suffering as divine punishment for moral transgressions; others see it as a necessary part of the soul's education and evolution. To find meaning in the suffering and adversity in your own life, look back to before they occurred, and then observe yourself now—stronger, wiser, perhaps more compassionate as a result of your struggles. You may see in your own life, and in stories that follow, how the path to Heaven may pass through Hell—and how we sometimes have to deal with the darkness before we can see the light.

Divine interventions operate outside the limited perspective of our personal desires. We may ask for healing, but we cannot dictate what form this healing will take. Hoped-for physical regeneration may fail, even as deeper wounds are healed on emotional or spiritual levels. Pain may purify our spirits and serve our ultimate destiny—we cannot always know what is for our soul's highest good.

Like all true mysteries, these stories yield no final answers to life's larger questions. Instead, they inspire hope and reawaken a sense of reverence, wonder, and awe. They remind us of a divine presence in our world and in our lives, as close as our next heartbeat, our next breath.

Join us now for a mystery tour through a living portrait gallery highlighting humanity's contact with a timeless power that continues to stir our imaginations and awaken our souls— a power that nourishes all living things, makes saints of schoolgirls and sages of kings, and turns everyday life into the most extraordinary adventure of all.

True Stories of Mystery and Miracles That Change Lives

God invented men and women
because God loves stories.

~Anonymous

One of the reasons religion seems irrelevant today
is that many of us no longer have the sense
that we are surrounded by the unseen.

~Karen Armstrong, A History of God

A single event can awaken within us
a stranger previously unknown to us.

~Antoine de Saint Exupery

Surrender in the Flames

A Gift from the Inferno

The night before the house burned down with Valerie Vener inside it, she and her college roommate had sat on the front porch discussing the worst ways to die. Her roommate feared drowning. Valerie's worst scenario was death by fire.

The following evening, the full moon of July 15, 1981, both of them were invited to a party. Valerie, exhausted, changed her mind at the last minute, went to bed at 8:00 P.M., and fell deeply asleep. The fire department later determined that the blaze started about 9:30 P.M. directly below her, in a living room uniquely insulated by plush furniture, Persian carpets, and two walls lined floor-to-ceiling with record albums.

The fire smoldered for half an hour in the contained environment, heating the room like a kiln, melting the records and unleashing thick, black, toxic smoke. As fire spread across the lower floor, poisonous fumes spread through the house and rose to fill the entire upper floor, including the room where Valerie slept. At approximately 10:15 P.M., a stifling heat and hellish stench awakened her. She sat upright in bed in an eerie darkness, woozy from oxygen deprivation and the heat, drugged by the toxic fumes she'd been breathing for at least half an hour. The light shining into her room illumined an ethereal realm of smoky vapor.

"I was in a dreamlike state," Valerie recalls. "Time had stopped. I felt both crystal clear and utterly disoriented. The environment was so bizarre. The usual laws of physics no longer seemed to apply. Logically, I should have panicked from the stench, abnormal heat, and darkness. But all I could imagine was that one of my roommates had left a pot burning on the stove."

Valerie started for the bedroom door to call downstairs, but stopped in her tracks when she spied several large, oval-shaped forms made of smoke hovering nearby. They appeared as pulsing, living beings—their outer structures enclosed a kind of circulatory system made of swirling smoke, Möbius-like threads spiraling up and down inside them like internal energy circuitry. "Their beauty was mesmerizing," Valerie recalls. She stopped before one of them and gazed in awe, not yet wondering what the smoke was doing in her room, until the overwhelming stench and the pain of breathing brought her back to a momentary sense of reality.

Valerie pushed at the door, already several inches ajar. It seemed heavy, as if some outside force resisted. Peering into the hall, she saw only impenetrable darkness. For the first time, fear pierced her dreamlike state. She did not yet realize that the house was on fire—only that something was terribly wrong. She stepped into a hallway so dark that she could not even see her hands, instinctively raised to protect her face from the extreme heat. Now she noticed a muffled, rumbling roar below, like a distant train.

She found her way down the hall to the stairs, where another wall stopped her with tangible force. It was a blast of searing heat, sucked up the stairs by an open window acting as a chimney. The first floor was now engulfed in flames. (The fire report determined that temperatures in the house ranged from 1,200° to 1,700°F.)

In toxic shock, her mind clung to the idea of a burning pot on the stove. She tried calling out with a rasping croak. But with each breath the repulsive stench and infernal heat blistered her nose and throat. Then, out of the darkness at the top of the stairs, a huge tongue of fire darted out at her, shocking her awake. Suddenly, everything was obvious. In terror, Valerie groped for the hall phone, lifted the receiver, and dialed "0."

"Operator," came the answer.

"I'm at 524 South Forest Avenue." Valerie gasped. "524 South Forest Avenue. On the corner of University. My house is on fire. I'm in the house. It's 524 South Forest Avenue."

"Ma'am, I'm sorry; I'll have to put you on hold for a moment."

Valerie dropped the phone. She didn't know she was being connected to the fire department—only that her house was burning down and she was being put on hold. She ran into her room, thinking she could climb out of her window. If she hung from the sill by her fingers before letting go, it might be a 20-foot drop to the street. With her years of professional dance training and her two-mile daily swims, she felt she could survive the fall without serious injury. Anything was better than burning.

She reached the window, but in trying to remove the screen, the window cracked and broke. Instantly, with a stunning power and finality, a wall of fire roared up outside from below, inches from her face, blocking her escape. She was in the fire's domain, under its absolute authority.

Now she heard voices in the street below, shouting, laughing, talking excitedly. Trapped in her room by a wall of fire, the sound of human voices beyond her reach increased her feelings of helplessness and isolation. Then she heard a shout from inside the house. "Valerie! Come downstairs! Follow my voice! Follow my voice!" She ran down the hall to the stairs, took one step down, and reeled back as a force field of rising heat singed her brows and lashes and burned several inches off her hair.

"Get out!" she heard a woman scream. "The walls are caving in. Get out."

"No!" a man shouted. "I can get her! She's upstairs!"

"Get out! Get out now!" the woman shrieked.

Then the walls and floor began to shake, and the voices stopped.

Valerie was trapped, and no one was coming to get her. Turning around, she saw flames darting from under the doors of the other two bedrooms. She stumbled back and stood in her doorway, looking into her room at the fire—it seemed to have a malevolent presence. She watched her plants shrivel and die in seconds, their life force consumed by the heat.

Blossoms of flame burst forth in spontaneous combustion, devouring the curtains, darting as if with intention across the room, leaping over her bed to engulf her writings and poetry stored under a bookshelf, igniting her paintings and burning them off the walls.

"The fire consumed my personal treasures one by one," she recalls. "My life was being sacrificed before my very eyes." The house, now a furnace, shook and roared. Valerie struggled to breathe as the fire devoured the remaining oxygen. Heat seared her lungs. The room was ablaze now—orange tongues of flame licked along the walls and ceiling, darting from under the doors, closing in from all directions. There was no way out. She could not be saved. Valerie knew she was going to die.

"In a moment," she recalls, "all the fear—the anguish of isolation and abandonment, the horror of dying—rose to an unbearable pitch. I realized that these core emotions had always been ever-present forces in my life, forces that I had, until now, been afraid to allow. In this extraordinary moment, I had no choice but to surrender completely to my inevitable death.

"With this surrender came an instantaneous change of perception. Suddenly, I had never seen anything more beautiful than the inside of a fire. Even the sounds were enchanting—the flames were dancing, thundering, and fluttering at the tops like thousands of bird wings. The fire had a wondrous presence. It seemed amusing that I could have been so terrified of such an exquisite phenomenon. Nothing had changed except my point of view, as a direct result of my surrender."

Valerie, absorbed in this beauty, found herself looking down with detachment at her body lying crumpled outside the doorway. Quite naturally, she continued to surrender, and her awareness continued to expand. She saw a large crowd of people and many fire trucks arriving outside—then she passed through a realm of gold, then into a marvelous and blissful blue, and finally, into an indescribable realm of white radiance.

Minutes later, the firemen made it upstairs, after their hoses cooled down the house. They found Valerie in the smoke-darkened hall and carried her outside. She had no pulse or breath. Of three paramedics who tried to revive her, two finally pronounced her dead of smoke inhalation. In the white light, Valerie knew nothing of the drama going on around her lifeless body.

"This radiance, so absolutely brilliant, left nothing to be desired," Valerie recalls. "There was nothing to reach for, no dilemma at all. I knew that this white light is what we try to describe in human terms as 'God.' It was also my core self. I saw with humor and compassion how 'Valerie'—the one who was identified with the body I had left behind—desired to do good, to control life, to survive. It was now obvious that 'Valerie' was never in control, could never be in control, and that the fear that drove the desire to control was absolutely unnecessary."

Then a bright entity of golden white light appeared, emanating absolute love. This being seemed more expanded than, yet not separate from, herself. She internally heard his perfect communication, "You were frightened, eh?" They laughed together at the joke of it all. Her surrender had only brought her closer to herself, a return to her origins in this radiance. In the end, this being gave her two choices: to return to her present body or take on a new one. "Either way, he said I was his—that I would always be his, and that he loved me. No ownership was implied in his words. Only perfect, eternal love."

Meanwhile Valerie's body lay in the front yard. Although she had been pronounced dead, the third paramedic refused to give up his efforts at resuscitation. He felt certain that she was *supposed* to live. He persisted alone for several minutes. Her heart began beating again.

Valerie violently awakened in an ambulance on the way to the hospital, in searing pain, her body blackened by toxic smoke. Incredibly, she had fallen in the only area and physical position in which she could survive until the firemen found her, with a carpet somehow wrapped around her vital parts.

In her 45-minute ordeal, nine pounds were cooked from her body. Her survival and full recovery, with minimal burns (mostly on her arms), and lack of brain damage from oxygen deprivation and toxic smoke inhalation, were called miraculous.

Valerie's experience, her trust in the power of surrender, and her new sense of self helped her get through her prolonged ordeal of recovery. Her struggle to remember and maintain her hard-earned wisdom in the face of severe emotional and physical pain helped her develop the ability to accept and embrace life even in its most difficult moments. She became attracted to meditation, divine worship, and other disciplines of attention that drew her back to the tacit memory of freedom experienced in the flames.

Today, Valerie Vener teaches others the spiritual lessons of surrender that she learned in the fire and in the light.

Conquistadors to Saints

The Healing Journey
of Alvar Nuñez Cabeza de Vaca

This account is based upon a report by Spanish soldier Alvar Nuñez Cabeza de Vaca, written with great care to the King of Spain in the year 1536.

In 1512, Alvar Nuñez Cabeza de Vaca fought in the Battle of Ravenna, where 20,000 men died. In 1521, the horrors of war again swept over his soul when he fought in the great Battle of Sevilla. Yet these traumatic events pale in significance beside an arduous journey he would undertake seven years later.

In 1528, Alvar marched into the sweltering heat of Florida with a company of 578 conquistadors, every man among them dreaming, like Cortez, of golden cities to conquer and possess. They asked the native peoples they found, whom they called Indians (Indios), where their great city lay, but after weeks of marching in full armor under the burning sun, they found not a city of gold, but "a large impoverished settlement of thatched huts, a place of unbearable squalor," according to *The Marvelous Adventures of Cabeza de Vaca*, by Haniel Long.

Incredulous, filled with that peculiar mix of shame and despair born of great folly, they turned back. By the time they reached the sea, they were starving—their numbers were reduced from 578 to 400, and their ships were gone. With a will to survive and with great labor, they built nine open boats and set sail for Cuba. But Cuba proved another unreachable dream.

The winds were unfaithful, and they drifted aimlessly. The sun, starvation, and the undrinkable sea decimated their numbers from 400 to 40. In such conditions, men did not die quietly or slip away in peace. They died babbling, delirious, and desperate, often weeping for their mothers. Others, maddened by sunstroke and a terrible thirst, leaped into the sea and drowned. To survive, some of the living ate the bodies of the dead. At last, they made it back to the Texas coast.

The Indians who found the 40 remaining castaways at first took care of them, believing they belonged to a race of gods whom their myths said would one day come from beyond the sea. But even gods must earn their keep, and at last the Indians told the Spaniards that they must use their godlike powers to heal their sick and dying.

"We laughed, taking it for a jest," Alvar writes, "and said that we did not understand how to cure. Thereupon, they withheld our food to compel us to do what they wanted."

They would not be fed until they performed miracles.

The past months had been a nightmare of death, madness, and starvation. Now they had to either heal the sick, or die. Alvar tells how he and his remaining comrades knelt in desperation over the sick and dying Indians whom they had to heal to save themselves—how they prayed with all their might. These were no ordinary prayers—they were no longer ordinary men. Now living ghosts from whom everything had been stripped away, devoid of possessions, their clothing shredded, their bodies emaciated, they had endured unbelievable suffering.

With nothing to rely on but grace, no one to lean on but God, they began their desperate prayers to heal. And heal they did. All the sick Indians were well by morning. The Spaniards, filled with wonder, believed that God had worked miracles through them.

These healings ignited a wave of faith among the Indians, who now came from surrounding tribes. More healings followed. On another occasion, five severely ill and paralyzed Indians were brought to them. Again, the Spaniards prayed and made the sign of the cross, "and in the morning," Alvar writes, "all woke up well and hearty and went away in such good health as if they had never had any ailment." The Spaniards—amazed and more than a little afraid—could not deny the mysterious power flowing through them, nor the fact that the sick, wounded, and dying were healed by their prayers.

What had turned these conventional Christian warriors, who despised all other races, into spiritual healers? Perhaps their suffering had opened them to God—or the inner stripping away of all they had once believed themselves to be, and their starved and wretched nakedness had released in them the power to heal. Their prolonged confrontation with suffering, death, and the power of Spirit would purge nearly all traces of their conquistadorian mentality—which in the end seemed no loss at all.

Though reluctant at first to heal these "savages," in time they were moved by the Indians' suffering and truly wished to heal them. They even began to pray for their spiritual as well as their physical health, for their souls as well as their bodies.

This group—the four that remained of the original 400 souls—consisted of Alvar, Alonso del Castillo, Captain Andres Dorantes, and a Moor named Estevancio, whose dark body bore the sun's fury as though it were moonlight. Together, they wandered from tribe to tribe, healing, wherever they went, the sick, the paralyzed, the injured, the dying.

Then one day, the Indians led them to a dying man too late, and found him already dead. "His lifeless body was surrounded by many people weeping," Alvar writes. "I found the Indian with eyes upturned, without pulse and with all the signs of death."

Alvar and his comrades prayed over the man and "breathed on him many times," as well as on the other Indians who had come to be healed. Soon after, to the astonishment of his family and tribe, the dead man rose, walked about, ate, and spoke with them, appearing "well and in very good spirits." All of the others were also healed.

The faith of these former conquistadors, and the power flowing through them, had triumphed over death itself. The Indians now came to them in an endless stream, their fevered eyes glittering like stars in their copper faces.

Alvar and his group were led from village to village as gods, caught up by a force that belonged to none and served all. The miraculous manifested for unknown reasons through four emaciated men. These former conquerors, who had come for gold and glory, had vanquished an unexpected adversary. Now they lived to serve others.

In one village, they stayed eight months, healing all who came to them. Alvar writes, "We never treated anyone that did not afterward say he was well, and they had such confidence in our skills as to believe that none of them would die as long as we were among them."

In time, these Spaniards began to feel overwhelmed, realizing the power to heal was an obligation, even a terrible burden. Yet their natures had changed. Love and human sympathy had been awakened in them. And they who once sought only gold were now willing to be endlessly used for the sake of others. They gave to all who came, holding back nothing, and healed freely those they would once have made their slaves.

In this way, years passed. Then, in Mexico, they encountered their former kind—conquistadors hungry for gold, who burned and plundered villages, who raped, murdered, and enslaved the so-called inferior races. But Alvar and his comrades now despised the bestiality of their countrymen and the suffering they inflicted upon the Indians who were now their friends. "The people had fled to the mountains," Alvar wrote, "out of fear of the Christians. This filled our hearts with sorrow— . . . the places burned down, and the people so thin and wan, fleeing and hiding, . . . their destitution so great that they ate tree bark and roots."

Alvar and his men confronted these conquistadors. "Thereupon," he wrote, "we had many and bitter quarrels with the Christians, for they wanted to make slaves of our Indians." These new conquistadors told the Indians that Alvar and his three comrades "had gone astray, . . . were people of no luck and little heart, whereas they were the lords of the land." Alvar was relieved to report that "the Indians decided these conquistadors were lying and gave their claims little attention, saying that we had come from sunrise, while the others came from where the sun sets; we cured the sick, while they killed those who were healthy. . . . Also that we asked for nothing, but gave away all we were presented with, while the others seemed to have no other aim than to steal what they could, and never gave anything to anybody."

In their healing journey of eight years, Alvar and his group had walked 5,000 miles and perhaps healed more than that many Indians of various injuries and diseases. They had been transformed beyond recognition, from conquistadors to saints.

Alvar, it seems, was changed more than the others, who, to one degree or another reverted over time to their former selves. Later on, his idealism and active compassion toward other conquered races alienated him from his own people. Alvar was betrayed by his soldiers, spent years in prison, and died in poverty.

As John Upton Terrell, one of Alvar's biographers, writes, "In the face of terrible disappointment and hardship, . . . he knew no bitterness, he never lost his courage, his spirit, nor his faith. . . . He practiced goodness and kindness. . . . He condemned his own people for the cruel and diabolical system with which they controlled the rich lands they had conquered only through brute force."

By his manner of living, healing, and dying, Alvar Nuñez Cabeza de Vaca became perhaps the greatest conquistador of all.

Mysteries of Heaven and Hell

Science's Magnificent Mystic

For many of us, the word "mystic" conjures up images of impractical, otherworldly souls with their heads in the clouds and their feet God-knows-where. But the early life of Emmanuel Swedenborg reveals an eminently rational man, a renowned technical innovator, and a scientific genius—an unlikely candidate for the legendary mystic he was to become.

In his home country of Sweden, Emmanuel was a respected Renaissance man. Among his many positions, he served as the king's appointed royal scientist and as a member of the Swedish House of Nobles, where he wrote legislative bills. Fluent in nine languages, he wrote primarily in Latin, the scholarly language of his day. In his spare time, he learned to bind books and make watches, cabinets, and scientific instruments. Also an astronomer, medical scientist, and mechanical engineer, Emmanuel ground the lenses to build his own telescope and microscope. He designed, among other things, an air gun, a submarine (never built), an airplane (a design actually built and flown two centuries later in the early 1900s), a music machine, a house heater, and a fire extinguisher. He also designed the world's largest dry dock; then, for the King of Sweden, Swedenborg supervised the transport of a fleet of ships 14 miles *over the mountains*, resulting in a crucial military victory.

When applied to Emmanuel Swedenborg, the terms "brilliant" and "practical" are gross understatements. By 1742, at the age of 54, he had mastered all known branches of science and developed several new ones. He had written 150 works summarizing the discoveries and knowledge in each of these varied fields, and then gathered their data into coherent systems (often making his own new discoveries along the way) before moving on to the next field. And after this man of unfathomable genius devoured and recapitulated all the human knowledge of his era, he decided to prove the existence of the soul.

In the process, he became a mystic.

After completing his exploration of the territory of the outer world, it was only natural for him to turn his infinite intellect to the inner world. As a scientist, Emmanuel knew he must look inward to discover the soul. So he began to analyze his dreams and to explore his own mind through a direct and deliberate meditative process. Along the way, he encountered elements of his "shadow side"—his arrogance and the "impurity of soul." (In fact, his insightful writings foreshadow the future science of psychology—Carl Jung would later owe Emmanuel Swedenborg an incalculable debt.)

As it happened, Emmanuel's inner explorations initiated a profound, at times violent, process of purification that finally gave way to surrender and to a genuine humility before God. Like many rationalists, Emmanuel had conceived of God as an abstraction. But over the course of a single night, his view was to change radically and dramatically.

It began as he lay in bed, having invoked a divine presence to help him in his quest for the soul. In his own words, "Immediately, there came over me a powerful tremor . . . together with a resounding noise like great winds clashing. I found that something holy had encompassed me; . . . it shook me and prostrated me on my face. I saw that I was thrown down and I found the words put into my mouth, 'Oh, thou almighty Jesus Christ, who of thy great mercy deignest to come to so great a sinner, make me worthy of this grace!' I prayed and there came forth a hand that pressed my hands. . . . I was sitting at His bosom and beheld Him face to face, . . . a countenance of such holy mien that cannot be expressed." It seemed Christ spoke to him, saying, "Love me truly" or "Do what thou hast promised."

Such blessed chastisements profoundly moved the stately scientist, transforming him for all his remaining years into a humble, even childlike, man of faith. He came to understand that the intellect of which he was so proud could not of itself produce everlasting truth, wisdom, or peace. These qualities, Emmanuel now realized, existed eternally, prior to the mind, and came only from God.

A singular vision had initiated Emmanuel Swedenborg's mystical journey. But the divine continued to intervene in his life, as spiritual seeds germinated within him, bringing in time profound revelations and insights. And a door to other worlds would soon open before him.

One night, an apparently human figure suddenly appeared to him in his room. "He said that he was the Lord God," wrote Emmanuel, "the Creator of the world, and the Redeemer, and that he had chosen me to explain to men the spiritual sense of the Scripture, and that He Himself would explain to me what I should write on this subject. That same night were opened to me, so that I became thoroughly convinced of their reality, the worlds of spirits, Heaven and Hell. I recognized there many acquaintances of every condition in life. From that day, I gave up the study of all worldly science and devoted my labors to spiritual things, accordingly as the Lord had commanded me to write. Afterward, the Lord opened daily and often my bodily eyes so that I could see into the other world and, in a state of perfect wakefulness, converse with angels and spirits."

This is the astonishing testimony either of an extraordinary mystic or a raving madman. Yet his whole life before this event was one of supreme ability and sanity. And the quality of his accomplishments and writings that followed also judge the matter in his favor.

Over the next 30 years, Emmanuel Swedenborg wrote 36 volumes, describing in meticulous detail, with a staggering breadth of vision unmatched in any literature of any era, various Heavens and Hells; the nature of God, angels, and demons; our relationship with all the above; what happens to us after death; and volumes more.

His inner life bore the fruit of mysterious powers, reported by many credible witnesses. Once, Queen Louisa asked Emmanuel to contact her recently deceased brother. Days later, he delivered a message to the queen—an intimate message from her brother that so shocked her she left the court immediately, pale and shaking. She later reported that Swedenborg had given her information that no living person could have known.

On July 17, 1759, Emmanuel attended a large dinner party in Göteborg at the house of a wealthy merchant, William Castel. At six o'clock, Emmanuel became extremely agitated.

Asked what was the matter, he described in detail a fire burning 300 miles away in the city of Stockholm.

News of his report spread through the town. When the governor heard the story, he summoned Emmanuel to his home for a detailed report of the fire. Emmanuel told him where, when, and how it started—even which houses were burned. Two days later, when messengers arrived from Stockholm, Emmanuel's report proved accurate in every detail.

At another party—as it happened, the very night Emperor Peter III of Russia was strangled in prison—Emmanuel became agitated and went into a trance. When he came to, the guests insisted he tell what he had seen. With great emotion, he described in vivid detail the death of the Russian emperor, asking the guests to note the time and date so as to compare it when reports arrived. Days later, Russian newspaper reports matched Emmanuel's vision.

At times, Emmanuel's humor had a moral edge. Declaring the futility of outward displays of piety, he taught that only charitable service ultimately mattered. He once attended a party with Archbishop Troilus, a passionate gambler in a card game called *tresette*, whose gambling partner, Erland Broman, had recently died. "Tell us about the spirit world," the archbishop taunted Emmanuel. "How does my friend Broman spend his time there?"

"I saw him but a few hours ago, shuffling his cards in the company of the Evil One," retorted Emmanuel. "And he was only waiting for Your Worship to make up a game of *tresette*."

Emmanuel Swedenborg wrote that angels and demons exist in their own realms and also within our minds—that our thoughts, feelings, and impulses emanate from these inner residents. We live, he wrote, in a space of free will between

Heaven and Hell; our spiritual challenge is to choose the good in any moment amid the tumult of these forces within us.

He saw the soul defined by choices and acts, not beliefs or professed ideals. He stated that the soul chose Heaven or Hell after death, as it tended to choose Heaven or Hell in any moment while alive.

Although a devout Christian, Emmanuel proclaimed (like most illumined beings) the universal validity of all religions, saying they "are like so many jewels in a king's crown." He said the true church existed wherever men acted in charity toward each other, and all would be saved, no matter what their faith, who lived by the principle of love. Without love, he observed, we are nothing.

He swore that the angels in Heaven revealed these truths to him.

Emmanuel Swedenborg's mystical writings achieved fame and notoriety in his lifetime. Yet he published and sold them anonymously, at less than printing costs and at his own expense. His sole purpose was to spread spiritual truth to as many souls as possible, as he had been assigned by Heaven. His authorship was, in fact, only discovered near the end of his life. His voluminous works, translated into 20 languages—still in print after two centuries—have influenced countless writers, artists, and mystics, among them Balzac, Hugo, Blake, Emerson, Thoreau, Whitman, Jung, D. T. Suzuki, Alan Watts, and many more. A worldwide church of Swedenborgian Christianity exists today.

Many inspired leaders have had premonitions of their deaths. But Emmanuel predicted the year, day, and hour of his death to his intimate circle. As Emmanuel lay on his deathbed, a clergyman named Ferelious came to administer last rites. Ferelious told him that many people believed he had created his spiritual writings from his own imagination, and that if this were the case, he ought to confess it before he died and depart with a clean conscience.

"Swedenborg thereupon half-rose in his bed," Ferelious writes, "and laying his hand upon his breast, said with some manifestation of zeal: 'As true as you see me before your eyes, so true is everything that I have written; and I could have said more had it been permitted. When you enter eternity, you will see everything, and then you and I shall have much to talk about.'"

After his death, the maid of the house in which Emmanuel Swedenborg lived said that he had seemed to be looking forward to the event with great enthusiasm—"as if he were going on holiday." After a lifetime of extraordinary service, and knowing full well his destination, perhaps he was.

The Price of Freedom

A Young Woman's Sacrifice

Irene Opdyke was born in 1921 in the Polish town of Kozienice. As a child, she played with friends of different religious faiths, including Jews—her parents raised her to believe in the equality of all people.

The eldest of five daughters, Irene left her family at age 17 and entered a nursing school in the town of Radom, near the Russian border. But soon her world, like that of millions of Polish people, would disintegrate in the brutality and chaos of war.

In 1939, Poland was occupied by both Russian and German soldiers. When the bombs began falling on Radom, 18-year-old Irene and a number of her fellow nursing students hid in the forest outside town. But that winter, Irene, hungry and cold, came out of hiding and re-entered the town, looking for food and warm clothes. She was caught, raped, and severely beaten by Russian soldiers who patrolled the town.

Then the Russians were driven out by the Nazis, who took Irene into custody once again. She was taken to the town of Ternopol and put to work as a waitress in a Nazi officers' dining room in a munitions factory.

Irene's circumstance, while unfortunate, was far better than that of many others—only 200 of the 18,000 Jewish residents in Ternopol would survive the six-year Nazi pogrom. At the factory, Irene was put in charge of 12 Jews who worked in the laundry room. Seeing that they were starving on their slave rations, Irene began sneaking them bread, butter, fruits, and blankets stolen from the Germans' warehouse. She smuggled one Jewish couple into the forests outside Ternopol, where many others were hiding. And, at great risk, she continued to take them supplies throughout the war.

Irene also began sticking the Nazi officers' leftover food through a hole in the fence that surrounded the Jewish ghetto. In this way, she fed people she would never meet through the long winter. She never saw anyone take the food, but it was always gone when she went the next time with more.

Luckily, Irene was beautiful, with perfect Aryan features—blue eyes, blond hair, and light skin. And Major Eduard Rügemer, who managed the factory, was captivated by her. An elderly man, thin, gray-haired, and nearing 70, he was, like many Germans in that time, "just following orders."

Major Rügemer made Irene part of his secretarial staff. In this circumstance, she now had to watch firsthand as Jews were beaten and executed in public—gunned down or hanged in the streets. One day, she saw a young SS soldier pull a baby from its mother's arms, throw the squalling infant into the air, and shoot it. She stood frozen, horrified. She recalls, "I could only stare and say, 'Oh, God, my God, where are you?'"

That night, in desperation, she prayed to God for guidance.

"In the morning," she says, "there was an answer in my soul, in my heart, that came like a whisper from above." That "whisper" told her she must devote herself to the welfare of the Jews. Irene knew she risked death by doing so—but without her help, their death was a certainty. She felt that God had put her where she was for a reason, "in the right place at the right time." Her prayer for guidance had been answered by a call to her humanity. Her mission was not to save herself, but to help save others. She now had to find a way.

"I had the opportunity," she says. "And God gave me the looks to do the job. I was playing a German fräulein . . . but I was a spy."

One day, she heard an SS officer tell Major Rügemer that the ghetto would soon be liquidated. All the Jews would be killed or put into death camps. Later, she rode through the town on her bicycle and warned as many Jews as she could. When she told her Jewish friends from the laundry room, they begged her to help them. She didn't know what to do. It had become too dangerous to smuggle them into the forest, and she had no place to hide them.

Once again, Irene prayed for guidance, and again her prayers were answered. Major Rügemer decided to move into a villa in town, and he asked Irene to be his housekeeper. When she saw the villa, she knew that she had found the perfect hiding place for her friends. When she told them what she planned to do, they warned her that they might all be killed, and her with them. But Irene, who had committed herself completely, only said, "I am in God's hands. His will be done."

The following evening in the munitions factory, Irene's small group of Jews hid behind a false wall they had constructed in the laundry room—the rest of the Jews from the factory were taken back to the ghetto. In the dark of the night, while the major slept, Irene sneaked them into the basement of his villa. When the sun rose the next morning, the final, brutal pogrom began—in a prolonged massacre, the Jews of Ternopol were forced to dig large pits, then were shot en masse, tossed in, and covered with earth. Many more were killed in the town's Jewish cemetery, and their corpses were scattered over the graves. Those not killed were sent to concentration camps.

But a dozen lives were saved through Irene's bravery.

For months, she hid her friends in the major's basement. And when he was out, they often went upstairs to help Irene cook, clean, and prepare for the major's frequent parties. Irene always locked the door from the inside so the major would not walk in and discover them. And at night, these fugitives hid in terrified silence while above them the Nazi officers dined, drank, laughed, and sang.

Then one of the women in the basement discovered she and her husband were expecting a child. Sadly, the others urged her to end the pregnancy, fearing that a baby's cry would give them all away. But Irene begged them to let it live, reasoning that to abort the child under these circumstances would be like giving the child to Hitler. Her insistence that "Hitler will not have this baby!" convinced them. (Today, that baby, Roman Haller, is a businessman living in Israel.)

On one horrifying day, Irene witnessed the public hanging of two families—one, a Jewish family, and the other, a Christian family who had hidden them. The Nazis first hanged the sobbing children while forcing the parents to watch; then they hanged the parents.

In a state of shock, Irene walked "like a zombie" to the

major's villa—and forgot to lock the front door. That afternoon, the major walked in unexpectedly and saw the Jewish women helping Irene clean the kitchen. The women ran downstairs. Without a word, the major turned and went to the library to telephone the gestapo. But Irene pursued him, knelt before him, clung to his legs, and kissed his hands, begging him, "Please, let them stay alive. It's my fault."

"Irene, you deceived me," the major said. "I'm old and tired. Tired of the war and tired of the killing. I don't want to see you dead. But I have my orders. I will go to my office to think." The major retired to his office and closed the door, leaving Irene praying outside. She did not see him again until that evening. He was drunk, but he made his meaning clear. The Jews could be spared—for a price.

"I was standing in front of him," she says, "waiting for the decision of life or death. He pulled me on his lap and said, 'I love you. You are mine. You have to be mine.' It was hard for me to make that decision. I was brought up in the Catholic faith, and you know, it was very difficult. . . . But it was, in a way, a small price to pay for so many lives."

In time, rumors of their affair spread through the town. The Nazis did not approve, and Irene was forced to leave the house. In a desperate move, Irene helped smuggle the now 13 Jews into the forest as they lay covered with straw in the back of a borrowed wagon. One of the Jewish men, disguised in a Nazi uniform, drove the wagon out of town.

Ironically, when the Russian soldiers returned to Ternopol and the defeated Nazis were fleeing for their lives, Major Rügemer went to warn Irene. He risked his own life to save her, taking her to the town of Kielsk, where his regiment was stationed.

Later, Irene joined the Polish underground. She tried to find her family and the other people she had known and cared for, but they had all disappeared.

Eventually, her partisan activities landed her on the Russian Red Army's most-wanted list. Now it was her Jewish friends' turn to hide Irene and to help her escape from Poland. They smuggled her into a displaced-persons camp and wrote a document testifying to the fact of her heroism—that she had saved their lives.

Irene never saw her parents again. But remarkably, nearly 40 years later, in 1984, she was reunited with her four sisters. By then, she was living in the United States as an American citizen.

Credited with saving the lives of 13 Jews—12 adults and a baby—Irene was later declared a Righteous Gentile by the state of Israel, one of 15,000 so honored at the shrine of Yad Va-Shem for saving Jewish lives. A tree was planted there to memorialize her courage.

Today, Irene Gut Opdyke lives in Los Angeles. She has started an educational foundation, mostly for children, teaching that tolerance, respect for others, and living one's highest principles can change the world.

"Courage is a whisper from above," Irene says today. "If you think only with your head, not with your heart, your head will tell you, 'Oh, that's dangerous, don't do this.' So you have to involve your heart. . . . I hope many generations will . . . remember that one person can make a difference."

The most terrible time in modern history brought out the best and bravest in one young woman. And as a result, Irene Opdyke not only experienced a divine intervention—she became one.

A Light in the Darkness

The Making of a Master Teacher

Si Tai Gong was born in the 1930s on a South Sea–island plantation camp. His father, a gentle field-worker, was an accomplished musician who played and sang in a local band. His mother devoted herself to caring for her children. Tai Gong's early years were happy ones, but when he was five, tragedy visited his family—a drunken doctor gave his father a penicillin shot and broke the needle off in his arm. Allergic to penicillin, his father came home from the fields and went into convulsions. The eldest brother ran for the doctor while Tai Gong and his family helplessly watched their father writhing on the floor. He died before the doctor came.

Now in dire poverty, the family moved into a simple house with outdoor plumbing. Tai Gong's mother, widowed with a large family to feed, made a desperate choice and married an airport worker, a violent alcoholic who soon began to terrorize the whole family. He beat them all, using whatever was handy—a leather strap, a cane, at times even a two-by-four. Tai Gong, who received the brunt of his stepfather's cruelty, was beaten, burned with a hot iron, kicked down stairs, stripped naked and made to weed the yard for hours in the hot sun, and even force-fed whiskey. The island missionaries and school-teachers who saw Tai Gong's bruises told him, "You must be a bad boy to have earned such beatings."

During this terrible time, Tai Gong would often wander alone through the forest and into the cane fields where his fa-ther had worked, to remember him and not feel so alone. Fre-quently ill from stress and physical abuse, Tai Gong had a recurring vision: He would climb on the back of a giant and fly across the island and over the sea. On several occasions, he awoke to find himself standing on the roof of his house under the night sky.

When Tai Gong was eight, his stepfather began locking him naked in a small pantry and leaving him alone in the dark-ness for days. At first, he cried in terror; then after a time, he began to hear voices—talking, whispering, singing. He listened to the voices and to the songs, and he began to hum, then sing along with the beautiful melodies he heard. The invisible voices kept him company; the music and his own singing soothed him.

One day, a luminous young girl—fair-haired, blue-eyed, and lit up like an image on a movie screen—appeared to him in the darkness of the pantry. "Why are you crying?" she asked him. When Tai Gong told her of his stepfather's cruelty, she looked deep into his eyes and smiled at him—he suddenly felt better. "You don't have to be afraid," she said. "Whenever you need me, I'll be there." Then she vanished.

After that, whenever Tai Gong grew afraid in the darkness of the pantry, this luminous girl would appear to comfort and reassure him. She also told him how to endure the pain when his stepfather beat him: "Think of me," she said, "and hum the songs. When you feel the pain, think of me." Then Tai Gong's angel whispered words it would take him years to understand: "Learn to forgive and to love."

During a year of frequent isolation in the pantry, Tai Gong discovered that the darkness contained a gift of light, for now he knew that he was never alone. He felt the girl's angelic presence near him, and a voice would sometimes warn him when he was in physical danger.

He ignored it only once—and fell out of a tree.

By age nine, Tai Gong spent most of his free time wandering alone in the island forest. Frail, sickly, and mistrustful of humans, his heart and mind were filled with hatred for his stepfather and for the missionaries who said he and his brothers and sisters deserved their beatings.

Then one day, an old Chinese man passing by Tai Gong's house found the boy tied to the rafters of the back porch as his stepfather thrashed him with a cane. The old man shouted at Tai Gong's stepfather, "Is this how you treat your son?"

"He's not my son!" the stepfather shouted back.

Without another word, the old man, a Buddhist priest, removed a knife from a sheath, climbed onto the porch, cut Tai Gong free, and took the boy with him to a temple near the sea, where Chinese monks practiced Shaolin kung fu and meditation. This elderly priest fed the emaciated boy and gave him a bitter herbal medicine to heal and strengthen him.

After that, Tai Gong went to clean the temple daily and watch the monks practice fighting with their hands and feet. He did his best to imitate their movements until the priest began teaching him. The temple became the boy's home away from home. Tai Gong studied for nine years, until he could move and fight like the crane, the tiger, the snake, the monkey, the mantis, and the dragon. The hours he had spent alone in the dark pantry, focusing on the pictures in his mind, had sharpened his powers of concentration and visualization and refined his intuitive abilities—all gifts of the darkness.

The years passed. Tai Gong traveled to California, joined the marines, taught advanced combat techniques, found a career as a successful nightclub singer, married, and had two children. Still, the shadows of his past haunted him, and the rage continued to burn.

Then in 1963, stirrings from the other world changed Tai Gong's life forever. In a recurring vision that appeared to him over a period of 30 days, he witnessed the crucifixion and agony of Christ. Night after night, he watched the horrified onlookers and indifferent soldiers, the weeping disciples, and the luminous figure of Mary standing at the foot of her son's cross. He experienced this vision as entirely real, with no emotional defenses to fend off the agony.

Against this backdrop, a long-suppressed memory of the luminous face of his angel in the darkness appeared, and her whispered words from his childhood came to him: "Learn to forgive and to love." This time, her words penetrated him to his core.

A prolonged period of crisis ensued as Tai Gong sought a new way of living. Like a baby learning to crawl, then stand, then walk, he began to practice and teach a way of life, love, and forgiveness, using the martial arts as a path to the Spirit within. In his own words, "God's light is moving into this world through an unbroken chain of beings who form a bridge between the human and spiritual realms. Angels and ascended masters may provide assistance, but it is up to us to carry the banner to the mountaintop."

The divine intervened in the life of Si Tai Gong in the form of an angelic young girl, an old Shaolin priest, and a vision of Christ. But in a larger sense, his loving father, abusive step-father, hardworking mother, and temple by the sea were all parts of the divine theater that shaped the life of Si Tai Gong, Grand Master in the art of Shaolin Temple Boxing, on his long and perilous journey from darkness into light.

Skinhead to Godhead

Redemption of a Racist

When he was 13, Richard Sabinski attended church three times. After each visit, he would talk about God with his friends. But Richard was a troubled and angry youth. Although he spoke of God with fervor, he hated all people of other races. At 15, his churchgoing days long past, Richard started doing drugs and getting into fights and into trouble. Pushing drugs by 16, he soon had three friends selling for him. Later, he bought a gun and pistol-whipped a drug buyer named Terry who refused to pay him for the merchandise. He then fired several shots into the side of Terry's car.

Terry escaped and called the police, who arrested Richard, then released him when Terry declined to press charges. A few days later, Richard saw Terry riding in a truck and began tailgating him. A high-speed chase ensued in which Richard fired his gun out of his window at the fleeing car. Richard was arrested again and sentenced to eight years in prison.

The overcrowded prison, brimming with racial tension, was a war zone where hatreds were color-coded and violence was a part of everyday life. Blacks, whites, and Hispanics fought territorial wars and formed gangs for protection. Skin colors became the uniforms of opposing armies, and racism became a bond of brotherhood. Richard's hatred of nonwhites now deepened to a burning focus—his gang became a potent symbol of his identity. In prison, Richard received a criminal education that would serve him upon his release less than two years later due to overcrowded prison conditions.

Back on the streets at 19, he returned to the drug business, now with hardcore members of his prison alma mater, fellow travelers on a dark path—armed robbers, drug users, violent felons. Richard attended one satanic ritual involving drugs, wild dancing, and formal prayers to Satan.

"By the time I was 23 years old," Richard says, "I realized I was an evil person. This reflection struck me out of nowhere— I was in my backyard, suddenly overcome by great sadness about my life and what I'd become. I knelt down and asked God for mercy. It was the first time I'd prayed in 10 years. The next day, I told several friends I was going to start over and become a new person. They laughed their teeth out," he reports.

Three days later, after finishing some Chinese food at a friend's house, Richard opened his fortune cookie to find the message, "Do not leave the righteous path you have chosen."

But Richard wasn't yet ready to hear this prophetic message. That same night, he and his friends went bowling and spied six Asian men a few lanes away. Richard's profound hatred welled up inside him—any skin color other than white made him see red. He and his friends approached the Asians and started a fight. But two Black men stepped in to defend the

Asians. Outnumbered, Richard and his friends left, raging about "niggers" and "gooks."

A few days later, Richard stood again in his backyard. "It was just getting dark," he said, "when I heard the sound of a bugle somewhere above me. I looked up and saw the sky split right in half. It was the eeriest thing I'd ever seen; one side of the sky was light and the other side dark. I knew without a doubt that God was asking me to change—giving me a choice. Again, I saw the darkness inside me, but this time I also saw a shaft of light, a ray of hope. I knelt down and again asked God to forgive me. All the violence, the hatred and craziness of my life flashed through my mind—all of it. I saw what a miracle it was that I had survived. I felt so grateful to be alive. I suddenly understood what a gift life is. And I knew that I wanted to do something good with mine."

Richard's vision changed his character overnight.

"The next day," he reports, "I went to the bus stop and saw a Black man waiting there alone. I looked at him and was amazed—I felt no hatred toward him. I saw he was a human being just like me. I'd never looked at a nonwhite person without that rage rising in me. Now, the rage was gone. I was so surprised. I almost started to cry. He turned toward me. I smiled and said, "Hello." It was the first kind word I had ever spoken to a man of color. Overnight, my heart had turned from stone to flesh. From that moment on, I haven't felt any racial hatred for another person."

Soon after that, Richard quit drugs, stopped fighting, and began to experience a new way of life—a brotherhood with all people. Still, he met with practical life challenges, with tests and trials. "I had to find a new way to make a living, to stabilize my life. I was poor for a while," he says.

During this period of soul-searching, Richard happened to see a Chinese man on television with fingers missing on each of his hands. The man had been tortured and persecuted for his religious activities. Deeply moved by this man's story, Richard realized that God, for reasons beyond his understanding, had given him a special compassion for the Chinese people. He resolved then and there to go to China to help the people there. Richard joined a local Chinese Christian church and was warmly embraced by his new community. He was baptized and learned to speak Mandarin. Since early 1997, Richard Sabinski has been living in and wandering through China, teaching English and telling of the miracles and grace made possible by the power of divine intervention.

Citizen of the Universe

The Transformation of Bucky Fuller

Until he was four years old, little cross-eyed Bucky saw the world as a blur of shapes and colors—he didn't even know what the members of his own family looked like. When he got his first pair of glasses, the sight of the world struck him with the force of a revelation. "For the first time," he said, "I saw leaves on a tree, small birds, . . . the stars, and the shapes of clouds and people's faces. It was a time of utter joy, as though all these things had been newly created just for me. I was filled with wonder at the beauty of the world."

When Bucky was 13, his father died after a series of strokes. The resulting family crises catapulted him out of the magical realm of childhood and into a harsher, more troubled world in which he often felt awkward and isolated.

Years later, through family connections, Bucky was accepted into Harvard University, where his quirky personality made him an outsider. A sense of alienation tormented this sensitive youth and brought out the reckless side of his character. That first year, as midterm approached, Bucky impulsively withdrew the funds his mother had saved for his education, went to New York City, lodged in one of its finest hotels, and attended the Zeigfield Follies. Captivated by the show's star, he returned the next night, sent roses and five bottles of champagne backstage, and in a grand self-destructive gesture, took the entire cast out for a party at one of New York's finest restaurants. In one evening, he squandered his college fund and ran up a bill it would take his family years to pay.

In the aftermath, Harvard expelled him for irresponsible conduct and his mother sent him to work as an apprentice mechanic in a Connecticut textile mill. A blessing in disguise, this stimulated in Bucky a natural aptitude for mechanical engineering. He threw himself into his work with a passion, sketching his ideas and designing new mechanical pieces for textile machinery. He received glowing work reports and was eventually allowed to return home, rehabilitated in his family's eyes.

At 20, Bucky met Anne Hewlett, the girl he would marry in 1917 and love until the day he died. When World War I began, he joined the navy and patrolled the New England coast searching for German U-boats. Though still a bit odd and erratic, he was a bright, likable young man with a zest for life and a creative knack for inventing contraptions.

When the war ended, Bucky returned home to his beloved Anne and their infant daughter, Alexandra. By that time, Alexandra had suffered bouts of polio and spinal meningitis that had left her partially paralyzed. To help cover the extra expenses, Bucky found a high-paying job. But three months after he had begun, the company shut down, leaving him penniless and unable to find decent work. Everything seemed to go wrong after that. At 27, Bucky began to look and feel like a failure. He'd never been a drinker, but now he became one.

In the midst of this difficult period, to distract himself from chronic depression, he decided to attend a Yale-Harvard football game with some old college chums. Before leaving home, Bucky, Anne, and Alexandra took a walk in the fresh air. Seeing her father's cane, which he used due to an old knee injury, Alexandra asked, "Daddy, when you come home, will you bring me a cane?" He promised that he would.

To his delight, Harvard won, and he spent the night drinking and celebrating. The next day, he phoned home from Pennsylvania Station to find Anne distraught. Alexandra had caught pneumonia and now lay in a coma. She was still unconscious when Bucky arrived. She awoke only once, looked up at him, and asked, "Daddy, did you bring me my cane?"

Bucky turned away in agony and shame, unable to meet her eyes—he'd forgotten all about it. She died that night in his arms.

Forty years later, he still could not speak of this incident without weeping. It would haunt him for the rest of his life. Bucky was devastated, driven nearly out of his mind with guilt and grief and stricken by his loss, his inability to provide for his family, his self-centered nature, and his failures.

That same season, Anne's mother, one of her brothers, and her brother-in-law also died. Bucky called it "a winter of horror." To escape his personal and financial abyss, he started a company to design and build construction machinery. Each day after work, he came home and drank long into the night.

After five difficult years, with the nation moving toward the Great Depression, Bucky and Anne had another daughter, named Alegra. His struggling company was bought out by a large corporation; he became an employee and was fired. Once again, Bucky became a pauper with a wife and newborn child to support. These blows destroyed his last shred of faith in himself. Believing he was cursed, fated to bring tragedy and suffering to those he loved, he fell into a suicidal depression.

On a bitterly cold winter evening in a mood of utter despair, 34-year-old Bucky Fuller walked out of his apartment and down to the shores of Lake Michigan, determined to throw himself into the frigid waters. "I've done the best I know how and it hasn't worked," he declared to himself. "I'm just no good." His own mother had believed he might turn out worthless, and had told him so—she had even tried to stop his wedding, warning her future in-laws that he was too irresponsible to support a family. Now, it seemed, she had been right about everything.

As Bucky stood on the windy shores of Lake Michigan, his mind suddenly cleared—he began a sober and spontaneous inquiry into his life, its worth and purpose, and the ultimate origins of his being. He determined then and there to discover the truth about himself and then act upon what he found—to live or die. If he was worthless, a "bad man," as some said, destructive to those he loved, he would end his life in those freezing waters. Anne would find someone better, Alegra was too young to miss him, and his in-laws could easily support them both if he were gone, he reasoned.

With a sudden urgency, questions arose in him. Was there a divine intelligence in the universe? Was his life of any value? Bucky resolved to accept only evidence of his own perceptions, not what he'd learned or been told by others. As his intense questioning deepened, as he considered the nature of God and reality, he experienced a sudden and overwhelming inner certainty that a Divine Intelligence existed, like God whispering in his mind. His engineer's vision saw proof of this not in beliefs or dogmas, but in the universe itself—in "the exquisite design of everything from the invisible microcosm of atoms to the macro-magnitudes of the galaxies, and all of them inter-accommodating with absolute integrity."

Next, he began a heartfelt inquiry into whether he could "be of any value to the integrity of Universe." As he reviewed his whole life and all he'd learned, an intelligent pattern began to emerge. And in a moment of supreme insight, he knew: "You do not have the right to eliminate yourself; you do not belong to you. You belong to the universe. Your significance will remain forever obscure to you, but you may assume that you are fulfilling your role if you apply yourself to converting your experience to the highest advantage of others."

These insights struck him with the force of a divine command—as if his soul had perched on his shoulder and counseled his mortal self. That night, Bucky Fuller went home a changed man. With a profound new sense of inner strength and purpose, he knew that to go on living he must consecrate himself to the highest purpose of serving others and his world, of working "for the total well-being of people everywhere."

Bucky knew he had no gift for reforming humanity; rather, his abilities were uniquely suited for reforming man's environment. He then decided he would no longer worry about money. "If the Intelligence directing Universe really has a use for me, it will not allow us to starve; it will see to it that I am able to carry out my resolve."

Within a matter of hours, a new vision of his life's purpose had unfolded in Bucky's mind; an inner revelation had completely reorganized his being. The only thing remaining was to act. He returned to Anne and told her what had occurred and how he intended to live. And this remarkable woman not only understood his vision but also agreed to his purpose. The radical nature of his transformation revealed itself in the way he went about changing his life, deepening his illumination begun on the shores of Lake Michigan. Determined to unlearn the mass of secondhand beliefs and opinions that filtered and distorted his direct perceptions, he now spoke rarely, and then spoke only essential communications to Anne and Alegra.

Anne became his voice to the outside world.

Driven by a profound urgency, Bucky moved his family to a cheap apartment in a poor section of Chicago and dedicated himself to prolonged contemplation and rigorous study, hoping to discover, he said, "the wellspring of true creativity and authentic life, to regain the sensitivities I was born with." To salvage every possible moment, Bucky began napping briefly when his mind began to flag, in time cutting his sleep to 2 or 3 hours out of 24. His friends and family thought his behavior wildly irresponsible, perhaps insane. Anne alone understood and stood by him, picking up the slack and defending him to the world.

As it turned out, Bucky's peculiar experiment released tremendous reserves of energy and creativity in him. Alden Hatch, his biographer and friend of many decades, writes, "From this intense period of silent thought emerged in embryo most of the great philosophical and mathematical innovations that have made his fame and moved the world forward. . . ."

Remarkable ideas, insights, and information began to pour through him, among them his radical architectural innovations. The solar-powered house-on-a-pole, his first famous invention, recycled all water and wastes or turned them into fertilizer. It weighed only 6,000 pounds and cost $1,500.

In 1929, Bucky broke his silence—his friends joked that he

never stopped talking again. In fact, he became a prolific lecturer and writer to explain his revolutionary ideas and inventions. He designed a car that traveled on land and water and that also flew. This aerodynamic Dymaxion car, with a land speed of 120 miles per hour, was 20 years ahead of its time. When his circular Dymaxion house was shown to the public, 30,000 orders flooded in.

But his most successful architectural design, for which he would become known worldwide, was the Geodesic Dome—the simplest and most durable, economical, and elegant architectural structure ever devised. It could be assembled in hours and withstand winds up to 200 miles per hour. The U.S. Marines purchased over 300 domes. The air force used them as Antarctic bases. His famed aluminum-skinned Kaiser Dome musical auditorium in Honolulu, roughly 50 yards in diameter, was constructed in only 22 hours.

Bucky also designed a self-contained, solar-powered pyramidal city of the future that floated on the sea. His lightweight transparent domes could cover conventional cities and create perfect atmospheres. A pioneer global visionary, he saw mankind as a crew of astronauts soaring through the galaxy on spaceship Earth—citizens not of nations but of the universe itself.

Needless to say, he was now able to afford a far more comfortable home and neighborhood for Anne and Alegra. Anne remained his one constant throughout his long, creative, whirlwind life. Now certain of God and of immortality beyond bodily death, Bucky made Anne this promise: He would die before her so that he could greet her on the other side.

One day, after lecturing in New York City, Bucky, now in his 80s, got a telephone call—Anne, back in Los Angeles, was in the hospital, seriously ill. He caught the first plane back, but by the time he arrived, Anne had lapsed into a coma. The doctors doubted that she would regain consciousness.

Once again, he had returned too late.

Perhaps Bucky may have recalled the heart-rending incident decades earlier—his forgotten promise to buy his dying daughter Alexandra a cane. Bucky set a chair by Anne's bed. She lay unconscious, her breathing faint. He spoke to her softly for a few moments.

Then, Bucky Fuller leaned back, closed his eyes, and quietly died.

Minutes later, a nurse came in and found him. Bucky had kept his promise. Anne, the love of his life, followed him several hours later. Perhaps Alexandra was there to greet them both on the other side.

Free as a Bird

A Gift of Love from Beyond

As far back as he could remember, Boyd Jacobson loved birds. Even as a young boy, raised and mothered in rural Washington by his great-aunt Karn, Boyd had spent many hours observing the birds of the great Northwest. He loved listening to their calls and collecting feathers, nests, and eggshells.

Boyd's bird-watching expeditions were limited to the fields and meadows near his own backyard, due to a difficulty in walking long distances. As a result of contracting Perthes' disease in infancy, Boyd's malformed right leg bone was shorter than his left. He could never walk barefoot without a painful limp. Even with lifts in his shoe, Boyd couldn't run or play sports without aggravating the pain in his hip. But riding a bike was easy, so he became an avid cyclist.

An artist and a free spirit, Boyd eventually moved to Marin County, California, where he worked as a film director. He often rode his bike up the steep and winding paths of his beloved Mount Tamalpais, a mountain deemed sacred by Native Americans who once populated its pristine slopes.

Boyd was married and life blessed him with a daughter, Karie. The marriage eventually ended amicably, and Boyd's relationship with Karie remained close and loving.

Then in 1989, around Karie's 17th year, Boyd met and fell in love with Allison James. Allison also worked in filmmaking. Within a year, they were engaged, and they shared a home near Mount Tamalpais with Karie and Boyd's "Mother" Karn. Allison found Boyd's off-beat, humorous character immensely appealing—so did most of his friends. Boyd was a witty, off-the-wall original who made people laugh, and his unconventional outlook and manner conveyed an expanded sense of reality.

Even as an adult, Boyd still had a thing for birds. He saw himself as a man but dreamt of himself as a bird. His friends related to him as Bird Man. One friend made Boyd a ceramic bird with Boyd's face on it that sat on a perch in a cage and sang when you flipped a switch. "When Boyd left a message on your answering machine," Allison says, "you heard only a birdcall and knew it was a 'Boyd call.' His business card even featured a cartoon caricature of himself as a bird."

After their engagement, Boyd and Allison decided to go to Bali to plan their wedding. Boyd wanted very much to walk barefoot on the beach with his love, without a painful limp, so he decided it was finally time to have the hip operation he needed to repair the degenerated joint. For this routine operation, he decided upon an old college acquaintance as his surgeon. After reassuring his loved ones that all would be well, Boyd Jacobson went under anesthesia. But he never regained consciousness, due to a tragic surgical mishap. His completely unexpected passing devastated everyone who had loved him, especially Allison, Karie, and Mother Karn.

Even more heartbreaking, Boyd had left without saying good-bye.

After he was cremated, half his ashes were sent to his family's plot in Washington. Allison and Karie decided to scatter his remaining ashes in his favorite meadow atop his beloved Mount Tamalpais. Two of Boyd's friends rode his ashes up on the back of his mountain bike along his favorite trail. Allison and Karie drove ahead to the top and chose a beautiful spot in the meadow near two granite boulders. After Boyd's friends arrived, they performed a simple ceremony then scattered his ashes across the meadow.

Several weeks after Boyd's death, Allison had a vivid dream: She was on foot doing an errand for her movie studio and heard Boyd's unmistakable birdcall nearby. She entered a store and followed his call to the back, where she found him. He spoke to her for a while and told her to "do the right thing." Before the dream ended, Boyd held out her cat Chelsea's food dish in one hand, saying that he knew she was hungry. Then, playfully, he held out his other fist, which he turned and opened. Sitting on his palm was a small white bird—a dream gift for Allison.

She awoke feeling strongly that she'd actually met Boyd's spirit. Chelsea was meowing hungrily, her cat dish empty. For Allison, Boyd's message, "Do the right thing," meant that she should take care of his mother Karn, then 87, for the rest of her life, as he would have done. Allison made an inner promise to Boyd to do just that. She later shared her dream with Karie and Karn.

Days later, Karie was going through Boyd's things in another room when Allison heard her exclaim, "Oh, my god!" Karie, holding out her closed fist, went up to Allison and said, "This must be for you." Then Karie turned her hand over and opened it—in her palm sat a small white ceramic bird. They both had goose bumps, and tears formed in Allison's eyes.

Then, two months after Boyd's death, Allison got a phone call from Glenn, a friend of Boyd's from out of town who had missed the memorial. Glenn was coming to town and wanted to visit Boyd's meadow on Mount Tamalpais. So Glenn, Karie, Allison, and her friend Barbara drove up together and parked the car at the trailhead.

Glenn and Karie took separate trails for some private time, so Allison and Barbara reached the meadow first and approached the first of two granite boulders marking his site. *There on the farthest boulder, six feet away, sat a large, beautiful, pure white bird, gazing directly at them.* Allison and Barbara froze so as not to frighten the bird away, then looked at each other in astonishment. They sat down near the closer boulder.

Immediately, the bird flew onto the closer rock, only a few feet from Allison. On impulse, she reached out her hand and made a "come here" gesture. With a hop and a flutter, the bird flew into Allison's lap. Instinctively, she felt that the bird was a message from Boyd, like the white bird in the palm of his hand in her dream and the white bird that Karie brought to her from his belongings. In that moment, she felt a profound shift in her grieving process—a torn place in her soul had begun to mend. It seemed that somehow Boyd had sent this bird as an emissary of comfort and a way to say farewell—evidence that his spirit was alive and free as a bird.

Allison sat still for 45 minutes, stroking the bird. Barbara as well as Karie and Glenn sat quietly with them. It felt like a spontaneous ceremony, an experience of grace and wonder. Finally, Allison said good-bye and thanked the bird, thanked Boyd, and thanked the universe; she then prepared to hike back to the car. Allison stood up slowly, expecting the bird to fly off. Instead, the bird hopped up and perched on her shoulder. Amazed, she headed down the trail with her feathered friend.

After some distance, Allison gently lifted the bird and put it on Karie's shoulder so she, too, could physically feel this living link to her father. Karie took about 20 steps down the trail, then stopped and looked back. As she did so, the bird flew back onto Allison's shoulder, where it stayed.

The afternoon grew chilly as the four of them approached the car, planning to drive down the mountain into Mill Valley for a warming cup of coffee in a local café. Allison once again told the bird good-bye—clearly she couldn't take it with her. But this bird was going nowhere. It remained steadfast on Allison's shoulder as she got into the car, drove down the mountain, walked into the café, sat down at a table, and had a cappuccino. The bird was still on Allison's shoulder when she and Karie walked into the house to tell the story and introduce Boyd's emissary to Mother Karn.

By 1998, Allison, Karn, and Karie had settled into their own separate homes. The white bird, now called Birdie, still lives with Allison, a part of the family. Allison built a comfortable indoor cage for Birdie but, from the beginning, let her feathered friend know it was free to fly as it wished. She often lets the bird out to have the run of the house, and Birdie often follows Allison outside when she works in the garden. Birdie has never flown out of Allison's sight.

After some research, Allison decided that Birdie was a great American king dove, but she couldn't tell if Birdie was male or female. Then, during the week of the first anniversary of Boyd's death, Birdie laid a single white egg; small enough to hold in the palm of your hand—or hide in a closed fist.

Birdie, a divine gift from Boyd, revealed to Allison more clearly than ever that the universe is a mysterious place and that death is not the end of life or love.

Conversion by Lightning

A Prisoner's Sudden Liberation

Huang Yao Rong was born in Szechuan province in 1930s China. His family, too poor to raise him, sent him to Hong Kong to live with his aunt, the wife of an officer in the Guomindang party, then fighting the Chinese Communists for control of China. In Hong Kong, Huang received a British education. After graduating from college, he returned to China to work for the Canton Railway.

In the early 1950s, the Communists won the revolution, defeating the Guomindang, who fled to Taiwan. Haung's political status was now tainted by his Guomindang uncle and aunt. To make matters worse, he had been baptized a Christian in 1946. Like millions of other politically suspect Chinese citizens, Huang lived under the party's close supervision.

Because his engineering skills were needed for China's modernization, he was allowed to work in relative freedom. But as stormy political movements swept through China, Huang was often publicly criticized and was twice arrested for alleged criminal political activities. On August 10, 1968, in the frenzied violence of China's Cultural Revolution, Huang was arrested as a spy. With his hands and feet bound and a dunce cap on his head, he was beaten and dragged through the streets before jeering crowds, then put in a makeshift military prison in his workplace. His fellow employees became his prison guards.

Millions across China suffered similar fates. Hundreds of thousands of warehouses, auditoriums, and buildings were converted into makeshift prisons after the established prisons were filled. Each morning and afternoon, Huang was forced to kneel, head bowed, in public meetings for hours at a time while he was verbally and physically abused. Each night, he was forced to write "self-criticism reports," confessing to political crimes he had never committed. Refusal to confess was considered proof of guilt, and was punished by beatings.

When Huang grew uncooperative, his hands, feet, three ribs, and an arm were broken, his lower vertebrae were fractured, and his skull was cracked. The skin on much of his body, raw and bloody from his beatings, stung with sweat in the summer's heat. Unrelenting nightly interrogations blended terror and pain as muscular youths pounded his chest and ribs, continuing even when he began vomiting blood. Unable to walk, he had to be dragged to and from his cell. Denied medical attention, Huang was forced to sit upright in his cell around the clock and was allowed a single one-minute bathroom break per day. He lost control of his bladder and bowels and soiled himself daily.

So passed his first 15 days of captivity.

Then, a monsoon hit Canton. Thunder and lightning shook Huang's cell and the fierce gusts shattered his window. Huang describes what happened next. "I was sitting against the wall. In the dim light, I looked down and saw myself covered with blood and filth. After all the beatings, I no longer had the shape of a human being. I knew if it continued, I would die. So I decided not to wait for death but to finish it myself, out of hatred for my enemies and to end my pain. Once this idea rose in me, I began to think of my wife and mother. My heart was in chaos. My emotions rose to a desperate pitch. Clenching my teeth, I took a shard of glass from the window broken by the crazy monsoon winds. My hands shook uncontrollably as I began to cut the artery in my left wrist.

"The next moment, thunder exploded nearby and a bolt of lightning flashed in my cell through the broken window. In that same instant, a bright light lit up my heart—this is the only way to describe it. I woke up. I saw clearly that my life was sacred, given to me by a divine power—I had no right to destroy myself.

"Many things were revealed to me in that instant. I saw the divisions and hatreds that had torn my country apart. My guards and torturers believed I was evil, as I believed they were. Our mutual hatred seemed justified. Now, I saw that as long as I hated them, the cycle would continue. Not even my death would end it. Only love could end hatred. And I could choose love. In that life-and-death moment, I realized no human effort, only a greater power, could save me and resolve my situation. I had not prayed in 20 years. Now, I knew the only way out of this alley of death was through repentance and prayer."

Abruptly, Huang's rage toward his torturers had vanished. He now saw clearly that these fanatical idealists, mostly in their teens and early 20s, had been raised in "revolutionary cradles" and taught to hate their enemies. Despite the terrible pain and cruelty they had inflicted upon him, Huang's heart overflowed with compassion. He now understood the meaning of Christ's words on the cross, "Father, forgive them, for they know not what they do."

Huang prayed through the night as thunder crashed, lightning flashed, and the rain washed in through the broken window. When the day broke, the storm outside and within Huang Yao Rong's heart had subsided. The suicidal despair and emotional agony of the past 15 days had been lifted from him, replaced by a newfound serenity, clarity, and confidence in God. Huang consciously sensed a divine power working on him from within.

Blessed with courage, he requested paper and pen, and with his broken hand, scrawled a letter to the head of the military control committee, describing without rancor his present condition and the torture he had endured. He felt no animosity toward them now, only their shared humanity. Soon, the young guards began to treat him differently—they gave him a chair during his interrogations. They beat him a few more times after that, but not harshly. The torture ceased altogether. He was fed better and was allowed to go to the bathroom whenever he needed, to shower, and to write to his family.

Huang spent five more years in prison before being pronounced innocent and released. Five years later, he was officially exonerated. Due to spinal and head injuries sustained during his torture, he eventually lost the use of the right side of his body.

In 1997, Huang, now living in the United States, visited Canton. There, one of his old friends and fellow workers told him the following story. Several months earlier, a former guard in their workplace prison, dying of brain cancer, had confessed to him that during the Culture Revolution he had severely tortured two individuals—one of them was Huang Yao Rong. "I have had no peace ever since," the dying man said. "I had to tell someone." He passed away several days later.

The friend asked Huang, crippled from his torture 30 years before, if he hated the people who had done this to him. "No," Huang replied, "If I hate, I lose my peace; if I forgive, I am given peace. How futile my hatred would have been toward a man who all these years suffered such remorse over his actions."

Huang Yao Rong now says, "Everything happened just as I have said. I have witnessed and experienced divine blessings beyond what I have the power to describe. Despite my severe physical handicap, I have found great happiness and peace. I have hope. I rely on the supreme wisdom of the divine to lead me through every difficult passage. I pray every day. I live to do God's work. I have sometimes made mistakes. But I have never forsaken my faith."

Today, Huang Yao Rong, who lives in San Francisco, speaks in local churches, sharing his story and message of forgiveness—demonstrating how we can, with the help of God, end the cycles of hatred and find inner peace through the power of faith, prayer, and forgiveness.

Brothers after All

A Moment of Grace in the Moment of Truth

Doug was born in rural Kentucky in the summer of 1956. His family rarely stayed in one place for more than two years, and by age 12, he had moved eight times to eight different states. In 1968, during the height of the Vietnam anti-war protests, Doug's family moved to Grand Forks, North Dakota, a farming town with a university and a military base.

Tensions ran high between the local military families and the student protestors, whom Doug resembled only by virtue of his long hair. This was enough to arouse the animosity of his teachers and his junior high school peers. When a number of the tougher students began a campaign of physical harassment to force Doug to cut his hair, he refused to back down. As a result, for the next three years, both in and out of school, he endured pain and humiliation in the form of frequent physical assaults by groups of local toughs and teenage gangs.

For years after, Doug lived on alert, with a clenching fear

and a burning anger. Then, in San Francisco at the age of 20, he began studying the martial arts. In his third year of intensive training, realizing he could now skillfully defend himself, he experienced an exhilarating sense of freedom. His fear of assault vanished, resulting in a reckless confidence—on a number of occasions he roamed through San Francisco's notorious Tenderloin district in the middle of the night, enjoying his sense of liberation in one of the city's most dangerous, crime-ridden neighborhoods.

He never even considered that he might be tempting fate.

Meanwhile, his buried anger manifested itself in an endless stream of martial art fantasies—mental rehearsals in which he visualized attacks like those he had suffered in earlier years now met with his newly cultivated fighting skills. Although philosophically disposed to pacifism, part of him secretly wanted a real-life payback against "the bad guys" for his years as a victim of violence.

Then, in 1978, while walking home from a friend's at 3:00 A.M. one chilly San Francisco morning, Doug rounded the corner onto his street and saw two young men, about 30 yards ahead, dressed in black from their shoes to their knit wool caps. He felt a sudden chill at the sound of a high-pitched ping as one of them tapped a foot-long metal pipe against a brick building.

"Okay, guys," he whispered, "just walk past my house and let me go inside." One of the men glanced back, saw Doug, and nudged his friend. Now, they both looked back and began calling out taunting, threatening words. Doug felt a surge of adrenaline and kept walking—as he had refused to cut his hair years ago under threats and violence, he now refused to flee from his own house.

The two men stopped in the next doorway to wait for him.

As he approached the two men, Doug's body felt electrified and his mind was uncommonly lucid. He felt certain he could handle the situation—they were two to his one but clearly overconfident; he was harmless looking, trained to fight multiple opponents, and had the element of surprise. With his senses heightened, Doug prepared for a fight he expected to last a few seconds.

As he drew near, he took note of their positions, visualizing how they would come for him and what he would do. *They would come out of the doorway—he'd throw his keys in the face of the one with the pipe and deliver sudden foot and hand strikes to stomach and head, as he'd practiced for years. In his mind's eye, he saw them fall to the sidewalk, writhing in pain, mouths and noses bleeding from ruptured internal organs.*

But in an instant, Doug experienced a radical reversal in consciousness that would change his life forever. The realization struck him that *he had the power to injure these strangers, but not the power to heal them.* A profound revulsion overwhelmed him—a sense of grief and remorse over what he was about to do. Suddenly, the scenario he had imagined, that was about to occur, made no sense. He describes what happened next:

"I now approached them with a kind of bemused bewilderment. My mind had shifted to an expanded perspective from which our little drama seemed utterly ludicrous. We three fools stood there among billions of people on earth, trapped in a silly game. It was obvious to me that we had no idea why we were doing this or even how we got on this planet. We'd never met, yet we were about to engage in mortal combat as if we were enemies. It was absurd! I felt a profound, exhilarating sense of brotherhood, even affection, for these two men. My fear and all plans of attack simply vanished. I didn't decide not to fight—the possibility disappeared from my mind in a kind of divine amnesia I can't explain to this day. I felt no fear, no sense of danger—only an absolute, joyous certainty that I loved these men as brothers."

This view was not a strategy or philosophy, but a realization. Doug, a trained fighter with no religious background or experience, did not believe that love conquered all or that thinking positive thoughts could resolve a violent confrontation. In his usual frame of mind, this behavior would have been unrealistic and dangerous. But Doug was not in his usual frame of mind.

The two men stepped out of the doorway toward him, one with the pipe raised just as Doug had visualized. He grinned at them as if greeting long-lost friends—in his profoundly altered state, it literally *never occurred to him* that he was in any danger, that these men, his brothers, might harm him. "I was overjoyed to see them," he recalls. With a huge smile, he looked into the eyes of a young black man about his age and said in a loud, affectionate voice, "Hey! How are you?" The man froze like a statue with his pipe in the air. Doug then smiled at his young Hispanic "friend" and said, "Good evening!"

Doug can still see the dumbstruck looks on their faces. "I think they felt that I loved them and they didn't know what to do—they'd been short-circuited. I walked on—it felt like floating—two houses past them to my front door, in no hurry at all. I went inside and stood in the dark. I was flooded with ecstasy, surrounded by a marvelous presence. I saw with utter clarity the world bathed in light . . . it was absolutely alive, divinely perfect. I knew all human beings were my brothers and sisters. I loved the whole world and everyone in it. As I basked in this remarkable state, I heard the two men run off down the street."

In the days and weeks that followed, Doug pondered this experience. What, exactly, had transpired? It was far beyond an expansive mood or a lucky break. The event had changed his life. A former atheist and skeptic, the incident awakened in him a profound curiosity about the nature of reality and about God. It soon led him to the practices of prayer and meditation, in a spiritual search to which he would devote many years.

As Doug Childers relates it, "That event taught me there is always a higher solution to any difficulty, and when things get difficult, I look for that higher road. I also learned beyond any doubt that a mysterious presence and power is available to anyone who opens to it. Finally, I came to understand that the greatest power we have is our ability to make simple, loving contact with other human beings."

Meeting hatred with love is one of the highest and most difficult practices of life. Doug would have been justified in defending himself and might even have taught these men a "lesson in manners."

Instead, he realized that they were brothers after all.

A Living Sacrifice

The Healings of a Holy Heart

Therese Neumann exhibited nearly every miraculous phenomena of sainthood in her utterly remarkable, closely observed, and thoroughly documented life. As a Catholic peasant farm girl from a small Bavarian village near the Czechoslovakian border, she led a typical life of chores, school, and church. The eldest of 10 children, she cared for a brood of younger siblings. At the age of 12, she began to hire herself out as a farmer and a domestic to supplement her large family's meager income.

Therese's childhood dream of going to Africa as a missionary ended when she was 20. First, she injured her back, and soon after, she tumbled down a flight of stairs. She suffered serious internal injuries, head trauma, and chronic convulsions so severe that they sometimes threw her from her bed. Months after her fall, her deteriorating eyesight failed completely.

She spent the next five years in bed—blind and crippled.

Therese spent these years of darkness and suffering in devotion to Christ, surrendering herself to God's will, and praying with great fervor to her beloved Therese of Lisieux, whose saintly life was associated with numerous miracles.

On April 19, 1923, the same day as Therese of Lisieux's beatification (formal declaration of blessedness), Therese Neumann, now 25, was lying in her bed in perpetual darkness when she felt a hand touch her. In that instant, her eyesight was fully restored. Soon after this, rose petals from Therese of Lisieux's grave, gathered by her father, were placed in the bandage around Therese's foot. Within several days, the skin, which had rotted away, was restored perfectly.

Therese Neumann wrote, "On May 17, 1925, the day of Therese of Lisieux's canonization (formal elevation to sainthood), I became aware of a great brightness before my eye. Indescribably beautiful and comforting for the eyes was this light. Then a voice began to speak: 'Wouldn't you like to be well again?'"

Therese answered, "Everything is agreeable to me what my loving God desires—to become well, to remain sick, to die."

The voice told Therese she would be healed but that she would receive more suffering, which no doctor would be able to cure, and that she could help to save other souls.

"Everything the good Lord wants is fine with me," Therese responded. She was instantaneously healed of her paralysis, her crippled legs, and her dislocated vertebrae. Although weakened from seven years of lying in bed, she now rose and walked using a cane.

On September 30, the anniversary of Therese of Lisieux's death, the radiant light appeared to Therese once again. The voice reminded her of sufferings to come, which she, like Jesus, must bear for the sake of others. "Always remain childlike and simple," the voice admonished.

After that, Therese was able to walk without her cane.

But then on November 13, 1925, Dr. Otto Seidl diagnosed Therese, now 27, with acute appendicitis. He ordered immediate surgery.

Therese told her priest, "You know, if I tell it to the little saint, she could help without the cutting."

"Do you really think Saint Therese works miracles for you?" the skeptical Dr. Seidl asked. In response, her family gathered rose petals from Saint Therese's grave and placed them on Therese's body, this time over her appendix. Then she, her family, and her priest prayed to Saint Therese for a miracle. To Dr. Seidl's astonishment, Therese was completely healed within minutes.

Dr. Seidl later testified, "There was no natural explanation for these extraordinary cures and the phenomena that followed them."

On March 28, 1926, directly after Therese had a vision of the Passion of Christ, wounds of the stigmata appeared on her body. At times, these stigmata glowed (as was captured in photographs). They would remain with her for the rest of her life and inspire many souls. Hard, nail-shaped protuberances also formed, running through her wounds, creating the uncanny appearance of actual nails driven through her hands and feet. Other wounds appeared: lacerations on her back and a crown of thorns around her scalp and even a deep wound in her side that became an open fissure, like the wound inflicted on the body of Christ by the Roman soldier's spear.

Over the years, many thousands came to see her; many miraculous healings were well-documented. Therese made clear that she did not heal by her own efforts but rather by the divine presence and power that emanated from her. She was a vessel of Spirit; yet on numerous occasions, Therese reportedly appeared to and miraculously healed people far away, even across continents, who wrote or prayed to her.

Like other saints on record, Therese was seen to levitate during her ecstasies—and on many occasions, she was witnessed in two different places at once. When she received communion, the wafer at times floated from the priest's hand, through the air, and onto her tongue. At other times, the wafer dissolved into thin air before she could swallow it. And in her frequent ecstasies, a wafer sometimes appeared on her tongue out of thin air. Many reliable witnesses testified to these remarkable phenomena.

But perhaps the most extraordinary and well-documented of all sacred phenomena associated with Therese is her total abstinence from any and all food *and* liquids other than her one communion wafer daily. *Therese Neumann did not eat or drink for the last 40 years of her life*—all the more remarkable considering the amount of blood she regularly lost and the continual pain she endured through her stigmatic wounds. She received her bodily nourishment from a higher power by invisible means, thus demonstrating the truth that we do not live by bread alone.

These are but a few of the miracles reported in the meticulously documented history of Saint Therese Neumann. No one, including Therese herself, understood specifically how these things were accomplished. But that they *were* accomplished is an established fact, observed by devotees and skeptics, doctors and scientists alike. In our century, modern science and timeless faith bore witness in silent awe to the miraculous life of Therese Neumann—a mystery that may never be explained.

Mind over Matter

From Sickly Child to Superhuman

On the sweltering evening of July 15, 1893, in the poorest section of Suwalki, Poland, Chaya Greenstein fell while carrying water home. She went into labor and soon gave birth to a three-and-a-half pound boy—three months prematurely. In those times, premature infants rarely survived, especially among the poor. So when this tiny child survived his first week, nursing with an eyedropper and sleeping in a cotton-lined bed the size of a shoe box, word spread. Three doctors who visited the child concluded that there was nothing they could do. Yet the baby, struggling for breath, too weak to cry out, clung to life. Finally, he was given a name—Yoselle, or Joseph.

Six years passed. Young Joseph, now a frail boy cared for by his mother—his father had died a year before—walked to school through the winter snow, his feet wrapped in rags. Pale and congested, an asthmatic like his late father, Joseph struggled to endure in the face of his physical infirmities. But in his

14th winter, after a medical examination, Joseph overheard the doctor tell his mother that he would likely not reach his 18th birthday. He watched his mother fighting to hold back her tears.

On the way home from the doctor's office, while passing a small array of circus tents, Joseph noticed a poster featuring a strongman with muscles like marble. Beneath the poster were the words "Champion Volanko." Enthralled by the picture—an image of health, strength, and vitality—he begged his mother to let him visit the show. Sadly, she had no money for admission.

Joseph somehow knew that he *had* to see this Champion. So when he spied some boys sneaking in under the tent, he did the same—and found himself face to face with a circus roustabout who began to beat and kick him. In the next moment, out of nowhere, Champion Volanko himself appeared, stopped the beating, and befriended young Joseph. The few words Volanko spoke struck the sickly youth with a force that would change the course of his life. "I was once more sickly than you," Volanko said. "The greatest athletes have often grown from the weak and infirm." Then he asked Joseph directly, "Do you want to die?" Joseph wanted very much to live and asked Volanko to show him how. So the strongman became a mentor to the weakling, a father to a fatherless boy.

That night, Joseph bid his mother a tearful good-bye. Filled with hope—for he had little else—Joseph left town with the circus as Volanko's helper and disciple. Sometimes the divine comes in the form of an angel of light and sometimes in the form of a Jewish circus strongman with a thick Russian accent and muscles like carved marble.

Joseph learned two important things from Volanko that he would always remember. First, he must assume no limitations;

second, he must stretch himself each day beyond what he believed he could do. When the muscular strongman stood in the snow lifting heavy weights, naked except for a loincloth, the skinny boy watched, enthralled by Volanko's vitality. Emulating Volanko, Joseph rubbed snow on his bare flesh and lifted empty buckets that Volanko gradually filled with sand—a handful more each day. From his teacher, Joseph learned to eat nourishing grains, to train hard, and to kill his illness before it had a chance to kill him. Volanko taught Joseph practical knowledge as well as spiritual wisdom.

"It is hard to be Jew, hard to be a man, but you must do your best," he told the boy.

Joseph learned about his mind and spirit as he learned to wrestle. As he practiced deep breathing, his wracking cough and his old life began to fade. He pushed beyond, more always, challenging the limits of his mind and body.

"Always think just one more, just one more," Volanko urged him.

In Ed Spielman's classic "biography of a superhuman," *The Spiritual Journey of Joseph L. Greenstein: The Mighty Atom*, he reveals how Joseph traveled across Europe and the East to learn mental disciplines and training methods that enabled him to perform extraordinary feats of strength never accomplished before and rarely duplicated since.

After Joseph and his wife, Leah, moved to the United States and settled in Houston, Joseph demonstrated such feats as biting steel nails in half; bursting heavy chains by expanding his chest; bending heavy iron rods with his fingers; making finger rings out of 20-penny nails; twisting two-inch steel bars around his arms; playing with 300-pound dumbbells as if they were children's toys; supporting a large horse, cow, and four men on his chest while lying on a bed of nails; pulling a 20-ton fire truck with 20 men on it around the block; driving 20-penny nails through a two-inch plank with one blow of his bare fist; bending iron bars over the bridge of his nose; straightening horseshoes with his bare hands, and then breaking them in two; swinging a "merry-go-round" of six people, all hanging from his long hair; and preventing two powerful automobiles from driving off in opposite directions by holding them back with a rope in each hand.

Yet even these amazing feats of power were not Joseph's most impressive demonstrations of faith in the divine power of mind over matter. After much preparation in strengthening his scalp, he fastened his hair to a rope and the rope to a chain, which he attached to a new Fairchild FC-2 airplane powered by a nine-cylinder engine identical to that with which Lindberg had flown the Atlantic 16 months before. Then Joseph accomplished something the experts said was not humanly possible: He stood on the runway behind the plane, which revved its engine to over 1,600 revolutions per minute, trying to take off. Joseph stood his ground and held the machine in place. (Later, a powerful young stuntman died attempting the same feat.)

Photos of Joseph Greenstein reveal a physically fit man of small stature—a few inches over five feet. His physique looks quite modest when compared to the hulking, high-tech muscles of today's bodybuilders and powerlifters. Yet none of today's strongmen can even approach Joseph's apparently superhuman feats. His abilities proceeded more from his faith and spirit than from his muscles. And the divine source of his power also provided incredible support and protection, clearly demonstrated by the following incident.

On October 12, 1914, a disturbed youth, enamored of Joseph's wife, Leah, fired a .38-caliber revolver point-blank at

Joseph. The bullet struck him between the eyebrows, knocking him off his feet. He lay stunned, blood running down his face, knowing he had been shot between the eyes. Finally, he put his thumb against the bullet hole to stem the flow of blood, rose to his feet, and staggered across the street to the pharmacy. As he went in, several patrons ran out—one fainted. The druggist, who had seen gunshot wounds, took one look and said, "You alive?"

"I'm talking to you, aren't I?" Joseph replied.

Later, in the emergency room, the doctor found the bullet flattened against Joseph's skull; it had barely penetrated the bone.

"I was shot between the eyes," said Joseph. "Why am I alive?"

The doctors had no explanation. The incident was investigated and reported by three Houston newspapers on Tuesday, October 13, 1914—the *Press*, the *Houston Chronicle*, and the *Daily Post*. The facts, as reported, were straightforward: A real bullet from a working pistol had been fired at close range into Joseph Greenstein's forehead. The result: a small indentation in his skull and hardly more than a flesh wound

From this apparent miracle, Joseph began to question his larger purpose in life. He shared the fruits of his contemplation with his wife: *"Leah, I was on the ground; I knew I was shot; then somehow I wasn't myself but something much more. I knew in that instant that I would not die, that I could not die— not yet. It is for a reason, Leah. Everything . . . Volanko, the bullet, everything."*

With this divine intervention, second only to his meeting with Champion Volanko, Joseph began his incarnation as the Mighty Atom, who would inspire people all over the world by demonstrating not merely the power of his body but the power of the human mind and spirit.

Once a premature infant fed with an eyedropper, Joseph

became not only the strongest man on Earth but also a loving and faithful husband, a father to 10 children, a showman, a citizen, an inventor, and a lecturer on physical culture and health—a man of his time and beyond his time.

By harnessing a force from beyond the physical realm, Joseph Greenstein, the Mighty Atom, showed a way to transcend apparent limits by uniting the powers of mind, will, courage, and spirit. Until Joseph passed away, he continued to inspire and teach all who came to him. The Mighty Atom's life and teachings would have made Champion Volanko, the divine strongman who intervened in his life, very proud indeed.

Vision Powers of Tunkashila

Preserving the Spirit of a People

Among all of the peoples on Earth, the Native Americans are known for their spiritual democracy. For they know that any person, young or old, can receive divine vision-guidance from Tunkashila, the Great Spirit who created and inhabits Earth and sky, thunder and lightning, wind and rain, and who pervades all living things. In the tribal tradition, a young brave would venture alone into the wilderness to fast and pray until he received a sacred vision by which he might live. The greatest warriors, healers, and holy men were those to whom great visions were given. The power of Tunkashila, it is said, pours through such a one like abundant rain.

So it was with Black Elk, the Oglala Sioux warrior, healer, and holy man. Born in 1863—a sad time for Native Americans, losing ground in their battle against the ever-encroaching white men—Black Elk grew up still hopeful that his people might survive as a great nation. From the beginning, his life was colored by the wrenching violence of that era. The Battle of a Hundred Slain, a Sioux victory over the white soldiers—a battle that crippled his father—was one of his earliest memories. "I remember that Winter of the Hundred Slain as a man might remember a bad dream," he later recalled. "It is like some fearful thing in a fog, a time when everything seemed troubled and afraid."

By the age of four, Black Elk first began to hear spirit voices calling him. When he was five, while riding his horse in the woods, he met his spirit guides. "I looked up at the clouds and two men were coming there, headfirst like arrows slanting down; and as they came they sang a sacred song and the thunder was like drumming. 'Behold,' they sang, 'a sacred voice is calling you; all over the sky, a sacred voice is calling.'"

Over the next four years, in this time of change, Black Elk continued to hear the voices calling to him from time to time, but he did not understand what they wanted from him. Then, in his ninth year, while he was eating in a tepee, a voice spoke to him loud and clear, saying, "It is time; now they are calling you."

He went outside to look, but he saw nothing. Suddenly, his legs began to hurt; the next day, he collapsed and became ill. As he lay in his tepee looking through the open flap at the sky, he saw the two men come down again like arrows from the clouds. Black Elk's first great vision had begun. "Each warrior now carried a long spear from which jagged lightning flashed. I went out to meet them, feeling light as a spirit. A cloud descended and lifted me into the air, where I was summoned before the six Grandfather Spirits. So I went in and stood before the six, and they looked older than men can ever be—old like hills, like stars."

These ancient sky warriors revealed to Black Elk many things about himself, his people, and their tragic future. They gave him gifts of power, among them a wooden cup of water in which he saw the sky, and a warrior's bow. The water was the water of life, whose power was the power to heal. The bow was a weapon of war, whose power was the power to destroy.

Black Elk then witnessed an apocalyptic vision that rivals in its mythic depth and complexity the great visions of the biblical prophets. It lasted for 12 days. When it ended, he found himself standing on the plain, far from his village. He walked quickly home, entered his tepee, and saw his parents sitting beside a sick boy who was covered with a blanket. That boy lying there was Black Elk himself. In the next moment, he found himself back in his body, under the blanket.

After Black Elk had rejoined his earthly form, his vision shone strong in his mind. "I could see it all again and feel the meaning with a part of me like a strange power glowing in my body." Being only nine years old, he could not yet fully understand all that he had seen—its meanings would unfold over time—but this vision would remain imprinted in his memory and spirit for the rest of his life. "Nothing I have ever seen with my eyes was so clear and bright as what my vision revealed; no words I have ever heard with my ears were like the words I heard. I did not have to remember these things; they have remembered themselves all these years . . . even now I know that more was shown to me than I can tell."

Haunted by all that he had seen, Black Elk spent much time in solitude, thinking of it. But he told no one. "I wanted to be alone; it seemed I no longer belonged to my people, but to the spirit world. . . . I could not make myself eat much; and my father and mother thought that I was still sick, but I was not—only homesick for the place where I had been."

Black Elk was destined to become, just like the visionary leaders before him, a warrior, holy man, and sacred healer of the Sioux nation. While still a boy, he took part in the battle of Little Big Horn, where General Custer made his foolhardy charge on the Sioux. And as a young man, he followed the great warrior Crazy Horse, the holy man and hero who always charged into battle ahead of his warriors, crying, "Hoka Hey! It is a good day to die!"

Crazy Horse had also received a great vision in child-hood—in his case, he was given the power to fight like a spirit warrior whom arrows and bullets could not touch. His vision had given him the power to avoid all wounds in battle. His skin was never broken, even though he often led the charge where the white soldiers' bullets were thick as rain. Like many spirit-led souls, Crazy Horse did not fear death; he had foreseen in a vision the exact manner of his death and met it bravely when it came.

Black Elk himself fought in many battles and healed many Sioux by the power that flowed through him. Some visions that foreshadowed what was to come were not of the spirit world, but nightmarish events in this world: One of the first braves to arrive after the Wounded Knee massacre, he found the bodies of several hundred of his tribe, mostly women and children, killed as they fled, scattered like dark patches in the white fields, slowly covered by flakes of falling snow.

"When I saw this," said Black Elk, "I wished I had died, too."

At last, the Sioux realized that the waves of white men would never end—that they would wash over the land, claiming it for their own—that the Sioux and other tribes would become like ghosts, their way of life snatched forever from their hands. But even when this world seemed senseless, the spiritual power of his childhood vision sustained Black Elk and gave him a sense of purpose and a reason for living. His visions and healing powers also gave strength to his people in this most tragic era.

Years later, he would tour Europe with Buffalo Bill's Wild West show and perform for Queen Victoria. In his heart, he remained a holy man and a healer seeking to keep the old ways alive so that the spirit of his people might survive.

Near the end of his life, Black Elk sometimes grieved, believing that he had failed to live up to his vision and preserve the sacred ways of his people. Even though he had the power to foresee many things, he did not see his own greatness or know that he had accomplished his purpose. By sharing his life in his spiritual autobiography—by revealing the visions that Tunkashila had granted him—Black Elk passed on knowledge that would help rekindle the Native American movement and generate a renaissance of Indian spirituality among generations of Americans. This great warrior, holy man, and healer fulfilled his divine destiny by helping to preserve forever—as long as the grass grows and the wind blows—the sacred ways and spirit of the Oglala Lakota Sioux.

When the Sun Danced

New Light on the Miracle at Fatima

In 1915, Lucia dos Santos, an eight-year-old shepherd girl in Fatima, Portugal, was reciting the rosary near her flock when a human form shimmering within a luminous cloud appeared to her. According to her testimony, the apparition visited her three more times that year.

If they had ended there, such visitations may have been dismissed as the active stirrings of a young girl's imagination. But the following year, the same shining form appeared to Lucia and to her two young cousins, Francisco and Jacinta Marto. The children had sought shelter from a storm in a small cave. While playing near the cave entrance, they heard a distant roar and looked out over the trees in the valley below to see a sphere of white light, like a glowing cloud, soaring toward them. When it stopped to hover nearby, they saw an angel within—an exquisitely beautiful young man.

"I am the Angel of Peace," he said. He taught them a

prayer, then vanished. In a rapture, the children repeated the prayer for hours until they swooned with exhaustion.

The angel returned that summer and urgently told them to pray. The following autumn, he again appeared in the cave and administered Communion before departing. Each time, over-whelmed by this mysterious apparition, the children fell into a deep trancelike state.

For a while, they kept these visits a secret. But in 1917, the three children's miracle became a series of mass events—super-natural encounters with an awesome power that directly im-pacted and transformed the lives of nearly 100,000 people, and indirectly, millions more. The following chronicle highlights these recurring visitations, each viewed by growing crowds of awestruck witnesses.

On May 13, the three shepherd children were surprised by a flash of brilliant white light. They walked toward it into a nearby hollow and were momentarily blinded by a bright glowing sphere, in the midst of which stood a tiny woman. She told them she came from heaven and asked them to return to the same spot each month thereafter.

A month later to the day, the children returned as re-quested. This time, 50 people accompanied them. The wit-nesses saw the children kneel and speak to thin air, their faces transfigured with unearthly light. The children all saw the Lady of Light as Mary, Mother of Christ. The meeting ended with a loud explosion. Then, a small cloud of light, visible to all, rose above the tree beside which the children knelt.

The following month, a crowd of 4,500 people watched the children converse with the air. Many heard a buzzing drone; the sun grew dim and lost heat; then a small luminous cloud materialized around the tree and, with a sharp explosion, departed toward the east.

The children revealed several prophecies made by the lady in the cloud, all of which came true. She told them that the present war would soon end (World War I ended a year later)—but added, "If people do not stop offending God, a worse war will begin during the reign of Pius XI." (World War II began in 1939, the last year of Pope Pius's reign.) The lady also told the children that "if Russia was not converted, she will spread her errors throughout the world." All these prophecies are documented in records made that same year.

On August 13 of that year, an estimated 18,000 people now gathered at the mysterious hollow. The three children were absent, confined by a skeptical official who pressured them to recant their story of Mary's miraculous appearances or else tell him the secrets she had revealed. When they refused, he separated them and told each that the others had been killed for refusing to talk. Still they remained silent. Meanwhile, the crowd at the hollow heard a loud thunderclap; then, with a bright flash, a luminous cloud formed, rose, and evaporated like mist. High above, the clouds turned the color of blood, then pink, yellow, and blue. The sun shone through, bathing the crowd in mists of rainbow light. Strange petals fell from the sky, vanishing before they touched the ground.

Six days later, Lucia and her cousins were tending their sheep when the temperature dropped abruptly. Once again, rainbow colors, witnessed by thousands, filled the countryside. The crowds who now followed the children saw a bright flash, and a luminous cloud enfolded the tree. In the center stood a radiant woman dressed in gold and white. Everyone fell to their knees, "their souls in rapture," according to reports. The woman spoke to the children and asked them to "make sacrifices for sinners." She then rose into the air and flew slowly east. All heard a roaring like the sound of great winds.

On September 13, a small army of 30,000 now-converted souls blanketed the meadows around the tree in the hollow where the children waited. Around noon, the sun dimmed, though the sky was clear. The air erupted with the cries of thousands as a luminous sphere approached from the east and descended to rest upon the tree by the children. The sphere became a cloud from which shining petals fell once again, melting away to nothing before touching the outstretched hands of the multitude. The lady in the center of the sphere spoke with Lucia, promising a miracle on the 13th day of October. She then ascended in her cocoon of light and before the eyes of the astonished onlookers, sped straight up and disappeared into the sun. Among the thousands of witnesses were two priests who had come specifically to expose the now-famous miracles as a sham. The two devout skeptics were converted on the spot.

By October 13, the day of the prophesied miracle, word had spread far and wide—70,000 people stood in the pouring rain beneath thick gray clouds surrounding the hollow where the children sat. At noon came a flash of light accompanied by "a strange sweet fragrance." The three children, their faces radiant, conversed briefly with the lady in the sphere of light.

Then the apparition ascended, the rain stopped, and the thick clouds parted dramatically. The sun now appeared as a shining silver disk. As thousands of witnesses later testified, the silver sun spun rapidly, throwing off brilliant beams of colored light in all directions. *Our Lady of Fatima* author William Thomas Walsh interviewed many witnesses and recounted the event as it was described to him. *"While they gazed, the huge ball began to 'dance.' . . . Now it whirled rapidly like a gigantic fire-wheel for some time with dizzy, sickening speed. Finally there appeared on the rim a border of crimson, which flung across the sky blood-red streamers of flame, reflecting to the earth, to the trees and shrubs, to the upturned faces and the clothes all sorts of brilliant colors in succession: green, red, orange, blue, violet, the whole spectrum. Madly gyrating in this manner three times, the fiery orb seemed to tremble, to shudder, and then to plunge precipitately, in a mighty zigzag, toward the crowd."*

Tens of thousands flung themselves upon the muddy earth, praying for their lives and their souls. At the last moment, the disk reversed its apocalyptic descent and the real sun, hidden behind it, appeared above. At tremendous speed, the silver disk ascended and flew into the sun. Incredibly, these events had lasted a full 10 minutes. The astonished multitude, drenched only minutes before, found their rain-sodden clothes *completely dried*. And hundreds of people had been miraculously cured of various injuries and illnesses—cancers, wounds, and crippling diseases. Many went home weeping, shaken to their cores.

Thousands of lives were profoundly altered that day, including those of people who had witnessed the miracle from as far away as 30 miles, from which distance the lights in the sky were clearly visible.

Forty-three years later—in 1960—a lawyer named Mendes, who was present at this "miracle at Fatima," testified to what many others also felt about its impact on their lives. "I still remember it today as vividly as at the moment it happened. I feel myself dominated by that extraordinary event."

Thousands of witnesses interviewed in a formal investigation undertaken by the Catholic Church described a wide range of phenomena. Some claimed to have seen two beings on a ladder descending from the sphere. Others saw the moon and stars appear in the sky, though it was midday. Miles away in other villages, people described objects and buildings reflecting the colors of the rainbow. Churches were filled to overflowing in every town.

Today, millions each year visit Fatima, Portugal, now a holy site where miraculous healings still occur. A final prophecy revealed to Lucia by the Lady of Fatima was sealed in an envelope and sent to the Vatican, with instructions that it be opened by the Pope in 1960. The envelope was, in fact, opened.

The secret has yet to be revealed to the world.

A Soldier's Healing

Vietnam Vet to Inspired Dramatist

Sean Kilcoyne was born in 1946 in the industrial city of Worcester, Massachusetts, to a blue-collar, Irish Catholic factory-working family. He attended church faithfully and served Mass as an altar boy for four years. Sean planned to be a priest, but changed his mind at the age of 12 after viewing the prospect of lifelong celibacy from the vantage point of puberty. Instead, he transferred his religious fervor into the secular arena and became the youngest Eagle Scout in Massachusetts's history.

As a teenager, Sean did summer work in factories, making nails and disemboweling chickens. He struggled through three high schools, finally graduated with honors, and was accepted into Holy Cross College. Feeling isolated in the elite upper-middle-class atmosphere, despite his election as school vice president, he quit after the first year and returned to factory work. Then, in 1966, he was drafted.

Like most Americans of that era, Sean had barely heard of

Vietnam. By now a lost Catholic with an innate spiritual opposition to war, he filed three appeals at his draft board to avoid military service. When the appeals were refused, he joined the marines, thinking the marines' discipline would improve his chances of survival. When Sean was ordered to Vietnam, he made a private vow that if he survived, he would create some meaningful art out of his war experience.

He arrived in Da Nang near Monkey Mountain as part of an ammunition convoy. That first day, his battalion drove into the countryside, past long lines of peasants on the side of the road carrying baskets and produce on their heads and bicycles. These wary peasants watched the soldiers with fear and resentment in their eyes. An eerie, unnerving scene followed—Sean saw soldiers swinging their rifles like golf clubs from the trucks. One broke a woman's arm; she wailed and clutched her maimed limb. Another soldier laughed and slammed his rifle butt into the back of an old man's head, knocking him down.

Repulsed by this inhumanity, Sean wept, feeling a shock of grief and fear that would haunt him far beyond the one year, one month, and one day of his remaining tour of duty in Vietnam. "The people I thought we'd come to help saw us as a malignant force—a significant part of their suffering—and they were right." The constant fear, the war's carnage, and a growing collective sense of futility, disillusionment, and betrayal took its toll on the young soldiers in this land far from home. They had entered a war where success was measured by body counts, where their lives were routinely gambled in reckless bids to increase already inflated statistics, where the enemy was a guerrilla army that attacked by surprise and then hid in its homeland's jungles.

The Vietnam War became notorious for creating a massive

culture of self-medicating drug abuse. Sean and his friends got drunk and stoned every night, and a substance-induced facade of sanity was maintained.

After Sean's service culminated in the Tet offensive, he returned home with a serious drug and alcohol habit. He walked his old neighborhood streets listening for the sound of gunfire that never came. His life had taken on a disorienting, surreal quality. One day, walking down a clean suburban street, he felt that all the houses were upside down. Alcohol seemed to help him manage his unnerving perceptions.

With dreams of changing the system, Sean returned to college on the GI Bill and graduated with a political-science degree. As director of research for urban affairs in the Massachusetts legislature, he led a team that co-authored a bill providing subsidized housing for the elderly. Sean seemed a natural for politics—until one day a reporter asked Sean if he planned to run for office. He replied, "I'm hesitant, but flexible." The next day, he read his own words in the newspaper and was disgusted by their "cunning ambiguity." Sean dropped out—he moved to Paris to write, make art, and pursue his drinking.

Within a year, he was living on the streets, warming his hands in the morning fires of ash cans. The war continued to fill his thoughts and haunt his dreams. Sean had left the war but could find no peace. So he moved to Guatemala and tried to lose himself in Mayan Indian villages. But one day, he woke up lying drunk on the ground in a jungle village and realized he was still trying to get back to Vietnam. It would take him years to understand why.

In 1976, Sean flew to Haight Ashbury in San Francisco. The Summer of Love had died and the Haight was now a paranoid pharmaceutical asylum. Sean recalls, "I drank and did drugs and hung out in strange bars with guys who locked themselves in their rooms, ate only cabbage, and worried about the FBI slipping microphones under their doors. Every day, I woke up, got drunk and high. By late morning, I'd be on the floor, howling under a mattress I'd pulled on top of myself. During the day, I walked the streets jabbering, angry, talking to myself about the lies, betrayal, and slaughter of the war. I was still in the jungle, on my way to becoming a village idiot. At night, I sat in front of my space heater, contemplating suicide. But refusing to die was the only thing that gave me a sense of power."

Then, one spring afternoon in 1978, as Sean walked aimlessly through the streets of San Francisco in a state of despair, he stopped at the curb for a red light on the corner of Ninth and Market Streets.

Both the light and his life were about to change.

Sean tells what happened next. "I looked up and saw a young angel, six inches tall, in white trousers, hovering in the air a foot off from my right temple. He was bare-chested, had white wings growing out of his back, and held a sledgehammer in his hands that he pounded silently on an anvil. Then I saw an identical angel off my left temple, also silently pounding a hammer on an anvil. In a flash, I felt a shock of awe as I saw my own darkness and fully opened to the wound at my center. I experienced the depth of desperation and savage anxiety that drove me out from under my mattress and into the streets.

"In that moment, I knew I wasn't alone—that my life wasn't going to end this way. As I gazed at these angels, incredible serenity filled me. These beings were aware of me, had come to help me, to protect me. I felt a quality of love and attention I'd never experienced before. These angels, pounding on their anvils, sent energy surging through my body. Somehow, this vision told me I had toughness and mettle. They saved my life."

The angels' intervention opened a calm space around Sean. He drank less as he pondered his vision and his life, examining his self-destructive patterns, considering how else he might live. He sought help at a veterans' hospital and began to confront his war trauma. Soon, Sean quit drinking and doing drugs and joined a therapy group with 20 vets. This was 1979, when the syndrome of post-traumatic stress disorder (PTSD) was just being identified. "Vietnam was the source of a sacred wound for many of us," he now says. "For years, it was my only connection with reality. I needed to somehow touch its significance, to keep it alive until I could deal with it."

Sean and others in his group joined a community-based veterans' organization called Swords to Plowshares. They began to devise tools for dealing with PTSD and worked with other traumatized vets—soldiers with "the thousand-yard stare" that came to be called frozen mourning. Sean later created a mental-health unit that contributed to our nation's understanding of PTSD.

As his healing continued, Sean recalled his former vow to make meaningful art out of his war experience; he also resolved to create a meaningful life out of his angelic vision. Fascinated with the mysteries of language, symbols, dreams, and sacred images—wanting to understand "the knowledge behind the knowledge," the hidden truths that give life meaning—Sean began creating ritual or sacred theater. First performing in the streets with other like-minded artists, he eventually began working with a professional group whose critically acclaimed pieces toured major U.S. and European cities. He also co-created a performance piece called *Angels/Anvils*, dedicated to his life-changing vision. On tour in 1989, *Angels/Anvils* received both popular and critical acclaim.

In 1990, Sean pursued his vision of "the theater of healing" by organizing a reconciliation ritual at the San Francisco War Memorial with both American and North Vietnamese war veterans, some of whom came from Vietnam to participate in the event. In 1991, during the Gulf War, Sean conceived and directed *The Boon*, a "performance grieving ritual" for war veterans and people of the Middle East, with Robert Bly, Malidoma Some, Mathew Fox, and others.

Today, Sean Kilcoyne lives and works as an avant-garde artist and "a grateful agent of conscious evolution." Of his life and work, he says, "On my way to die, I was brought back and given a life. I keep faith with my vision by healing and creating. This is the source of the meaning in my life and the inspiration for my work."

Hope and a Prayer

Divine Help in a Desperate Moment

The car, cruising down Monterey Boulevard, swerved suddenly onto the Highway 1 exit ramp and sped out of town into the night. The driver, Lee, a 40-year-old South Vietnamese soldier, turned to his lone female passenger, a 20-year-old foreign student from Beijing. "I have a gun," he said. "Do what I say or I will kill you!"

Lee was a busboy in the Chinese restaurant where Jenny worked as a waitress. One of her co-workers always drove her home after work. But Lee, who had offered her a ride home tonight, had another plan. Jenny watched her abductor in terror as he turned to her, his face illuminated by the dashboard lights. His left eye gleamed crazily—his right eye was gone, a maimed slit of pink flesh, ruined in the war.

Lee spoke again, his voice harsh. "I'm going to rape you and dump you in a field. Obey me if you want to live."

Jenny had come to America seeking a new life. Now, on

this dark night, it seemed the remainder of her life might be counted in minutes as Lee's car sped along the pitch-black highway.

"I don't want to die!" she murmured, her eyes filling with tears.

Desperately, Jenny searched for options, knowing she was no match for this experienced combat veteran. Looking down at her door, she considered leaping out of the car, but at this speed, the fall would surely kill her.

Seeing her gaze toward the door, Lee roared, "You can't open the door. It's an automatic lock!"

Jenny had ridden in few cars and didn't know whether to believe him or not. Then, oddly, a minor incident from a week before flashed through her mind. Jenny, still struggling with English, working two jobs, missing her family, and feeling out of place in America, must have let her sadness show in her face, because a young woman she was waiting on at the restaurant said to her before leaving, "You seem unhappy—you really ought to try praying. It works."

Jenny had found these do-gooder words irritating and irrelevant—she would have preferred a generous tip. What was the use of mumbling superstitious words to some imaginary God? In China, the Party had taught her that religious people were weak and fearful—mental cripples believing in fairy tales. She believed, like Marx, that religion was the opiate of the masses.

Now, abducted by a dangerous madman in a speeding car on a dark highway, about to be raped and possibly murdered, the idea of praying to a powerful being who might help her in this terrifying situation seemed compelling and perhaps her only remaining option. "Deciding to give prayer my first and maybe last try, I closed my eyes and prayed desperately, 'Dear God, if you exist, please help me!' I aimed my prayer like an arrow straight to God. To my surprise, I began to feel a calm strength entering me."

As Jenny prayed, the car suddenly lurched and the tires squealed. She opened her eyes to find that Lee had inexplicably swerved off the highway onto an entry ramp heading back into town. He turned onto a main thoroughfare and they drove through the city under bright streetlights in evening traffic. Though baffled, she continued praying, eyes open, searching the road, her mind crystal clear: "Please God, give me strength!"

As they approached an intersection, the light turned red. Incredibly, Lee pulled to a stop—right across the street from a police car with its blue and red lights fluttering. A police-woman stood on the roadside writing a ticket for the car she had pulled over.

Jenny knew this was her moment of truth. If God had helped her to this point, she must now help herself. Filled with strength, still praying, she grabbed her book bag and pulled on the door handle, not knowing if it would open. It did. Lee reached out and grabbed her arm, but she pulled away with all her might and ran across four lanes toward the policewoman, feeling stronger than ever before.

When the light changed, Lee's car pulled away with squealing tires. The police caught him half an hour later.

"This experience shook my belief system like an earth-quake," Jenny says today, 12 years later. "I grew up in China during the Cultural Revolution. I watched my family and country destroyed. I never saw God help anyone. My high school science curriculum included philosophical arguments for atheism: 'The world is matter, and consciousness, only a by-product of matter, is extinguished at the moment of death. So-called miracles and supernatural powers are coincidences based on pseudo-science and superstition—peasant mentality.'

"But a divine power saved my life—I have no doubt of it. All my philosophical arguments blew away like dust in the wind. I began to understand that not everything can be scientifically explained and measured, reduced to atoms, chemical elements, and basic particles.

"This incident was a turning point in my life. Indirectly, it taught me that the most important things in life—kindness, love, faith, integrity—can't be found in a test tube. Yet these qualities are real; they can move mountains or save lives. I wasn't surprised when my parents and friends called my experience luck and my belief in God an illusion. I only know that I was about to die. And when I prayed, a power and calmness came over me, my kidnapper turned off the highway, drove me back into town, and stopped in front of a police car.

"Now I know I'm watched over, that a divine power exists. And the more I align myself with this power by living with integrity and faith, the better my life becomes. It's almost . . . scientific."

Faith That Moves Mountains

A Camel Herder Becomes a Prophet

On an otherwise ordinary day, an angel appeared to a young merchant and former camel herder, known by all in the city where he was born. The angel's words filled him with awe and dread—it told him that he was to defy his people's ancestral religion, to denounce 360 deities carved in stone and worshipped for centuries, to declare himself the prophet of a single God, to abolish a way of life upon which countless lives and beliefs were founded—and establish a new religion out of nothing. Surely, he would be met with incredulity, rejection, violent persecution, and exile. Could his seemingly mad quest bring anything but failure—or at best, a martyr's death?

Or would this mortal, obedient to the divine command of an angel, achieve a victory beyond any that reason could have foretold?

He was born in Mecca in A.D. 570. His father died before his birth. His devastated mother, unable to nurse him, named him Muhammad and gave him to a nursemaid—a shepherdess in a band of Bedouins. Muhammad spent his first five years with these nomads, living a hardy, open-air existence following the grazing flocks through desert grass and scrub, sleeping in tents beneath a vast desert sky. Once weaned, he drank camel's milk and ate mostly rice, dates, wild birds, and locusts fried in oil. From the beginning, the desert claimed Muhammad as its own. He would always be a Bedouin at heart.

At age six, he returned to his mother, but she died later that year. He ended up living with an uncle, a caravan merchant. In the years that followed, Muhammad traveled throughout Arabia with his uncle's caravans, learning the wisdom of the desert, the ways of business, and the art of war as they fought off bands of marauders. His travels took him into close contact with various tribes and religions—Judaism, Christianity, and the Arab sects who worshiped hundreds of gods and goddesses in the form of stone idols. These experiences made a deep impression on this thoughtful, introspective youth. From these early threads, the tapestry of his fate was woven.

He grew into a handsome young man admired for his strong character, moral integrity, and sharp mind. But he had come to a merchant's life more by chance than choice. Disinterested in money and drawn to solitude, he left the caravan to work as a shepherd in the desert for months at time.

When he was 25, Muhammad took a position in a trading company owned by a beautiful woman 15 years his senior. Her name was Khadija. For two years, he led Khadija's caravans throughout Arabia, rising to the position of company manager. Not surprisingly, Khadija fell in love with him. Finally, she proposed to him through an intermediary. Their marriage, which blessed them with six daughters, would last until Khadija's death 21 years later.

But almost as soon as the wedding ceremony had ended, Muhammad's mind again turned inward. His encounters with so many cultures and religions had planted hidden seeds within him that began to grow. He found himself pondering how the 360 stone gods in the temple of Mecca could save souls. Such questions drew him to once again search his own soul in the solitude of the desert.

Muhammad began spending his days in a cave in the hills outside Mecca, fasting, praying, and meditating. Sleeping little, he began to enter altered states and have waking visions—to experience the inner life of a mystic. At times, violent trembling seized him and he lost consciousness. A practical man of robust health who had endured many grueling journeys across the desert, he found these phenomena strange and disturbing. But these inner quakes that he feared might be harbingers of failing health were actually the premonitory tremors of a great awakening.

One night in the holy month of Ramadan in his 40th year, while fasting and praying in his desert cave, Muhammad heard a voice calling him with great urgency. Looking up in the darkness of his cave, he saw an angel standing before him, emanating a dazzling light. Muhammad fainted with fear; when he awoke, he found the angel still standing there.

"Read, thou," the angel commanded him in a voice of stern authority.

"I cannot," Muhammad stammered, for he could barely read.

"Read, thou," the angel commanded him again in verse, "in the name of the Lord who created all things, who created man from a clot. Read in the name of the Most High who taught man the use of the pen and taught him what before he knew not."

In awe, Muhammad repeated these words, memorizing each one. Then the angel said, "Muhammad, thou art the messenger of Allah, and I am his angel, Gabriel."

With that, the angel vanished.

In stunned exaltation, Muhammad went and told Khadija what had happened. She embraced him and unequivocally expressed her faith in his vision and his mission, saying, "Rejoice, dear husband. He who holds in His hands the life of Khadija is my witness that thou wilt be the messenger of His people."

But Muhammad could not accept his own vision. How could he, an ordinary man so far from perfection, be such a messenger? He feared that he might be deluded or perhaps insane. Days passed. He waited for another sign, for further confirmation so that he might believe in himself and know how to proceed. But no sign came.

At last, he returned to the cave on Mount Hira, seeking the angel Gabriel. He waited and prayed, but to no avail. In despair, haunted by terrible doubts and assailed by fears of madness, Muhammad climbed onto a precipice and prepared to leap to his death. At that very moment, the angel appeared before him again and, raising his hands, repeated, "I am Gabriel, and thou art Muhammad, the Messenger of Allah." Muhammad froze on the edge of the chasm in a spellbound trance. Hours passed. That night, one of Khadija's servants came and found Muhammad still perched on a crag, lost in ecstasy, and led him home.

After that event, Muhammad began to quietly spread the revelation of his new faith among only a few close friends and family members. But in this tightly knit culture, word spread quickly. Before long, his persecution began—gossip, brutal beatings, plots against him, and attempts against his life. Over time, his honesty and virtue, the words of scripture revealed through him, and the mysterious workings of fate brought about the conversions of several of Mecca's greatest warriors. All this greatly strengthened the fledgling faith of Islam and drove fear into the hearts of its enemies.

People demanded that he perform miracles as proof of his divine mission. Muhammad answered that he had not come to perform miracles; he had come to preach the word of Allah. Challenged to move a mountain, he gazed toward it but it did not budge, so he spoke the now-famous words demonstrating his wisdom, humor, and humility: "If the mountain will not come to Muhammad, then Muhammad will go to the mountain."

From beginning to end, Muhammad acknowledged himself as an ordinary man, full of faults and limitations—a man chosen by God, for reasons he did not understand, to deliver a new revelation of Islam, which means "submission to God." Islam required faith in God, charity, purity, and a life free of idols, lived with the courage of a warrior in battle, with prayer as a cleansing immersion in His spirit.

The citizens of Mecca were roused to fury by Muhammad's attack on their cherished idols—and by his declaration that there was but one God, named Allah, and that he, Muhammad, was His prophet. Forced to flee across the desert to the city of Medina, he began his mission anew, once again a lonely prophet with a handful of followers in a city of unbelievers.

Over time, the angel Gabriel revealed scripture to Muhammad, which he recited aloud and which Khadija and others wrote down. This scripture became known as the Holy Koran (Quran). The Koran was Muhammad's defining miracle—the writing of this masterpiece of poetic religious scripture by a simple, semiliterate man might in itself have earned him fame as a prophet. But this feat was only one chapter in the life of Muhammad.

Persecuted as a heretic for nearly two decades by the people of Mecca, including many of his own relatives and former friends, the once young Bedouin became in old age a fearless military general. More than once, Mecca's army laid siege, seeking to destroy Medina, where Muhammad and his followers lived—their war would not end until Muhammad or Mecca fell. In the final battle, while outnumbered three to one but filled with the power of Allah, Muhammad and his followers descended like a storm upon the Meccan army and destroyed it. This battle turned the tide.

Within one century, Islam's armies conquered the Arabian continent city by city, turning its legions to the worship of Allah, the God of Abraham, Moses, and Christ. Spreading more rapidly than any religion in history, Islam is today one of the three great world religions, revealed through an ordinary man, a camel herder whom Allah made his prophet by the power of divine intervention.

How Death Teaches Life

Revelations from the Eyes of an Infant

Grace sometimes appears in the form of adversity. This was the case for author and healer Chris Griscom, whose painful encounters with death changed the course of her life. Like many of us in the Western world, Chris was blessed with relative freedom from the devastating forces of war, famine, and plague that still afflict millions worldwide. But in the 1960s, while serving in the Peace Corps, Chris came to know many souls who walked in the valley of the shadow of death.

Before she began working with indigenous peoples in El Salvador, Bolivia, and Paraguay, death kept a respectable distance. "Death was a foreign language to me, an abstract idea," she reports. "I had never experienced its sounds, its smells, its devastation, or imagined that it would shape my destiny. But in parts of Latin America, death is right in your face, right in your heart."

One day, in a small village in El Salvador, Chris, still

cloaked in innocence, met death in the form of an infant girl whom she held while waiting for the overworked doctor to attend to her. Chris looked down into the eyes of this strangely quiet child cradled in her arms, unprepared for what was about to happen. "Suddenly, those eyes swept past me, or through me, into some unimaginable void, and with an unforgettable shudder, she died. In one timeless flash of perception, my brain recorded every minute detail—the final expulsion of air, the smell of already putrefying flesh, her empty eyes, and an inexplicable sensation of a weight change in my arms."

With a scream, Chris flung the lifeless child into the doctor's arms and fled. Unprepared for such an intimate encounter with death, her entire being recoiled with the feeling— "Not in *my* arms!" Unable to erase the imprint or forget the moment, she felt "a profound sense of contamination." This incident shattered her youthful innocence, ended her denial of death's reality.

The next night, Chris awoke in the darkness to see the dead girl's spirit form facing her. Surrounded by brilliant light, this apparition communicated a profound message with great compassion before fading back into the night: "The choice of my death was my own; the time of my death was my gift to you." Chris's vision and her haunting sense of a timeless connection to this child whom she had known only minutes on this Earth left her "in a breathless state of expanded awareness and awe" and with an absolute certainty that "we are more than these bodies."

The child's funeral was held in a small, one-room adobe house. Her tiny body, dressed in white, was surrounded by flower petals. "As I stepped forward to enter," Chris recalls, "her mother rushed up and gave me such an urgent embrace that I gasped in surprise, for her tear-drenched face was full of light-ness. . . . She ushered me up to the coffin and . . . said joyously, 'God has taken her. She is with God!' Stunned, I looked around at all of the people gathered there, and I saw with my heart that they had apparently surrendered this child, . . . celebrating her reunion with God. In that moment, I consciously became a seeker of life's spiritual truths."

Death became Chris's greatest teacher. As she later writes, "No grand intellectual truth or concept could compare to the breathtaking power of surrender I witnessed in that village of Dulce Nombre de Maria, El Salvador." She adds, "Whether the fates deemed me a slow learner, or God just wanted to test my capacity to surrender, I was to hold other innocents at the mo-ment of death. . . . Each time I felt an excruciating pierce to the heart, followed by an increasing capacity to surrender to God. I witnessed, as well as experienced, depths of sorrow and pain . . . transmuted into heights of ecstasy. Faces of light. Faces of God. Surrender was the vehicle of that transformation. The shock of death brought me to life."

Chris was to become intimately acquainted with the angel of death, who would open her to an expansive life and teach her other lessons about the courage to surrender: At age 40, in a Mexican hospital while being treated for a relatively minor wound, Chris was given an anesthetic to which she was al-lergic—her heart and breathing stopped. "My awareness under-went the most fantastic energetic explosions as it pulled up and out of my body and entered into a dimension of light."

In this—the first of six near-death experiences Chris Griscom would encounter—she was unconscious and near death for an hour. When she returned, further tests revealed a severely damaged left ventricle. Her doctors recommended bypass surgery but the operation had to be postponed due to a severe case of typhoid fever Chris had contracted.

It turned out to be a blessing in disguise.

"As often happens during episodes of profound illness," she says, "a strange clarity or expansion of awareness enabled me to perceive my light body as distinct from the one lying on the bed. Guided by this clarity, . . . I superimposed the heart of my light body onto my damaged physical heart so as to re-imprint the structure of that heart."

To some this may seem a metaphysical abstraction; yet within three days, the doctors were shaking their heads, saying, "This can't be—we have a different electrocardiograph reading."

For Chris, this incident demonstrated that she had "tapped into the light energy that holds the blueprint of the physical body and merged into (her) physical cells, exciting them to create something completely new." While this may also seem far-fetched, recent discoveries in cellular biology show that our cells can instantaneously and measurably respond to our visualizations, and by this means, we can intentionally stimulate remarkable healing processes that appear, in many respects, miraculous.

Today, Chris Griscom, mother of six, teacher, healer, writer, and founder of the Light Institute in Galisteo, New Mexico, writes, "All of (the body's) expressions are party to the energies that move through it. We can become aware of these energies and influence them. Our bodies are capable of feats of which we have not yet even dreamed."

Unexpected Journeys

A Businessman Explores Out-of-Body Realms

In the spring of 1958," wrote Robert Monroe, "I was living a reasonably normal life with a reasonably normal family."

At the time, Robert, a successful businessman and writer of music for television and radio, owned five radio stations with offices on Madison Avenue. Then, with no preparation and without apparent reason, Robert was catapulted beyond his body into ethereal realms usually reserved for great saints and mystics.

Although he could not explain how or why his uncommon adventure began, he knows precisely when. One Sunday afternoon, with his wife and two children at church, Robert lay down on the living room couch to take a nap. "I had just become prone," he wrote, "when a beam or ray seemed to come out of the sky to the north at about a 30 degree angle from the horizon. It was like being struck by a warm light. . . . The effect when the beam struck my entire body was to cause it to shake violently—to vibrate. I was utterly powerless to move of my own volition. It was as if I were held in a vise."

This same phenomenon repeated itself nine times over the next six weeks—gentle relaxation became a sudden violent trembling. Fearing epilepsy or a brain tumor, Robert went to his doctor, who pronounced him in perfect health. But that very night, after he lay down to sleep, it happened again. This time, he decided to observe, rather than fight, this phenomenon. The vibrations swept up and down his body for five minutes, then slowly stopped. Whenever it happened after that, he simply witnessed it as objectively as he could. He observed an image of a "flaming electric ring" passing from his head to his feet, sweeping up and down in "a great roaring surge." Robert reported that he could feel the vibrations in his brain.

One night, after the now-familiar phenomena occurred, Robert suddenly found himself floating near the ceiling. Disoriented, he first thought the ceiling was a wall. Then he turned over, looked down, and saw his wife in bed with a man lying beside her. It took him a moment to realize . . . the man was him.

Until now, he had feared he might be out of his mind; now, it appeared he was out of his body. Thinking that he must be dying, he "dove back in," opened his eyes, got up, moved around. He felt fine, although stunned by the undeniable reality that "he" was something other than, or at least not limited to, his body.

The vibrations came six more times before he dared to try to leave his body again. At his next attempt, he went out effortlessly. So began the "astral" career of Robert Monroe, a modern pioneer who would explore more uncharted, nonphysical realms and spaces than any man since the great seventeenth-century mystic Emmanuel Swedenborg.

Over the next four decades, Robert Monroe was to become the world's premier out-of-body (OOB) researcher. In his meticulous journals and books, he recorded thousands of OOB explorations, detailing the realms he visited and discoveries he made in his excursions through time and space. He also described various entities he met, from highly evolved spiritual beings and guides to other astral adventurers, lost souls, lucid dreamers, ordinary sleepers in OOB dream states—and even the spirits of the dead.

On one such journey, Robert was drawn to a bedridden boy around 10 years old. The boy, ill and afraid, was aware of Robert's presence. Robert attempted to comfort him, then left, promising to return.

"Several weeks later," Robert wrote, "I left the physical. . . . The same boy moved into view. He saw me and moved close to me. He was bewildered, but not afraid."

Robert instinctively knew the boy had died.

"What do I do now?" the boy asked him. "Where do I go?"

At a loss, Robert put his arm around the boy's shoulder and told him that some "friends" would soon come and take him where he needed to go.

"The next day," Robert said, "the newspaper carried the story of the death of a 10-year-old boy after a lingering illness. He had died in the afternoon, shortly before I had begun the experiment."

What makes Monroe's work especially compelling is the objective methods and technology he used to investigate and verify these decidedly subjective experiences. In the early years, he corroborated events however he could. Once, while sailing out-of-body down the main street of the town where he lived, he noticed a white car up on the grease rack of a local service station, with both back tires removed. Immediately upon returning to his body, he got in his car and drove to the station. There he found the same white car suspended on the racks, the back tires off just as he had seen.

Over years of research and experience, a bigger picture began to emerge of the multidimensional nature of the universe and the various spiritual beings, including ourselves, who inhabit it.

Robert Monroe's three books, beginning with *Journeys out of the Body*, describe a universe of intersecting realms inhabited by nonphysical beings, essentially spirits, who incarnate, or take on bodies, for purposes of higher education, spiritual growth, or even sheer adventure. The human journey begins, he says, with a soul's disorienting descent into the depths of matter, to the point of total identification with the body and the physical world. Yet the soul is infused with a desire to re-ascend, via spiritual growth, to the blissful freedom of its ultimate "home" in the light that many call God.

In 1971, Robert Monroe founded the Monroe Institute, a research center devoted to the study of out-of-body phenomena. This was the first time such studies had ever been done using scientific controls and technology—many of which Monroe invented himself.

Over the next two decades, tens of thousands of volunteer researchers, wired and monitored, made hundreds of thousands of "journeys," within their minds and often out of their bodies, afterward reporting their findings in great detail. Monroe used this research to map various states of consciousness and to train others to alter their own consciousness at will. And the technology he helped create is today being used in a wide variety of fields, from health and medicine to higher learning.

Robert Monroe left his body for the last time on Saint Patrick's Day 1995. He never determined the source of that beam of light that triggered his astral career nor the identities of the spiritual entities who assisted and guided him (though he did suspect that one of these entities was himself, far in the future). But his experiences, research, and writings have enlarged our understanding of our spiritual nature and the universe in which we live. They also offer a plausible explanation of our purpose here on earth, while providing an intriguing map and guidelines for our ascent into realms beyond the body.

An Unlikely Pilgrim

One Woman's 28-Year Trek for Peace

Mildred Norman was born on a small New Jersey chicken farm in 1908. A review of her youth provides few clues to the divine destiny that lay ahead. Her family attended no church and adhered to no particular religion. She graduated from high school, got a job, wore makeup, bought nice clothes, drove a fancy car, went out on dates, and wrote amateur plays for a local Grange group.

The momentum of conventional living carried Mildred into marriage just as America fell into the Great Depression. Her husband had trouble finding work, and later, due to different fundamental values, their paths eventually diverged and the marriage ended. In this time of crisis, Mildred began to question her entire existence and its meaning. It was a turning point and a time of preparation for her life to come.

The seeds of her future were beginning to sprout; out of

her inner search came new directions along the mountain paths she would hike—the solitude in the midst of nature's companionship brought clarity as she prepared for something she couldn't yet name. In one six-month period, Mildred ended up hiking the entire length of the 2,158-mile Appalachian Trail—the first woman to do so.

Near the end of that journey came a revelation that was to shape the rest of her life. In her journal, she wrote, "At the age of 30, out of desperation, and a deep longing for a more meaningful way of life, while walking alone in the woods one night, I came to a moonlit glade and prayed. In that moment, I felt a complete willingness, without any reservations, to give my life—to dedicate my life—to service. 'Please use me!' I prayed to God. A great peace came over me." By morning's light, her old life was finished.

But Mildred Norman's spiritual preparation had only begun.

Nothing in her early years had foreshadowed this transformation. Many family members, friends, and neighbors, dismayed by the changes in her, dropped out of her life. What followed was 15 years of testing—a war between what she called her "lower, self-centered nature" and her "higher, God-centered nature."

Struggling to integrate the spiritual awakening that came to her that night on her Appalachian journey, Mildred spent more and more time serving—working with senior citizens and the emotionally disturbed and volunteering for various peace organizations. During this time, she slowly rid herself of unnecessary possessions, attachments, and useless activities. A pacifist and early advocate of voluntary simplicity, she pared her life to the bone. She now owned only two dresses—one to wear while the other was in the wash.

Her years of preparation culminated one morning in a second illumination, on her daily silent walk in nature. "All of a sudden I felt more uplifted than ever before—I knew time-lessness, spacelessness, and lightness—I did not seem to be walking on the earth. Every bush, every tree seemed to wear a halo . . . a light emanation around everything and flecks of gold fell like slanted rain through the air. The most important part was not the phenomena . . . it was the realization of the unity of all creation."

With this realization, the preparatory phase of her life ended and a new life began. She changed her name to Peace Pilgrim and resolved to walk across the length and breadth of North America, speaking of peace among nations, peace between individuals, and the all-important inner peace.

Her life became a pilgrimage.

In the years that followed, she divested herself of all possessions except for the clothes on her back—no coat, no sleeping bag, no money—only plain, rubber-soled shoes, long pants, and a simple tunic. In her pockets she carried her only earthly belongings: a folding toothbrush, a comb, a map of the area where she was walking, and her current mail. She wore the tunic over a long-sleeved shirt in winter and over short sleeves in summer. On the back of her tunic, Peace Pilgrim had printed the words "10,000 miles for Peace." Later, it changed to 25,000 miles—a number she far surpassed in her 28-year pilgrimage during which she crossed each Canadian province once and the entire United States nearly seven times.

As a pilgrim, she relied on the goodness and generosity of

others and the grace of God. She never asked for food or lodging but ate only what others offered freely. She took her rest in country fields, parks, bus stations, and homes across North America. Everywhere she walked, she spoke of peace, inspiring her listeners to consider their highest ideals and to begin or to continue living them.

"Peace," as she was called, walked south in winter and north in summer; she had her share of sweltering days, frozen nights, and mortal dangers. But her faith in divine providence sustained her. When a hulking, half-crazed teenage boy attacked her, she made no effort to defend herself. She showed him only love and compassion and was soon reassuring this lost young man that there was a way for him to find inner peace. Eventually, he did. Another time, a man invited her into his car, they talked a while, and he invited her to get some sleep. She curled up trustingly and did just that. When she awoke several hours later, he confessed to her that he'd planned to rape her but her trust rendered him unable to go through with it.

On another occasion, she faced yet another disturbed man attempting to assault an eight-year-old girl. Peace stood her ground, gazing at him without anger or criticism, until he finally turned and left. Peace often said, "There is a spark of good in everyone, no matter how deeply it may be buried. It is the real you." It was this divine spark that she addressed in every person she met.

And once, on an isolated road, she was caught by a sudden snowstorm—a blizzard so dense and fierce that she could not even see her hand in front of her face. Close to freezing, she surrendered to God's will and stumbled on. Soon, she found the railing of a bridge. Groping her way down the snowy embankment, she crawled underneath the bridge and found a cardboard box filled with wrapping paper. She curled up inside it and went to sleep.

Peace woke to a blue sky and sparkling sun. Another day had begun.

"Aren't people *good!*" she loved to say. And everywhere she went, people proved her right, opening their hearts and their hearths to her. In this way, for nearly three decades, Peace Pilgrim lived as a divine servant in the world, touching and inspiring thousands on her journey for peace. Today, she is known by millions worldwide for her simple yet profound message: *"This is the way of peace: Overcome evil with good, falsehood with truth, and hatred with love. Live according to your highest light, and more light shall be given."*

Bridge between Worlds

A Healing Vision on the African Plain

In 1956, at the age of four, Malidoma Patrice Some was kidnapped from his family and village by a French Jesuit missionary. With West Africa under French occupation, the Jesuits kidnapped many such children, hoping to raise an army of native missionaries to convert the African people from their tribal traditions to Christianity. Malidoma would spend the next 15 years in captivity, indoctrinated by the Jesuits to be a priest.

The day of his kidnapping, he was taken to a Jesuit mission and locked in a concrete room with a metal door. When he protested, a missionary whipped the frightened boy until he collapsed unconscious on the floor. He awoke weeping for his mother. The beating taught Malidoma the consequences of protest and made him obedient as a slave.

At 12, he was sent to a large boarding school, a stone-and-concrete fortress housing over 500 boys ages 12 to 21. They were taught to speak French and forbidden to speak their native tongues. By then, few of the boys could remember their tribes or families, whom they learned were "damned and degraded beings living in sin."

The stick and the strap were often-used teaching tools. In time, the cruelty of the missionaries made the boys cruel to each other. Dormitory life, with its numerous bullies and sexual predators, was a hellish realm. Younger, weaker boys were routinely molested. Malidoma was even molested by one of the missionaries. Over time, this brutality destroyed his faith in God. Once, when he was nearly drowned in a river by an older student, Malidoma tried praying to the God of these missionaries. But, he says, "It was like praying to the same one who had caused my misfortune."

At 20, Malidoma fled from the boarding school into the jungle, rejecting the role of priest for which he had been groomed. He could not imagine luring his long-lost family and tribe into a religion that had caused him so much suffering. He walked for 11 days along the dusty roads and slept under trees and in the bush. Finally, dirty, starving, and exhausted, he reached Dano, the village where he was born. He managed to locate his old home. Finding no one there, he sat down under a nearby *nim* tree and fell asleep.

He awoke surrounded by curious children. Soon, a young woman passed by, entered the house, came out to give him a drink, and then went back inside—brother and sister did not recognize each other. Then, a frail old man arrived on a bicycle; they exchanged greetings, looked curiously at each other, and the old man went inside—father and son did not recognize each other.

Finally, an old woman walked up with a bundle of wood on her head. She looked at Malidoma strangely—came near him and hovered, regarding him intensely—she walked forward and backward, engaged in inner struggle, looking back and forth from the river to Malidoma. Then, dropping her bundle of wood to the ground, she screamed, "Malidoma! *Patrere!* Malidoma!" Recognizing her own son, Malidoma's mother rushed and knelt before him. She grabbed his hands and, with tears streaming down her face, began wailing, her grief mixed with joy.

Malidoma's unexpected arrival produced a crisis in his family and his village. He had returned to his people as a stranger raised by their oppressors, no longer one of them. He did not speak their language or understand their customs. But slowly, as he had once learned a foreign tongue and Jesuit ways, Malidoma began to relearn Dagara, his forgotten native language. Within six months, he could speak it passably well. His foreign education also proved useful—he could write letters for villagers to family members in faraway places. But he still felt lost, drifting between two worlds with no firm foothold in either one. His despair and alienation only intensified his wish to belong.

As his anguish reached a crisis, the village elders proposed a solution: To find his spirit and rejoin his people, Malidoma must undergo the Dagara tribal initiation, a dangerous, sometimes fatal, ordeal. Dagara initiation expanded one's awareness beyond the ego or separate self, beyond the ordinary world, allowing the initiate to merge his own spirit with the universe of cosmic forces. The ordeal could open a doorway to the supernatural hidden in everyday life. But initiates passed through this doorway only by confronting terror and death.

The morning came when Malidoma and 63 youths from five villages went with their families to the edge of the bush. They stripped off their clothes and said good-bye to their families, knowing they might never see them again. Then, naked and singing, they followed the elders into the trees. Many hours later, they arrived at a secluded spot in the savanna.

The six-week initiation involved prolonged bouts of singing, dancing, fasting, meditation, and instruction by the elders, who terrified and dazzled the youths with their displays of shamanic power. These rituals and ordeals—they spent one night standing buried up to their necks in a pit—opened doors to the "other world." Malidoma's first vision, vividly described in his memoir, *Of Water and the Spirit*, came after he meditated for nearly two days on a *yila* tree.

"Out of nowhere," he writes, "in the place where the tree had stood, appeared a tall woman—an extremely beautiful and powerful entity. I could sense the intensity emanating from her—an irresistible magnetic pull. She lifted her veil, revealing an unearthly face. She was green, light green. Even her eyes were green, though very small and luminescent. She was smiling and her teeth were the color of violet and had light emanating from them. The greenness in her had nothing to do with the color of her skin. She was green from the inside out, as if her body were filled with a greenness that was the expression of immeasurable love.

"Never before had I felt so much love—a love that surpassed any known classifications—we dashed toward each other and flung ourselves into each other's arms. . . . While she held me in her embrace, the green lady spoke to me for a long time in the softest voice that ever was. I cried abundantly . . . not because what she told me was sad, but because every word produced an indescribable sensation of nostalgia and longing."

Hours later, healed and restored, Malidoma awoke from his vision to find himself hugging the *yila* tree. In a form he intuitively understood, the Divine, in maternal form, had given him a blessed vision of cosmic love. Such experiences, far beyond his normal state of awareness, baffled him. Later, one of the elders counseled him, "You do not need to understand everything right away. You have the rest of your life to comprehend what occurred. So be patient. Be happy you did not stay behind." He referred to four youths who had died during the initiation.

He tells of another vision and the realization it left him with long after its light had faded. "Slowly, like the dawn breaking, I began to see light . . . like an aurora borealis, shot through with areas of dark and ones of extreme luminescence—the light was so powerful that it would have fried my sight into blindness under ordinary circumstances, but somehow I was able to gaze at the skies of the underworld and survive. In that moment I saw that the light we encounter on the road to death is our own being, coming home to itself. This light is our own natural and eternal state."

Malidoma's encounter with the Divine world triggered a wholesale reorganization of his psyche, cleansing him of much confusion and healing him of deep wounds acquired through his bitter life experience. For the first time in 15 years, he was no longer an exile. He had come home at last.

Malidoma Patrice Some has shared with the West his story of exile and return and the richness of his culture that imbues everyday life with spiritual meaning and presence. His story reveals that, in a sense, we have all been held captive, cut off from the spirit world and the wisdom of our ancestors. Like Malidoma, we each confront our own initiations that test us, teach us, and guide us home to the place within where Spirit dwells.

The Power of Love

Saving Grace in the Dutch Underground

Jack Schwarz, born in Dordrecht, Holland, later emigrated to the United States to establish himself as a pioneer and expert in the fields of holistic self-health and human energy systems. He has achieved worldwide recognition for his demonstrated ability to voluntarily control and regulate his body's "involuntary" functions, such as pain, bleeding, breathing, heart rate—all documented in various scientific studies by Elmer Green, M.D., of the Menninger Clinic, and by other independent medical laboratories.

And as his wife, Lois, and close friends testify, Jack lived for many years eating only two or three small meals per week and sleeping less than two hours a night while maintaining his abundant energy and busy schedule.

Jack's first initiations into the world of energetic-healing abilities came at age nine, when he hugged his ailing mother, then ill with tuberculosis. After this simple embrace, she began to recover with unusual rapidity and insisted that Jack's touch was the cause. Whether or not her perception was accurate, this incident created in Jack a curiosity about energy and healing and opened his mind to the idea that such things might be possible and that such unusual abilities might exist within himself.

A few years later, while working in a clothing store as a window dresser, Jack would routinely stick many straight pins into his lapel to keep them handy as he pinned outfits on the window mannequins. One day, a friend came up behind him, reached around, and gave Jack a playful-but-forceful slap on the chest—accidentally driving the pins deeply into Jack's flesh. Jack went to the washroom, pulled the pins out one by one, looked at his bleeding chest, and *willed* the bleeding and pain to cease. Both stopped immediately.

Excited by this discovery, Jack began experimenting on himself, deliberately piercing his own body with pins—and later with large knitting needles. He found that he was able to control both pain and bleeding. As time passed, Jack discovered he could also consciously accelerate the healing time of cuts and wounds and resist infections as well.

But years before he became renowned for such abilities, Jack faced a life-and-death challenge—and experienced a divine intervention—that revealed to him the greatest power of all.

In 1940, the shadow of Nazi storm troopers spread across the face of Europe. When the war broke out, Jack, then 16, became a member of the Dutch underground. When the Nazis took over Jack's hometown of Dordrecht, they confiscated, as usual, the census records in order to learn the location of all able-bodied young men who were to be sent to work in slave-labor camps.

When the storm troopers came to the Schwarz household,

the family hid Jack behind a false chimney. But after a careful search, the soldiers found him and took him to a railroad station to wait for the train that would carry him to the labor camp. The next morning before boarding the train, Jack saw his father, a small man, push his way through the masses of people and the Nazi guards to take Jack his suitcase. He later wrote, "This was the first time I realized how much my father loved me."

Ironically, on the way to the labor camp in Hamburg, the Allies fired upon the train; many of the young men were injured and some near Jack were killed. On arriving at the labor camp, word got out, perhaps through an informer, that Jack was a member of the Dutch underground. He was taken to a bare room for interrogation. There, a Nazi guard tied him up, tore off his shirt, and began whipping him with a cat-o'-nine-tails, flaying the skin from his back.

Jack, already adept at self-hypnosis, had by then taught himself to control his bleeding and dissociate his mind from physical pain. Being young, proud, and cocky, he first thought he would "show them." But the prolonged whipping was too much, and he finally fainted.

While unconscious, Jack experienced a profound vision— far more vivid than his waking life or his dreams: He found himself standing in a crowd of faceless people before Christ on the cross. With his face full of love and agony, Christ looked down at them and said, "My God, why hast thou forsaken me?" In Jack's vision, Christ spoke not to God but to the people in the crowd and to Jack himself. In that moment, Jack knew he was being called to live Christ's way of love. He also understood that all human beings were actors playing their roles perfectly in the Divine Theater.

The consequences of that visionary realization were immediate: Jack returned to consciousness filled with love and compassion for all souls. And as the guard began to whip him again, Jack turned his head, looked into the guard's eyes, and said in German, "I love you."

He meant it with all his heart.

Dumbfounded, the Nazi dropped his whip and ran from the room. Later, another soldier took Jack back to his cell. He was left alone after that. Several months later, to his amazement, Jack was sent to Holland on an assigned task, apparently expected to return voluntarily. Jack accepted wholeheartedly this opportunity to escape, and he remained in Holland, serving in the Dutch underground until the war's end.

Years after the war, Jack emigrated to America.

In 1958, Jack Schwarz founded the Aletheia Institute in Mendocino, California, where, for more than 40 years, he has helped men and women of all ages explore and develop their own capacities for energy healing, regeneration, voluntary control, and self-discovery.

Awakened to Heal

Internal Energy Creates a New Life Purpose

For years now, the Chinese government has studied unique individuals with a variety of extraordinary powers. They are called special-ability people. Some of them have developed their remarkable abilities through advanced internal-energy practices called *Qi Gong*. Most, however, have acquired their powers spontaneously, by mysterious means.

Mei Mei Xiang is an example of one such person.

Before moving to Beijing, Mei, an elementary school teacher, lived in Northeast China with her husband and son. A modest person, she was well-liked by her students and neighbors. One afternoon in the mid 1980s, Mei rode her bicycle into the city to attend an annual fair, a traditional celebration honoring the ancestors. There was music, food, dancing, and people in colorful costumes, dressed as heavenly spirits, ancestors, and historical figures.

Riding home afterward, Mei grew tired and stopped for a

short nap at the foot of Lady Mountain, known for centuries by locals as an abode of the goddess *Quan Yin*. She arrived home after dark. That same night, she experienced sudden and severe stomach cramps. The next day, when they grew worse, she feared it was food poisoning from the fair. She was about to go to the hospital when the cramps suddenly stopped—a strange rushing force filled her belly then flooded her body. Her skin tingled with electricity. She felt feather light and exhilarated.

The force lifted her up—she found herself walking effortlessly on her toes in an intoxicated state, then dancing giddily around her house. To release the storm of energy that threatened to overwhelm her, she went out and began to walk, then dance, still on her toes, across a field, into the streets, even through traffic. Mei ran and skipped down the crowded sidewalk without bumping into anyone, feeling weightless, guided with unerring precision by the powerful force. She felt her body both absorbing and radiating energy.

Every day after that, waves of energy flooded through her in cycles, building to an almost unbearable intensity, at which point she was compelled to release it through vigorous movements and dancing. Her friends, family, and neighbors grew puzzled and worried about her. Many thought she had gone mad. Mei herself did not understand what was happening. But she felt extremely clear, happy, and energetic. Although at times she feared being overwhelmed by the intense energies flooding through her, she sensed that something important was happening to her and intuitively trusted what was occurring.

This process lasted 100 days and was accompanied by states of exultation, inner voices, remarkable visions, and fantasies. Mei felt she was in contact with the spiritual world. On the 100th day, Mei prepared fruit and food and told her husband, "Today, everyone is here: Buddha, Quan Yin, the Heavenly Emperor and Heavenly Mother. I must prepare food for our guests." For the first time since her experience had begun, Mei felt emotionally and psychologically stable—able to control the energy flowing through her. Her fears of being overwhelmed by the force began to subside.

At this point, the force began producing new phenomena—now she heard ancient music that sent her into deep trances or moved her into ecstatic states as she began to dance. Many people who saw her found her dancing eerie, yet beautiful to watch. Mei also found she could now look into people's bone structures and see the energy flow in their bodies. On other occasions, she could see faraway people or events. And her hands were charged with electrical energy—once, on the bus, she grabbed the metal handrail and everyone suddenly let go, some crying out from the shock. She could sometimes open locks simply by touching them.

When she went out in public, she often heard a cacophony of people's thoughts crowding in on her, or she saw images, symbols, and nonphysical entities, even fairy-tale and mythic characters from ancient times. At other times, she was overwhelmed by information pouring through her too rapidly to process, as if an inner floodgate of knowledge had opened within her. "At that time," Mei says, "I traveled many places in my mind—sometimes I was on top of a mountain; other times I was underwater or in a different city. I often felt confused, but a voice was always with me, reassuring me. Every day, I went to the park to dance to the music only I could hear. I had to do this to survive my strange experience."

One day, while cooking meat for her family, a voice told her, "You cannot eat this food." After that, she could not eat killed flesh. When she saw a piece of meat, she saw the creature as it had been in its living form.

Then one evening, the voice told her, "It's time for you to heal people and serve society." So Mei began a new experiment with the energy flowing through her, to see if she could use it to heal. She found that when she stood before a sick person and thought, "I want to heal this person," her hands raised automatically to massage the air inches from the place that needed healing. She felt energy pour through her into them, and many reported that their pains and ailments disappeared.

Initially, Mei's strange behavior had made her well-known as "the teacher who went crazy." Now, she became famous throughout her city as a healer. As she came to better understand the principles and methods she had applied spontaneously, she began teaching others to heal. Eventually, she moved to Beijing and opened a *Qi Gong* clinic and school.

Mei calls her art *Yu Zhou Zi Ran Gong*—Skill of Universal Nature. Having learned to control and conduct what at first was an overwhelming flood, she can now tap into this Universal Nature and access information and energy. Mei believes that the spirit energy called Qi is unlimited, existing everywhere and in everything. And to whatever degree the channels of our minds and bodies open, energy pours through us to heal and balance our beings and awaken our higher human capacities. Even though such "religious" ideas are officially frowned upon by the Communist Party, many Party officials come to Mei.

Mei Mei Xiang attributes the awakening of her gifts to the goddess *Quan Yin* and to Buddha, whose presence and form she feels. Today, she uses her extraordinary, spontaneously awakened abilities to heal others and serve society, just as her inner voice instructed.

Kingdom of Compassion

A Warrior Becomes a Buddha

Three hundred years before the birth of Christ, the invincible armies of Alexander stormed across the ancient world. But Alexander's dreams of world conquest died on the shores of the Ganges—the river he would never cross. Two years later, another great warrior rose from obscurity to conquer the same territory that had defeated Alexander the Great. The warrior's name was Maurya, and his ever-expanding kingdom, the Mauryian empire, would come to be known as India.

As the years passed, Maurya's kingdom passed to his son Bindusara, then to his grandson Asoka, a battle-hardened warrior whose driving ambition rivaled that of Alexander. King Asoka spent his early years at war, conquering his neighboring provinces. Then, in the eighth year of his 40-year reign, Asoka defeated the nation of Kalinga—a staggering victory in which 100,000 Kalingans were slain and 150,000 were taken captive.

Many thousands of Asoka's own men died, and thousands of wounded on both sides perished in the days that followed.

Kalinga was now Asoka's. Yet his moment of supreme triumph produced an unprecedented and wholly unpredictable result: As he gazed upon the field of slaughter, contemplating its godlike harvest of dead, Emperor Asoka was overcome by a grief and remorse that changed not only his life but also the future of India.

In that moment of profound mourning, he understood the value of all living things, the primal horror of war, and the petty hunger for earthly glory that had lured him to this act of supreme folly. The revelations that came to him on that corpse-laden plain forever seared his soul, opened his eyes and heart, and released in his mind a ray of light seen in few kings before or since.

It was Asoka's last battle. That day, he renounced forever the use of war as a tool of the state. He now understood the sole task worthy of a true emperor—to influence his subjects by his own example—by ruling with justice and mercy, and living with love. To this purpose, Asoka devoted the rest of his life.

"When a country is conquered," he later wrote, "people are killed, they die, or are made captive. Thus arose His Sacred Majesty's remorse for having conquered the Kalingas. . . . Today, if a hundredth or a thousandth part of those who suffered in Kalinga were to be killed, to die, or to be taken captive, it would be grievous to His Sacred Majesty. . . . If anyone does him wrong it will be forgiven as far as it can be forgiven. . . . For His Sacred Majesty desires safety, self-control, justice, and happiness for all beings."

Asoka embodied these words in 10,000 noble deeds,

which he performed over the next 33 years of his extraordinary reign. In the classic memoir *Autobiography of a Yogi*, Paramahansa Yogananda relates just a few of the deeds that made Asoka the greatest king India, and perhaps the world, has ever seen: "Emperor Asoka erected 84,000 religious stupas [shrines] in various parts of India. Fourteen rock edicts and 10 stone pillars survive. Each pillar is a triumph of engineering, architecture, and sculpture. He arranged for the construction of many reservoirs, dams, and irrigation sluices; of highways and tree-shaded roads dotted with rest houses for travelers; of botanical gardens for medicinal purposes; and of hospitals for man and beast."

The effects of Asoka's divine realization—like the sermons carved in stone through which he preached his message of compassionate justice—spread across his vast empire and down through the centuries. Even today, although little-known outside of India, Asoka's transformation continues to influence our world.

His championing of Buddhism, then barely two centuries old, helped this fledgling religion flourish and spread to become one of the great world religions. By outlawing the killing of animals for sport and making ahimsa—noninjury to man and beast—his national policy, Asoka fostered nonviolence as a religious principle among India's many faiths and spread philosophically based vegetarianism throughout Indian culture and from India to the western world, where it blossoms even today.

To establish compassionate justice as the foundation of his kingdom, Asoka ended the use of torture, which his warrior-grandfather Maurya had honed to barbaric perfection. Asoka also created and sent to every province a multitude of new public officials called Officers of Righteousness. Their sole mission was to prevent wrongful punishment and imprisonment and to promote "welfare and happiness among servants and masters, Brahmans and the rich, the needy and the aged."

Remarkably, every soldier in his vast army was instructed in the Golden Rule—that one must treat others as one wishes to be treated, which Asoka referred to as the Law of Life. Even when defending his kingdom from invaders, Asoka used force only as a last resort, when moral reasoning and peaceful negotiation had failed.

His example has inspired countless Indian men and women through the ages, including Mahatma Gandhi; Jawaharlal Nehru, India's first prime minister; and his daughter, Indira Gandhi, India's first and only woman prime minister. Though himself a Buddhist, Asoka preached universal tolerance among all religions. He inscribed on his instructive monuments, "All sects deserve reverence for one reason or another. By thus acting a man exalts his own sect and at the same time does service to the sects of other people." Asoka also demonstrated a deep support for the integrity of all religions by ordering his Officers of Righteousness to defrock all monks, even Buddhists, who failed to live the tenets of their faith—setting high standards still relevant and needed today.

This is the glory of Emperor Asoka, who began his career as a warrior, was converted by despair and illumination on the field of battle, and won his greatest spiritual victory by making himself a servant to the needs of his people. Asoka's supreme embodiment of the universal principles he taught mark him as a true bodhisattva, a Buddhist saint, and a visionary of the past, present, and future, whose light can guide today's leaders—and tomorrow's.

Madonna in Light

Seeing Is Believing—An Uncanny Visitation

In 1919, just outside Cairo, Egypt, a wealthy and devout Muslim donated a piece of land to the city for the purpose of building a Christian church. What made his donation even more unusual was that he had been directed to make it by the Virgin Mary, who had appeared to him in a particularly vivid dream. Five years later, with the church completed, Mary again visited the Muslim gentleman in a dream and promised to appear in the church the following year.

If Mary appeared as was promised, she was not seen by a living soul.

Forty-three years passed; the devout old Muslim and his prophetic dream were by then forgotten—until the night of April 2, 1968. Two Muslim mechanics working late in the auto repair shop across from Saint Mary's Church of Zeitoun went out for some fresh air. Looking up, they saw a glowing female figure standing on the church top by the central dome. Confused, they first thought the woman was a nun contemplating suicide. One of the mechanics ran to fetch the church pastor while the other called an emergency squad.

When they returned, the figure was gone.

Others must also have seen the figure, for word quickly spread that a luminous lady had appeared on the church. Small crowds began to gather each night, waiting expectantly.

One week later, on April 9, the woman, emanating an aura of white light, reappeared—this time before a small gathering. From then on, her brightly glowing figure, clothed in flowing robes of light, appeared randomly and frequently on the church's roof at night. Word of mouth and news reports spread the story, and the crowds grew.

It was not long before photographs of startling clarity captured the unearthly visitor.

The apparition, whom many believed to be Mary, manifested itself dozens of times in the first two months, each appearance lasting from 10 minutes to several hours. These appearances weren't merely a local event covered in the back pages of the town newspapers—the city had to tear down several old nearby buildings to accommodate crowds that gathered nightly, often numbering in the tens of thousands and at times reaching 100,000.

One remarkable aspect of this phenomenon was its dazzling and varied displays of light. Before Mary's arrivals, bright flashes played about the cathedral or plummeted cometlike from the sky. In sudden bursts of radiance, "doves of light" fluttered about the dome or soared far out over the city. Radiant stars at times surrounded the apparition. On other occasions, the entire dome was illumined—one witness described it as "engulfed in a brilliant blue white light, as if it were melting. . . . The edges of light on top of the lighted dome appeared to roll inward so that one's eyes were directed to the very center."

These phenomena were extensively witnessed, photographed, and documented. Bishop Samuel, official investigator for the Coptic Christian Church, witnessed the apparition numerous times, and he later filed a detailed report for the church archives. Deeply moved by his experiences, he wrote, "The scene was overwhelming and magnificent. The apparition walked toward the west, sometimes moving its hands in blessing and sometimes bowing repeatedly. A halo of light surrounded its head. I saw some glittering beings around the apparition. They looked like stars."

Bishop Athanasius, sent by the Coptic Pope Kryllos VI to investigate and report on these appearances, was equally impressed. "There she was," he wrote, "five or six meters above the dome, high in the sky, full figure, like a phosphorous statue, but not so stiff as a statue. There was movement of the body and of the clothing. . . . One would estimate the crowd at 100,000. . . . Our Lady looked to the north; she waved her hand; she blessed the people, sometimes in the direction where we stood. Her garments swayed in the wind. She was very quiet, full of glory. It was something really supernatural, very, very heavenly."

The "lady of light" made hundreds of appearances over a period of two years and finally disappeared in 1971. All told, hundreds of thousands of people witnessed the apparition; innumerable photographic records exist, along with detailed testimonials by news reporters, Church officials, and thousands of citizens of different faiths and social positions. Although the precise nature of these visitations remains unknown, their reality is beyond dispute—another unsolved mystery in the X-files of the spiritual realm.

Our conventional assumptions about the nature of reality and about the kinds of beings that inhabit or appear in this world are called into question and perhaps expanded by these sightings of an ethereal lady, bathed in light, on a church top in the city of Zeitoun.

Transformation at Lourdes

Healing a Physician's Soul

Born in France in the late 1800s, Alexis Carrel, like many of his contemporaries, received a religious upbringing. But after years of medical school, where he learned to apply rigorous critical analysis to every question, Alexis found his childhood faith implausible—he had acquired the skepticism of a confirmed rationalist.

As a physician, Alexis rejected belief in miracles. And when he began to hear stories of miraculous healings of numerous afflictions—healings attributed to the waters of Lourdes—he decided that such phenomena must be psychosomatic in origin. No true organic disease such as cancer or tuberculosis could be cured by faith alone—of this he was certain. Yet as a scientist, he was honest enough to realize that disbelief without investigation was little more than negative faith, the other side of the same irrational coin.

Because Alexis valued, above all else, the power of reason,

he traveled to Lourdes in 1903 in order to investigate these phenomena directly, examining patients before and after they went to the holy grotto. His first afternoon there, he met A. B., a young medic and past classmate volunteering as a stretcher bearer, carrying cripples to the waters of the grotto. As he and Alexis discussed cases they had each seen, A. B. mentioned a nun who had been cured that very afternoon of an old ankle injury. But Alexis, who had examined her and found that her injury was not organic, attributed her cure to autosuggestion.

Then A. B. sadly mentioned a boy with terminal cancer. The boy had left that morning, uncured, with his brokenhearted father. "You see," said Alexis, "Lourdes is powerless against organic disease."

A. B. quickly responded, "I have seen cases, just as serious, cured." He then described a string of such cases. Alexis held to his position—as a scientist, he refused to accept as fact anything he had not seen with his own eyes and thoroughly investigated before and after.

"What kind of a disease would you have to see cured to convince you?" A. B. asked.

After considering the patients under his care, Alexis said, "There is one patient who seems closer to death at this moment than any of the others. Her name is Marie Ferrand, an unfortunate girl in the final stages of tuberculosis. I know her history—her whole family died of the same disease. She has tubercular sores, lesions of the lungs, and now has a peritonitis diagnosed both by a general practitioner and by the well-known Bordeaux surgeon Bromilloux. Her condition is very grave. . . . She may die any moment. If such a case were cured, it would indeed be a miracle."

Marie Ferrand would be their test case. They immediately

went to her bedside in the hospital of Our-Lady-of-the-Seven-Sorrows, to find that her condition had deteriorated. "Her pulse was excessively rapid, a hundred and fifty beats a minute, and irregular," wrote Alexis. "Her heart was giving out. Her abdomen was also distended, with solid masses and fluids filling her belly, her legs swollen, her nose and hands cold, and her nails and ears had turned a greenish hue.

"Advanced tubercular peritonitis," Alexis told A. B. "The fluid is almost all gone. You can feel the solid masses at the sides—death is near."

Another doctor examined her and agreed. "She might very well die at the grotto," he told Alexis softly. Alexis considered his ethical vows—if she was to die in any case, he would do his patient no harm by this investigation. And it might serve the higher good of science. He went ahead to the pool and was waiting there when Marie arrived on a stretcher with A. B.

In his book, *Man, The Unknown*—based on detailed notes he took as the events occurred—Alexis described what happened next: "The ministering priest was kneeling down, facing the line of patients and the crowds beyond. He lifted his arms and held them out like a cross. He was young; his fleshy white face, dripping with sweat, was covered with red blotches. Only the childlike expression in his eyes and the evident intensity of his faith saved him from absurdity. 'Holy Virgin, heal our sick!' he cried out, his child's mouth twisted with emotion . . . the crowd responded with a cry. . . . Here and there, people held out their arms. The sick half-raised themselves on their stretchers. The atmosphere was tense with expectancy. . . . A forest of arms was raised. A wind seemed to blow through the crowd; intangible, silent, powerful, irresistible, it swept over the people." Alexis noted that he felt a catch in his throat and a tremor through his spine. And to his surprise, he suddenly wanted to cry.

After examining other patients in the line, he returned to find Marie Ferrand—still hovering at the point of death. Fearing to immerse her in the grotto lest it hasten her demise, they instead poured water from the grotto over her head. Alexis now looked closely at Marie and noticed that "the harsh shadows on her face had disappeared . . . her skin was somehow less ashen." He assumed his perception of her improvement to be a psychologically induced hallucination, based on hope and suggestion—interesting in itself. He recorded the observation in his notebook, along with the time—20 minutes before three o'clock.

Alexis continued to observe his patient intently, with all the objectivity he could bring to bear, and noted that "there was a distinct improvement of her general appearance. The face of Marie Ferrand slowly continued to change. Her eyes, so dim before, were now wide with ecstasy as she turned them toward the grotto. This change in her visage was undeniable." As yet, this proved nothing.

Then, to his astonishment, Alexis noticed something else: The blanket covering Marie Ferrand's distended abdomen was gradually flattening out. "Look at her abdomen!" he cried, unable to contain his excitement. "The bell of the basilica had just struck three . . . minutes later, there was no longer any sign of distention in Marie Ferrand's abdomen," he wrote. Even as Alexis watched and continued recording his notes, he felt that he was losing his senses—what he was seeing was impossible. Marie Ferrand's breathing normalized and her heartbeat became regular.

"How do you feel?" he asked her.

"I feel very well," she answered. "I am still weak, but I feel I am cured."

"There was no longer any doubt," Alexis wrote. "Marie Ferrand's condition was improving so much that she was scarcely recognizable. . . . In a few minutes she raised her head, looked around, moved her limbs a little, then turned over on her side, without having shown the least sign of pain. . . . A dying girl is recovering!"

Alexis went to report the event to Dr. Boissarie, chief doctor of Lourdes clinic. After listening to his colleague describe what had transpired, Dr. Boissarie said, "This inexplicable power in Lourdes has cured cancers, tumors, and even tuberculosis. We have seen it many times and must concede it. This is not the first time that a tubercular peritonitis has disappeared. I have several records of it in my office." He then recounted several dramatic cases of other dying patients healed at the grotto.

When Marie Ferrand was returned to the hospital, Alexis performed a thorough examination—the hard masses in her abdomen had vanished. Except for the weakness generated by her prolonged illness, and her still swollen legs, she seemed completely normal. She was cured. Two other doctors also examined her and reached the same conclusion.

This healing that occurred before his eyes caused a crisis in Dr. Alexis Carrel's soul. He tried by every means to discount it, yet none of his arguments held up against the evidence of his own experience and scientific investigation. He knew of other doctors who had gone to Lourdes who were so disturbed by the evidence of mysterious healings that they refused to admit having been there. Now, he understood their dilemma.

Long into the night, Alexis paced up and down by the grotto, wrestling with a spiritual dilemma that had become intensely personal. If he reported what he'd seen and had verified, he risked ridicule—the loss of prestige and respect among his colleagues. Yet if he denied or withheld the truth, as he was tempted to do, he risked losing both his integrity and self-respect.

Through a sleepless night, Dr. Carrel weighed his career against his soul. As dawn approached, Dr. Alexis Carrel began, for the first time in many years, to pray. As he did so, something inside him was reconciled, resolved, and healed.

The incident at Lourdes was a turning point in the life and career of Dr. Alexis Carrel. In the following years, he spent much time researching and investigating the phenomenon of miraculous healings. His thorough report, when it was finally written and published, included the fruits of these years of research as well as an account of the event at Lourdes that had changed the course of his life. As he had feared, his report did result in controversy and public attacks on his character. Yet he courageously defended himself and his findings in the press.

Many years later, Dr. Alexis Carrel—then a famed surgeon awarded the Nobel Prize for his medical research and discoveries—wrote, "We must liberate man from the cosmos created by the genius of physicists and astronomers, that cosmos in which, since the Renaissance, he has been imprisoned. We now know that we . . . extend outside the physical continuum. . . . In time, as in space, the individual stretches out beyond the frontiers of his body. . . . He also belongs to another world."

That other world, where the laws of known physics are transcended by laws yet unknown and by events we call miraculous, was revealed to a skeptical young surgeon by the healing of Marie Ferrand in the grotto at Lourdes. But Marie was not the only person transformed that day. Her healing had become his own.

Grandmother's Guidance

A Dream That Spared Generations

Ever since she was a girl, Jean Munzer has known that she and her family owe their lives to a spiritual visitation that occurred in a dream to her mother, Clara. The incident, which took place before Jean was conceived, also involved Jean's grandmother, who at the time had been dead for more than 20 years.

Clara was born in Vienna, Austria, in the early 1900s. She never knew her own mother, who died while giving birth to her, or her father, who died of an infection a year later. Clara was raised by her maternal grandparents, who owned a prosperous store.

As a teenager, Clara worked in her grandparents' store—that's where 15-year-old Siegfried Gruen first saw her. He approached her and placed on the counter before her a book of poems he had written.

"I write poems, too," Clara said.

So began a friendship and a lifelong romance that would last for more than 60 years.

During the three years after their first meeting, Clara and Siegi were inseparable. They pledged their love to one another despite her grandparents' disapproval. Their objections were conventional—they were prospering middle-class business folk, while Siegi came from a poor family. And Clara was too young. But no reasons could halt their blossoming love.

Even when Siegi, a singer, actor, and poet, went to America in his 18th year, he wrote Clara nearly every day—a practice he would continue for six years. He lived with his uncle in Michigan and worked in his uncle's shoe store. A gifted singer, he eventually sang in the Detroit Opera. But after fulfilling his dream of becoming a U.S. citizen, Siegi returned to Vienna to fulfill another, more important, dream—to marry Clara and take her back with him to America.

But another obstacle presented itself—although Clara's grandparents had resigned themselves to her marrying Siegi, they wanted her to remain in Vienna, fearing that if she went to America they would never see her again. Clara herself did not want to leave Vienna or her grandparents, though she desired to marry Siegi. So a solution was proposed: In order to keep Clara near, her grandparents offered to set Siegi up with his own business in Vienna. Clara fervently campaigned for this plan and at last persuaded Siegi, who was willing to sacrifice his American dream for love. It seemed the matter was settled.

But on the night before Siegi was to sign the contract for his new business, Clara had an extraordinary dream: Her dead mother, whom she had never known, appeared vividly to Clara and urgently told her that she must leave Vienna and go to America with her future husband. Clara was not given to psychic or paranormal experiences. Yet this dream seemed much more than a dream to her, and it affected her deeply. She awoke firmly convinced that her mother had in fact come to her, for reasons beyond her understanding, to deliver a message of great importance and urgency. She knew that she must obey.

Early that morning, Clara ran to Siegi's house and told him that he could not sign the business contract—that they *must* go to America together. Siegi, surprised by her sudden change of heart and the unusual event that prompted it, happily agreed. Clara and Siegi were married soon after, and when they emigrated to America, several of Siegi's relatives went with them.

Several years later, Hitler invaded Austria. Most of the family members of Clara and Siegi who remained in Vienna were taken to concentration camps, where many of them died.

Today, Jean Munzer considers this story to be much more than a family heirloom. She believes that her mother's dream made her family's future possible, and it had a profound influence on Jean's life work. "My parents and my father's family who came to America were saved by my mother's dream," Jean says with certainty. "Myself, my children, their children, and all our future generations owe our lives to a dream warning given to my mother, Clara, by my grandmother, who had long before passed from this world.

"That dream was the first and only psychic experience that my mother would ever have. But what an important one it was for our family. My mother's story has illumined my life. It has shown me that other realities exist besides the one we see, that spiritual protection and guidance are available to us in this life and beyond, and that we can trust our inner wisdom in whatever form it comes."

Since 1978, Jean Munzer has served as the director of the Metaphysical Center of New Jersey. She lectures throughout the world and her work has been included in eight biographical references, including *Who's Who in the World* and *Foremost Women of the Twentieth Century.*

Martyr of Mystery

The Celestial Origins of a Modern Religion

Joseph was born in Puritan Vermont on December 23, 1805. Growing up, Joseph endured extreme poverty, suffering, and instability as his parents moved to a series of farms, trying to eke a living out of poor soil. When he was seven, his entire family contracted typhoid fever and survived. When the disease infected Joseph's leg bone, a local doctor recommended amputation.

Young Joseph adamantly refused.

The only way to save his leg, the doctor said, was to cut it open and snap off the diseased bone fragments, piece by piece, with forceps. Joseph endured the excruciating operation without any anesthetic. His mother, who had fled to the woods, came back upon hearing his agonized howls, but Joseph ordered her out. His leg was saved but he walked on crutches for three years and retained a slight limp for the rest of his life.

In 1916, the family moved to a small New York town.

They had suffered the deaths of three children and a series of devastating swindles. Joseph's parents grieved for each loss but found comfort in their deeply personal religion—they rarely attended a formal church. Their trials had only increased their faith in God. By age 12, Joseph regularly prayed, contemplating the wickedness of the world and the weight of his own sins.

When he was 14, while praying in the woods, Joseph heard the voice of Christ speak his name and forgive him for his sins. A devout and God-fearing boy unlikely to tell falsehoods, especially where God was concerned, Joseph related how a pillar of brilliant light shone down from the heavens, engulfing him, and how he saw two beings standing above him "whose brightness and glory defied all description." Then he lost consciousness and awoke lying on the ground. "My soul was filled with love," he wrote. "For many days I rejoiced. . . . "

Still, Joseph remained an ordinary youth. He did his share of fighting and, later, drinking, though no more than others his age. But at the age of 19, as he lay in bed praying before going to sleep, Joseph experienced one of the most vivid divine interventions recorded in modern times. He wrote, "While I was thus calling upon God, a light appeared in my room . . . until the room was lighter than at noonday, when immediately a person appeared at my bedside, standing in the air, for his feet did not touch the floor. His person was glorious beyond description . . . his countenance like lightning. When I first looked upon him, I was afraid, but the fear soon left me. He called my name and told me he was a messenger sent from the presence of God, that his name was Moroni, and that God had a work for me to do."

The angel told Joseph he would be both blessed and cursed "among all nations" and that a book "of the everlasting Gospel" written on gold plates was buried nearby—which he must translate. This wondrous and terrifying being commanded Joseph's obedience and warned of dire consequences should he fail to carry out God's word. Then, a tunnel of light opened above and the angel ascended "right into heaven . . . until he entirely disappeared."

Joseph lay in the darkness, "marveling greatly at what had been told to me by this extraordinary messenger," overwhelmed and astonished, contemplating all he had seen and heard. But there was more to come. The angel appeared three times that night, repeated all he had said, and added a final warning that Joseph must never try to profit by the golden plates or use them for any other purpose than to glorify God. With that, the angel ascended.

From a timeless place, the cock crowed, greeting the coming dawn. Exhausted, Joseph went to work in the fields, so weakened by his encounters that he could barely lift his hoe. His father sent him home, but as he tried to climb a fence bordering the field, he fainted. He was awakened by the voice of the angel Moroni calling his name, and looked up to see the illumined heavenly messenger hovering over him. The angel again repeated all he had said the previous night, then commanded Joseph to go and find the golden plates and then to tell his father all that had occurred.

Joseph found the buried plates but was unable even to touch them. The angel told him to return to that spot once each year for the next four years. Only if he purified himself of the wish to profit by the plates would he be able to take them and fulfill his mission.

Three times Joseph went to where the plates were buried. Each time, the angel Moroni told him he still harbored a secret greed and was not yet worthy to serve the Lord. A fourth year passed. Joseph, now 23, had grown up to become a strikingly handsome, charismatic man, 6 feet tall and a renowned wrestler, with wavy auburn hair and piercing blue eyes. Yet his mission now transcended earthly glories.

On Joseph's fourth visit to the plates, on September 27, 1827, the angel Moroni told him he was at last worthy to take the plates. Joseph dug them up—a stack of sheets made of copper and gold, thin as pages of a book yet heavier than stone, weighing perhaps 60 pounds and covered with indecipherable hieroglyphs. Word of Joseph's miraculous find immediately spread through the town. On several occasions, attempts were made to steal his heavenly treasure—a mob even broke into the house one night—but the plates were well-hidden.

That same year, Joseph married Emily, a woman who matched his strength and who believed in him and in his mission. It was Emily who helped him to translate the plates—she in fact wrote down the words of the Book.

The strange translation process involved something like ancient magic or future technology—Joseph would put his face into his hat and, gazing into two diamond-like lenses that had come with the plates, would see words appear on the plates or in his mind's eye. As he spoke the words aloud, Emily wrote them down.

The spiritual and literary quality of the text would be remarkable for a brilliant scholar, let alone an untutored 24-year-old farmer. It read like scripture; Joseph soon began attracting followers. He allowed only a select group to view the golden plates—each witness signed a document swearing that he had seen and touched them.

In June 1829, as Joseph and three disciples prayed in the

woods, the angel Moroni descended, as was his custom, in a pillar of light and proclaimed Joseph's translation of the plates to be true scripture. Again, each witness signed a document testifying to the event's authenticity.

Joseph would allow eight more witnesses to see and handle the plates; these eight also signed documents swearing to the truth of the plates' existence. When the Book of Mormon was completed in 1829, the angel Moroni once again returned and, the plates having served their purpose, he took them away. Despite the physical absence of the golden plates, the wisdom they contained formed the foundation of the early Church of Jesus Christ of Latter-Day Saints, which continued to grow.

In later years, some of those who had seen the plates rejected and opposed Joseph—one became his bitter enemy—yet not a single witness ever recanted his testimony. All swore throughout their lives, and several on their deathbeds, to the truth of the existence of the plates and to the visit of the angel Moroni, declaring them to be wonders of God.

By his mid 30s, the poor, half-educated farm boy from Vermont had become a revolutionary prophet of a new religion with thousands of followers, the mayor of his own city (the largest in Illinois), the virtual head of an independent militia, and in 1844, a candidate for president of the United States. In the face of Joseph's growing power, angry mobs arose throughout the state. Federal militias sent out against the Mormon militia of 5,000 soldiers threatened a full-scale war in Illinois. To avert a bloody conflict, the governor called on Joseph and his Church leaders to surrender and submit to the law of the land, offering them his personal guarantee of safety. Joseph and his men surrendered in good faith.

But on their way to jail, Joseph said, "We are like lambs led to slaughter." And so they were.

On June 27, 1844, an armed mob with coal-blackened faces stormed past the federal troops guarding the jail. Joseph and his comrades heroically confronted the mob. Joseph himself leaped through the jailhouse window into the gunfire, crying, "Oh Lord, my God!" as he was shot down.

Though widely misunderstood, hated by some and feared by others, Joseph's personal presence had become a spiritual force. Men could hate him from a distance. But in his presence, even his bitterest enemies came to grudgingly admire, even love him. And many former enemies sincerely eulogized him after his death.

Joseph Smith's murder ensured the flowering of his new religion, as if his martyr's blood had eternally watered its roots. His Church, with fewer than 20,000 members at his death, now has more than 4 million. Today, copies of the hieroglyphics made from the original golden plates are kept in the historical department of the Church of Latter-Day Saints in Salt Lake City, Utah.

The origin of their language has yet to be identified.

Voyager Within

Jung's Courageous Journey into the Psyche

C arl Jung is best known as a renowned psychiatrist and author, explorer of dreams and of human nature. Many also know him as the originator of a new psychology—one which embraced the soul and declared Spirit as a living force at the center of the psyche. Yet few are aware that Jung's contributions resulted from his own personal encounters with a divine force.

Born in Basil, Switzerland, in 1875, Carl was deeply influenced by his father, a church pastor who had lost his faith. His sensitive temperament came more from his mother, an intuitive woman given to spontaneous outbursts of profound insight, around whom mysterious events seemed to happen—like the time a solid oak table in front of her emitted a sound like a gunshot and split down the middle, against the grain, or when a thick steel knife in a breadbasket loudly exploded into neatly sheered fragments. Such events, which had no rational explanation, served, in part, to generate the first stirrings of Carl's inquiries into life's deeper realities.

Carl's destiny was also influenced by a rich internal world of vivid dreams and fantasies, and he would devote his entire life to exploring this inner realm of inexhaustible mysteries. "Man's psyche," he later claimed, "is as infinite within as the universe is without."

Fascinated by the supernatural and the possibility of life beyond death, and curious about the human soul, Carl was drawn to an exciting new science called psychiatry, then in its infancy. After completing his doctorate, he took a position in a mental hospital in Zurich, where each day he confronted the haunting specter of minds destroyed by every kind of madness.

Psychiatry at that time was mainly concerned with identifying, naming, and cataloging the various types of mental illness. Patients were regarded as merely pitiful objects to be studied— soulless wrecks from whose shattered lives useful knowledge might be extracted. But Carl saw his patients as complex human souls, each containing a unique, if hidden, story, each guarding a mystery waiting to be discovered. He said that for each person, this hidden story is "the secret . . . the rock against which he is shattered." He began to search for that story in each patient, convinced that it held the key to their healing.

Throwing himself passionately into his work, Carl delved into his patients' psyches and into his own, emphasizing the importance of the human relationship in the healing process. He believed that a physician should not hide behind a mask of superiority. "A doctor is effective only when he is affected," Jung wrote. "Only the wounded physician heals."

The publication of his first book brought him to the attention of another great man then making a name for himself—that man was Sigmund Freud. The two began to correspond, each recognizing and respecting the other's genius. So began a professional and personal relationship marked by both fruitful collaboration and historic conflict.

Freud called Carl his "crown prince and heir." But Carl's mission lay waiting in his own uncharted depths. He felt compelled to uncover the spiritual implications of mental illness, while Freud dogmatically emphasized the sexual source of all psychological disturbances. To Freud, the idea of spirit was a delusional construct masking sexual repression. But Carl considered spirit, or soul, the essential core of man's being. Their increasingly diverging visions would become irreconcilable.

Freud insisted that Carl's radical ideas were wrong—dangerously close to mysticism. His increasing efforts to discourage Carl from pursuing his own vision forced Carl to choose between the embrace of a revered authority, father figure, and mentor, and the call of his own destiny. After long and agonized soul-searching, Carl chose the lonely path to greatness.

The split between them, when it came, plunged Carl into a state of profound uncertainty, self-doubt, and intellectual paralysis. Now shunned by most of the international psychiatric community, Carl lost his footing and felt himself falling into an abyss. His descent was marked by cataclysmic dreams and terrifying visions. In one, he saw a rising flood submerge the European continent, destroying nations and drowning multitudes before turning into a sea of blood. (After World War I began the following year, he saw his vision as a premonition arising out of what he would later call the collective unconscious.)

At first, Carl feared he might be going mad, perhaps entering a psychosis that would destroy him. Even so, as a dedicated scientist, he kept a journal of his inner process, thinking to leave a record behind so that at least some human knowledge might be salvaged from his destruction. For months, he struggled against these inner visions and forces.

Finally, Carl realized he must explore the very shadows he most feared. If he lacked the courage to face his own demons, how could he ever hope to heal others? Thus, Carl Jung began a conscious, deliberate, often terrifying journey into the psychic underworld that would last for years. It was a desperate, sometimes terrifying, period full of apocalyptic visions, fears of madness, and spiritual encounters with the denizens of the Heaven and Hell within his own psyche. In the process of exploring this inner landscape and struggling to understand all that he encountered in these inner depths and heights, he became perhaps the first scientist-shaman.

At his time of greatest peril, as his inner forces threatened to overwhelm him (he kept a loaded revolver in a drawer near his bed and had considered suicide), an inner guide appeared to him—a wise old man who called himself Philemon. In long internal "conversations," Philemon counseled Carl, displaying profound and original insights that often surprised the psychiatrist—the "scientist" speculated that Philemon must be a facet of his own mind, yet the "shaman" within him related to Philemon as an independent and superior entity.

Carl wondered at the nature of this mysterious figure. Was Philemon merely an imaginary creation? Or was he something more mysterious? He came to understand that Philemon was both a part of his psyche *and* a being with an individuated existence of his own. Carl fully accepted this unique relationship and later referred to Philemon as his "guru," a guide on his journey through the unconscious. Whatever his ultimate nature,

Philemon and the forces he represented transformed Carl Jung's relationship to psychiatry and to his own psyche—and perhaps saved his life. With Philemon's help, Jung the scholar/scientist, crossed the shaman's bridge between worlds and passed through an inner abyss into the life of an illumined mystic. And as a result of these years of inner work, Carl emerged as a prolific figure of colossal genius.

New energy, ideas, and insights came flooding through him. He began to write for the first time in nearly a decade. In time, he would produce over 30 volumes of astonishing scope and depth—firsthand reports of a man who had traveled to the innermost regions of the psyche and returned with undreamed-of riches. Among these was an original psychiatric model of the mind that included the soul—that viewed man's psychological processes in the light of his spiritual nature.

One night in the second half of his life, Carl woke to see a greenish-gold figure of a crucified Christ hovering over him, "marvelously beautiful," bathed in bright light. This central religious figure impacted Carl deeply. Ever a scientist, he sought to grasp the meaning of this vision held within his psyche. He came to understand his vision of the Christ as an alchemical symbol of the union of spirit and matter in human flesh, that meeting of opposites we must integrate in order to be saved or become whole. Carl the scientist had provided keys to unlock the spiritual treasures of the world religions.

His vision led him to study ancient alchemical texts. Before Carl single-handedly cracked this code, alchemists were thought of as crude scientists, or magicians, seeking to change lead into gold. But Carl discovered that they were in fact a secret brotherhood of mystics driven underground by the Inquisition—their true goal was spiritual transmutation, changing the "lead" of unconsciousness into the "gold" of transcendent awareness. He found in these alchemical works clear confirmation of many of his psychological theories. His wide-ranging explorations resulted in his classic theories, taught today in nearly every school of psychology and psychiatry worldwide.

At the age of 69, Carl Jung suffered a heart attack. He found himself a thousand miles in space, with Earth below, bathed in blue light. "The most glorious thing I had ever seen," he said. In this vision—one of the most significant of his life—he landed on a black meteorite where "a black Hindu sat silently in lotus posture upon a stone bench" before the entrance to a temple. As he was about to enter the temple, he felt everything he had been, done, experienced, known, and accomplished—all his hopes, desires, and goals—stripped away from him until only his essence remained.

He later wrote, in *Memories, Dreams, Reflections*: "I had the certainty I was about to enter an illumined room and. . . . I would at last . . . know what had been before me, why I had come into being and where my life was flowing." But before he could enter, he saw his doctor rise up as a spirit from Earth, framed "by a golden laurel wreath." He had been sent to take Carl back. The next instant, Carl found himself back in his body, sick at heart—he had longed to enter that temple where the riddle of his life would be solved.

During his weeks of recovery, Carl experienced a series of exalted visions. "These were states of ineffable joy. Angels were present, and light. . . . Night after night I floated in a state of purest bliss, 'thronged round with images of all creation.'" At this point, the most productive period of his life's work began. "A good many of my principal works were written only then," he recalled. "And something else, came to me . . . an affirmation of things as they are, an unconditional 'yes' to the conditions of existence, . . . of my own nature."

Carl Jung died shortly before his 86th birthday, productive to the very end. His writings, born of his journey into the wilderness of the human psyche, mark him as one of the towering figures of our age. His life-changing encounters with the spiritual forces and entities he discovered there—forces at work and at war within each of us—have helped illuminate humanity's path to the spiritual treasures waiting within our own inner worlds.

Our Lady of Guadalupe

A Sacred Image Changes History and Baffles Science

An extensively documented series of miracles began in the early years of the sixteenth century, on the Saturday morning of December 9, 1531, the day of the Feast of the Immaculate Conception.

Juan, a short, middle-age Aztec peasant, trod the rugged Mexican landscape beneath the cold blue vault of Heaven. The sky soon paled and morning stars appeared as pinpricks of light. As he reached the shoulder of Tepeyac Hill, nine miles from Mexico City, he heard music of unearthly beauty resound "like a choir of mellifluous birds." Ethereal and enchanting, it stirred the silence of his soul and filled him rapture. Looking up at the hilltop from where it came, he saw a vision of heavenly splendor, a luminous cloud from which rays of light streamed out in the colors of the rainbow.

Then, the music suddenly stopped and he heard a woman's

voice call to him from the top of the hill, her voice sweet, affectionate, insistent: "Juanito," she called, as if familiar to him. "Juan Dieguito. . . ."

Juan's heart instantly knew what his mind could not fathom: He rushed to the top of the hill, reached the promontory, and found an angel of God—a girl perhaps 14 years old, her slender body emanating a mysterious light. He stopped, struck speechless. He later reported that such compassion as he had never known before shone in her eyes as she gazed at him, beckoning him forward. He took a few faltering steps, then fell to his knees as she spoke words he would never forget: "Know for certain, dearest of my sons, that I am the perfect and perpetual Virgin Mary, Mother of the True God, through whom everything lives, the Lord of all things, who is Master of Heaven and Earth. I ardently desire a temple be built here for me, where I will show and offer all my love, compassion, help, and protection to the people. . . . Here I will hear their weeping and their sorrows, and remedy and alleviate their sufferings, necessities, and misfortunes."

She told Juan to tell the bishop of Mexico City of her wish to build a church on that spot. Juan, a poor Aztec peasant who spoke no Spanish, hurried to the bishop's house to do the will of the Mother of Christ. He waited on a cold patio as Bishop Zumarraga summoned an interpreter. When the translator came, the bishop listened to Juan politely, then casually dismissed him. Stories of angelic visitations are suspect in any age.

Dejected, Juan returned to the summit where the Lady waited for him. Seeing her radiance, he again fell to his knees, touched his head to the earth, and confessed his failure, begging her to send another man more worthy than he—one who would be believed. But Juan could not dissuade her.

The next morning, he returned to the bishop's home and knelt, distraught, pleading, with tears in his eyes. Through the translator, Juan Gonzalez, the bishop thoroughly questioned Juan about his vision. Juan answered sincerely, with convincing detail. Bishop Zumarraga found himself strangely moved—he did not know what to think. Was this peasant crazy? Or had he truly been chosen by God for some mysterious purpose? Finally, he told Juan that he required a sign; let the Lady decide what kind of sign to give—but he, the bishop of Mexico City, could not build a temple based on fantasy.

Mary was waiting again on the hilltop for Juan when he returned. "That is very well, my little son," she told Juan. "Return tomorrow and you will have the sign he requested. Then he will no longer doubt you."

Juan returned home to find his uncle mortally wounded, shot with an arrow by his own people for collaborating with the Spanish missionaries. In a weak voice, Juan's uncle begged him to fetch a priest to hear his confession and administer last rites. Juan started for the city. For the sake of his uncle who had raised him like a son, he would put off his meeting with the Lady until after he had brought a priest. But as he skirted Tepeyac Hill, he saw the Lady descending in a luminous cloud to meet him where he would pass by.

"Listen well and let it penetrate your heart, my little son," she said. "Do not be weighed down with grief or fear any illness or vexation. Am I not your Mother? Are you not under my shadow and protection, in the folds of my mantle? Your uncle will not die—at this very moment, he is cured," she said.

She then sent Juan to the top of the hill to gather flowers. A joyous Juan rushed to the barren hilltop he had seen only the day before—to his astonishment, masses of brightly colored flowers now grew out of season in the frozen December soil—even Castilian roses from Spain.

He gathered them in his *tilma*—a long poncho of woven cotton—until it hung like a sack on his belly. He returned to the Lady, who told him that the bishop would accept the flowers as the sign he was looking for.

Buoyed up with faith that his uncle was now well, Juan hurried off to see the bishop. At first, the bishop's servants refused to let him in; they pushed and taunted Juan, then tried to grab the flowers. But the flowers shrank into Juan's *tilma*, melting away from their grasping hands—strange behavior for flowers in any season. Awed, they sent word to the bishop, who ordered Juan to be brought to his quarters at once.

Bishop Zumarraga was visiting with a group of important officials, among them Bishop Ramirez and the governor of Mexico as well as Juan Gonzalez, the interpreter. Juan Diego told them of the Lady and of the strange flowers grown overnight, then let the flowers spill out of the folds of his *tilma* onto the floor. Their perfumed smell filled the room. All stared down at them, amazed. And when they looked up at Juan, their eyes fastened on his *tilma*. Every man went down on his knees in awe.

Juan, mystified by their behavior, looked down at his *tilma* and saw *an image of Mary emblazoned on it with uncanny perfection.*

Modern experts say the 56-inch-tall image on the *tilma* of Juan Diego equals in artistry and beauty the works of da Vinci, Raphael, and Rembrandt. But the manner of its appearance on the *tilma* is more miraculous than its eerily vivid lifelikeness. For Bishop Zumarraga testified that he saw the image of the Mother of Christ appear on the *tilma* at the very moment he looked up from the flowers. Four centuries would pass before modern technology would unravel even more mysterious aspects of this unparalleled work of spiritual and artistic perfection.

On that same morning the flowers appeared to Juan, a beautiful woman illumined by a celestial radiance suddenly appeared to Juan's dying uncle. In a few moments, he rose, miraculously healed, and knelt before her. She told him she had sent Juan to the bishop and about her sacred image. She told him her name—the Ever-Virgin Mary *Tequetalope*, an Aztec word meaning "Who saves us from the Devourer." This last word of her name was phonetically translated into Spanish as *Guadalupe*.

The church was indeed built. On December 26, 1531, a multitude of thousands escorted the *tilma* with its sacred image to the newly built chapel on Tepeyac Hill. During the celebration, a group of Mexicans fired arrows into the sky. One pierced a man's neck, killing him. His corpse was carried into the chapel and laid beneath the sacred image. The crowd prayed aloud to Mary for a miracle. Minutes later, the man opened his eyes and rose, healed. Spaniards and Mexicans—mortal enemies—now embraced one another with joyous affection.

Word of Mary's miraculous appearance and her resurrection of the dead swept across Mexico. Millions who had bitterly fought the spread of Christianity now flooded in to worship her sacred image. Within a few years, over nine million Aztecs and millions more of every race, district, and tribe were converted to the new faith. An "unavoidable" bloodbath between the Spaniards and these conquered peoples was averted by the power and presence emanating from the miraculous image of Our Lady of Guadalupe.

In the next four centuries, an estimated *billion people* went to venerate the sacred image. Thousands of miraculous healings of every kind of affliction were recorded. The image, kept for a century in the damp chapel, exposed to the elements and the smoke of votive candles—touched, rubbed, kissed, and embraced by *millions*—proved itself virtually indestructible. According to one chemist, the "corrosive hydrocarbons, ionizations and soot [in the small chapel] . . . should have blackened the picture beyond recognition." Yet even today, it shows no signs of age, wear, or damage, nor have its bright colors faded over the centuries. A *tilma* normally rots in 20 years—this one remains perfectly preserved after nearly five centuries.

On November 14, 1921, a time bomb hidden in a large flower vase directly beneath the image exploded, blowing chunks of marble and masonry from the walls, shattering the stained glass windows of the basilica, and twisting a thick iron cross on the altar. Yet the miraculous image several feet away was not only unscathed *but the thin sheet of glass covering it was not even cracked*. And none of the many worshippers gathered there, who witnessed this miracle, were seriously injured.

In 1936, two colored fibers from the sacred image, one red, one yellow, were examined by the director of the chemistry department of the Kaiser Wilhelm Institute in Heidelberg, Germany. Remarkably, he concluded that there was "no coloring agent of any kind in the fibres." The source of color in the fibers was untraceable, being neither animal, vegetable, nor mineral dye. *Yet no synthetic coloring existed before the 1800s.*

In 1946, a microscope examination of the image revealed that it has no brush strokes. The image is not painted on. It appears to be a kind of living photographic image created three centuries before photography was invented.

On May 29, 1951, an enlarged photograph under magnification revealed, in the eyes of the sacred image, the face and bust of a bearded man. A special investigation was begun by order of the archbishop of Mexico City.

On December 11, 1955, the investigating committee announced that the face in the eyes of the sacred image, as if reflected there, had been positively identified from a painting as the face of Juan Diego.

On July 23, 1956, oculist Dr. Rafael Lavoignet examined the eyes of the tiny image with an ophthalmoscope. His verdict: "In the cornea of the eyes, a human bust can be seen. The distortion and place of the optical image are identical with what is produced in a normal eye. . . . On the surface there shines quite distinctly the silhouette of a human bust. The head is turned three quarters towards the Virgin's right and slightly bent forward . . . as though at the moment of the Image being impressed, a man facing the Blessed Virgin, and reflected in the cornea of her eye, had himself been photographed in this indirect way. The image of the bust shows a distortion in exact conformity with the laws of such a reflection in vivo."

Oculist Dr. Javier Bueno confirmed this report, adding, "The silhouette of the same bearded man is reflected in the nasal region of the right eye, and also appears in the temporal corner of the left eye. The distortion of the reflected image is even more striking for its perfect obedience to the laws of curvature of the cornea." The precise nature of corneal eye reflections was not scientifically verified until the 1880s—300 years after the image's creation.

In 1962, an optometrist and his wife analyzed a photograph of the eyes of the sacred image magnified 25 times and discovered *two more faces*. The true-to-life manner in which all these images are "reflected" in the corneas could not have been produced by sixteenth-century technology. And these figures match almost identically those of Bishop Ramirez and translator Juan Gonzalez in Miguel Cabera's eighteenth-century painting of the image's miraculous appearance, faithfully rendered according to original documents.

On May 7, 1979, the image was examined via infrared technology by professor Philip Callahan, an authority in the field of infrared radiation and the study of its effects on molecules and also an accomplished painter. His conclusions are summarized by author Francis Johnson in his marvelous book *Our Lady of Guadalupe*. "The picture, . . . its colour rendering and the preservation of its brightness over the centuries are inexplicable. There is no sizing and no protective over-varnish present on the image. Without sizing the tilma should have rotted centuries ago, and without protective varnishing the picture should have been ruined long ago by prolonged exposure to candle smoke and other pollutants. Under high magnification, the image shows no detectable sign of fading or cracking—an inexplicable occurrence after 470 years of existence."

The story of the sacred image of Our Lady of Guadalupe is one of the strongest cases in history, documented by personal testimony and scientific investigation, of supernatural intervention by a divine power. Twenty million people each year visit the sacred image and many mysterious healings still occur. And after nearly five centuries, the Catholic Church is moving closer to declaring as formally blessed the humble Aztec peasant Juan Diego, who lives forever in the eyes of Our Lady of Guadalupe.

Addict to Artist

A Lost Soul Finds New Purpose

Andy Lakey was born in France in 1959 to a half-Spanish, half-French mother and an American father. His family later moved to Ohio, then Japan, then Kansas, and finally to California. Maybe it was the instability or not fitting in—or maybe there are no "good" reasons at all—but by the time Andy graduated from high school and joined the navy, drugs had become an integral part of his life. He didn't last long in the navy, though he managed to leave with an honorable discharge.

Andy soon found a lucrative occupation as a car salesman. But as his career ascended, so did his drug use. Cocaine, which he smoked in a freebase pipe, was his drug of choice. By 1986, at the age of 27, Andy was making $85,000 a year, much of which went up in smoke. He was going nowhere, in the fast lane.

Then, on New Year's Eve, Andy Lakey received a house call from God.

It came like a bolt of lightning. While greeting the New

Year by freebasing cocaine in a friend's apartment upstairs from his own, his heart suddenly began rapidly palpitating and he felt extremely ill.

"I felt certain I was going to die," he says.

Staggering out of the room, Andy collapsed in the hall, then somehow stumbled downstairs to his apartment. Leaving the door open behind him, Andy got into the shower, still fully clothed, and turned on the cold water, hoping it might revive him. With the water pouring over him, feeling frightened and alone, he bowed his head against the wall and prayed for the first time since he was eight years old.

"I still remember the prayer," he says. "I said, 'God is good. God is great. God, if you let me live, I will never do drugs again.'" These were desperate words muttered by countless other addicts, but Andy meant them with all his soul. And he added, "I will also do something to help humankind."

"Almost instantly," he reports "I felt a twirling sensation, like a little tornado or whirlpool around my feet. . . . There were seven figures, and as they twirled up toward my knees, my thighs, my waist, and up to my chest, the twirling got faster and faster.. . . . When they reached my heart, they came together as one and put their arms around me. . . . Now there was only one figure. . . . It embraced and lifted me into another dimension. There were a thousand planets with 10,000 poles of light extending through them and into . . . a galaxy of brightness. Inside each pole were millions of tiny figures . . . including me, waiting to enter. . . . Every pole was filled with millions of souls in perfect columns and perfect harmony. But I could not get into a pole."

At that point, Andy woke up in the emergency room—his friend had found him unconscious in the shower and taken him to the hospital just in time. The doctor told him that due to the massive amount of cocaine in his body, his heart had started to fail.

Andy woke up totally free of his years-long dependency on drugs.

This near-death lesson, with its staggering vision, was not lost on him. Andy vowed to change his life. He started by finding a new job, since most of his business acquaintances were also his party friends. Meanwhile, he began to contemplate the meaning of his vision—a vision he resolved to bring into this world—first by drawing it, then by painting it. This project became an obsession to which he devoted every spare moment, every night.

On his 30th birthday, Andy quit work to become a full-time artist. "The only problem," he relates, "was that I never learned how to paint." This small obstacle would not deter him. He created an art studio with a friend and, as a show of commitment, bought $5,000 worth of supplies and became a full-time artist-in-training.

One morning some time later, Andy awoke and felt something was shifting. He went to his studio, sat before one of his paintings, and began to pray. When he raised his head, he saw a ball of light come through the wall and enter his forehead. "The ball enveloped my body, filling me with pure love, pure energy. . . . I found myself communicating with three men. They were definitely my angels. . . . They had beards, whitish hair, very light in color, very bright. . . . They were giving me information telepathically and told me exactly what I was to do: I was to paint 2,000 paintings by the year 2000. These angels would take care of everything. . . . I knew they would give me my art technique; they would teach me to paint."

The angels vanished but kept their word. Soon, through a series of fateful coincidences, Andy Lakey stumbled onto the highly unorthodox technique that marks his paintings—the paint rises off his canvases, thickly textured because it is often applied directly from the tubes.

In little more than a month after this second vision, Andy had completed six canvases. On the day that he put three of these paintings on display at a local bank, a Canadian art collector came in, stared at them for an hour, and ended up hiring Andy to do a giant painting in his home. An art consultant, impressed by Andy's unique style—his almost three-dimensional paintings are as tactile as they are visual—suggested that he create paintings for the blind. After she tipped off a local TV news crew about this talented angel artist, Andy Lakey's career took off.

Peter Jennings obtained and donated one of Lakey's first paintings to New York City's nonprofit Lighthouse, an organization for the visually impaired. Other admirers and owners of his work include Ray Charles, Stevie Wonder, Jimmy Carter, Ronald Reagan, and numerous other high-profile public figures along with a host of other people who are deeply moved by his work.

Ten months after he began painting, with around 50 paintings under his belt, Andy had a one-man exhibition in a local gallery. Every single painting sold. He began donating paintings to hospitals, schools for the blind, and other charitable institutions and now donates 30 percent of his work. Even the pope formally accepted one of Andy's paintings as a gift; it now resides in the Vatican.

Thousands of people have written, faxed, and called Andy Lakey, many reporting different forms of healing, revelation, and transformation in connection with his work. In 1993, Andy, who had by then completed 1,678 angel paintings, went on *The Oprah Winfrey Show* and shared his vision with millions of viewers.

Although some suggest his vision was no more than a drug-induced hallucination, his transformed life and the dramatic emergence of his unique artistic gifts suggest otherwise.

"I don't have the answer," says Andy, now married and the father of four. "I'm just doing what I was instructed to do. Once you love yourself and you love others, it's as if the world knows this, and the world will take care of you and love you back. When I look up at the night sky, I see the stars totally differently . . . they're a reminder of what's really out there. In my heart and spirit, I see bright planets and poles of light. I see angels flying through the universe, doing the work of God."

Andy Lakey has found a vision worth living for.

The Incorruptibles

Vitality and Healing Powers of Saintly Corpses

For centuries and throughout the world, millions of people have witnessed—and numerous scientists have investigated—the bodies of saints and laypersons from many cultures who show no signs of decay for weeks, years, and in many cases, for centuries after their deaths. Without human intervention, such corpses have endured conditions that rot the wood, corrode the metal, and disintegrate the clothing in which they are interred. The bodies of Saint Francis and Saint John of the Cross remained perfectly intact even after being covered with corrosive lime to hasten their dissolution. Their flexibility, physical texture, and appearance is such that they seem to be asleep rather than dead. Cumulatively, these men and women are traditionally referred to as the incorruptibles.

Although the Catholic Church considers incorruptibility "an accessory to sanctity" rather than a miracle, a variety of mysterious phenomena have occurred to and around these apparently vital corpses. Some spontaneously bleed, emit perfumed oils and fragrance, and, stretching the limits of credulity, a few of them, sealed within glass caskets, are reported to have opened and closed their eyes, moved their limbs, or changed the positions of their bodies centuries after their deaths. Witnesses who have testified to these events rank among the most highly respected in their times—monks, cardinals, priests, and popes; noblemen and -women; scholars and writers; government officials and heads of state; doctors; scientists; and others. Yet to this day, the fact of the incorruptibles and the extraordinary phenomena that surround them defy scientific explanation.

Thousands of spontaneous healings, many of them investigated and documented, have reportedly occurred in the presence of the incorruptible saints. Yet while the healings may be documented fact, their source remains open to speculation. Some call them miracles. Others reduce them to the placebo effect. Yet such words hardly begin to explain the mystery of the phenomenon. Perhaps after reading the stories that follow, you can choose your own explanation.

The following incorruptibles are only a few of many existing today.

Saint Catherine of Bologna died in 1463. Eighteen days after her death, the nuns first noticed a sweet fragrance filling the cemetery. They traced it to Catherine's grave, exhumed her, and found her body in a state of radiant physical perfection, emanating the delightful fragrance. In 1500, Saint Catherine appeared in a vision to a nun, Leonora Poggi, asking that her body (still flexible and lifelike) be placed in a special chapel in a sitting position. It was done. There she has remained for 500 years, sitting in a throne in the Sanctuary Church of Corpus Domini in Bologna, Italy. Today, she remains well-preserved, although four centuries of smoke from candles and oil lamps have darkened her skin.

Saint Charbel Makhlouf, a monk from a village in Northern Lebanon, died at age 70 of a fatal seizure while saying mass. Father Charbel was quickly buried without a coffin, according to custom. For the next 45 nights, many witnesses saw a brilliant white light emanating from his grave. The excitement it generated caused monastery officials to apply for ecclesiastical permission to exhume and examine Father Charbel's body.

In the meantime, heavy rains fell. Four months later, in the presence of the order's superiors, Father Charbel was exhumed and found entombed in liquid mud in the rain-soaked grave, perfectly preserved and in a state of lifelike flexibility. He was carefully washed, newly clothed, laid in a coffin, and set in a private chapel. Witnesses soon noticed a liquid, apparently perspiration and blood, exuding from the pores of Father Charbel's lifelike skin. It saturated his new clothing, which had to be changed twice a week. Nearly 30 years passed.

On July 24, 1927, two physicians from the French Medical Institute of Beirut examined Father Charbel's body. These physicians as well as the judge of the ecclesiastical commission, the defender of the faith, a notary public, and the superiors of the order all documented Father Charbel's perfectly preserved state. The body was placed in a new tomb sealed with masonry, and the burial site became a shrine for visiting pilgrims. There, in the years that followed, many healings occurred to visitors and pilgrims.

Twenty-three years later, a strange liquid was discovered leaking from the tomb, across the floor into the oratory. So, on April 22, 1950, ecclesiastical authorities, officials, and physicians gathered for the exhumation. Father Charbel was found perfectly preserved, his flesh and limbs flexible and lifelike, his pores still exuding the same mysterious liquid.

Between 5,000 and 15,000 pilgrims from around the world now visited Father Charbel's shrine daily, seeking cures for various afflictions. After the 1950 exhumation, the monastery began to investigate and record all the miraculous healings that occurred there, documenting over 1,200 cases in the next two years. Alessandro Obeid, blinded with a torn retina, regained his sight after seeing a vision of Father Charbel at his shrine. Maria Abel Kawary, dying from a gastric ulcer, was restored to health after praying at the shrine. After Mountaha Daher, a tragically deformed hunchback, prayed at Father Charbel's shrine for her needy relatives, all deformities miraculously disappeared from her body, so that her appearance became normal. These and many other such cases were investigated, verified, and documented by medical authorities.

Finally, in 1965, after long and rigorous investigation, Father Charbel was beatified (declared blessed) by Pope Paul VI. His body, exhumed again, had finally "complied with the laws of nature"—only his bones remained, tinted red, a color they have kept since. In 1977, the miraculous monk was canonized, becoming Saint Charbel.

His shrine is still a site of spontaneous healings.

Saint Andrew Bobola of Poland remains one of the most extraordinary cases of preservation on record. He died a grisly death in 1657 when Russian Cossacks beat him; dragged him for miles behind their horses; burned, choked, and partly flayed him alive; cut out his tongue; drove wooden splinters under his fingernails; mutilated his face; chopped off his hands; and finally killed him with a sword. Forty years later, his interred body remained undecayed. In 1737, his still-preserved body was examined by physicians Anexander Pascoli and Ramond Tarozzi of the College of Physicians in Rome and medical professors in the University of Rome. Their dissertation stated that the extreme mutilation of the body should have caused its rapid deterioration. Yet it remained flexible, lifelike, and of normal color, the blood still freshly congealed over its wounds. It was examined again in 1827 by Dr. Marco Cingelo Marcangeli, a hospital medical director and professor of theoretical medicine at the University of Rome, who confirmed its preserved condition as "nothing less than miraculous."

Saint Andrew's body, now dark and rigid, lies on display in a crystal reliquary below the main altar of the Church of Saint Andrew in Warsaw, Poland. Over 400 miraculous healings have been documented at his shrine.

Saint Rita of Cascia, who lived from 1381 to 1457, is associated with numerous spontaneous healings of those visiting her incorrupt body. At the moment of her death, her cell filled with a perfumed fragrance and brilliant light emanated from a wound on her forehead. Today, over four centuries later, her incorrupt body periodically emits a delightful fragrance. Formally examined in 1627, her flesh was natural in color, soft to the touch, and as flexible as in life. At times, her body has inexplicably changed position and her uncannily lifelike eyes have opened and closed spontaneously. Documents also record that she has been seen moving from side to side and has even levitated in her sarcophagus in the sight of witnesses. Miraculous healings still occur at her shrine in Cascia, Italy.

Paramahansa Yogananda, an Indian saint best known for his classic memoir *Autobiography of a Yogi*, brought one of India's ancient spiritual traditions to America in the 1930s and introduced the science of yoga to tens of millions. Few people, however, appreciate that when he died, his body also transcended the usual process of decomposition—a relatively modern case of incorruptability.

Yogananda died on March 7, 1952, and was interred in Los Angeles's Forest Lawn Memorial Park. Three weeks later, his body still showed no signs of physical deterioration and "his unchanged face shone with the divine luster of incorruptibility." The following material comes from a notarized letter written by Harry T. Rowe, Forest Lawn's mortuary director. Rowe writes, "The absence of any visual signs of decay in the dead body of Paramahansa Yogananda offers the most extraordinary case in our experience. . . . No physical disintegration was visible in his body even twenty days after death. . . . No indication of mold was visible on his skin, and no visible desiccation (drying up) took place in the bodily tissues. This state of perfect preservation of a body is, so far as we know from mortuary annals, an unparalleled one. . . . At the time of receiving Yogananda's body, the Mortuary personnel expected to observe, through the glass lid of the casket, the usual progressive signs of bodily decay. Our astonishment increased as day followed day without bringing any visible change in the body under observation. Yogananda's body was apparently in a phenomenal state of immutability. . . . No odor of decay emanated from his body at any time. . . . The physical appearance of Yogananda on March 27, just before the bronze cover of the casket was put into position, was . . . as fresh and as unravaged by decay as he had looked on (March 7) the night of his death. For these reasons we state again that the case of Paramahansa Yogananda is unique in our experience."

To this day, such phenomena remain unexplained.

Remember the Music

A New Life beyond Fear of Death

When Carol Benjamin was 9 years old, music entered her life in the sensuous shape of a cello. For 25 years, her music graced the practice halls of her home, her schools, the Oberlin College Conservatory of Music, and finally, the Fort Wayne Philharmonic Orchestra in Indiana.

Carol's early life seemed blessed with talent, music, and love. At 23, she met and eventually married a kind and gentle man named David. Despite his struggle with chronic depression, they lived and loved in a world of music, literature, and the outdoors. But in their 12th year of marriage, David died suddenly and all semblance of sanity, meaning, and justice departed Carol's world. "Part of me wanted to die, too," she says. "It was like a temptation from the other side, like standing on a high cliff and looking down."

Within three years of David's death, Carol learned that she

had cancer of the liver. Rejecting the option of a transplant, she found a surgeon willing to try to remove the tumor. To prepare for the surgery, she began to train daily: She swam, meditated, and watched her diet. Facing her mortality for the first time, she tapped into what she calls warrior energy. With seven-eighths of her liver to be removed, she would have only a 50-percent chance—a coin toss—of surviving surgery. So Carol put her things in order, made out a will, left copious instructions, and wrote to every friend she had ever known to complete any unfinished business.

At one point while under general anesthesia, the oddest thing happened to Carol: She found herself standing at a threshold between worlds, hearing a conversation between two groups of beings—she heard rather than saw them. As if her fate were being discussed in some kind of cosmic courtroom, she heard one group say, in essence, "She's done what she came to do and she should go now."

"You're right," the other group responded, "but we think she can do more." Carol had a clear sense that either way would be okay—it was out of her hands. Suddenly, a hand came from behind and turned her around, away from the threshold, back toward life.

But she hovered on the edge of death for four weeks.

Carol's doctor told her sister, Marla, to prepare herself—it was unlikely that Carol would live. But she did live, fighting her way back to a relatively normal life. She moved to Boulder, Colorado, and continued working at a profession she had learned during her years with David—as a physical therapist. She even got a puppy.

But Carol was living on borrowed time. Her liver grew

back to its normal size, yet surgical scars now blocked the bile ducts. With each passing month, her skin yellowed as she grew weaker and more ill. Carol's physician urged her to consider a transplant. Without it, he said, she had only a few more months.

The evaluation process for a liver transplant involved exploratory surgery to determine whether the cancer had spread. If it had, there was no hope; if it hadn't, she would qualify for the lifesaving surgery.

While lying in bed in the pre-op ward, Carol again encountered a being from the "other" world. "This time," she says, "it seemed more like an angelic intervention: Eight of us were scheduled for a variety of operations that morning. The charge nurse announced the surgery order for each of us; I was number six.

"I had closed my eyes and was resting, trying to meditate. At one point, I opened my eyes and saw a figure standing before me at the foot of my bed—an androgynous being about nine feet tall, wearing a flowing white gown—he appeared to be about 19 years old, yet ageless. He noticed me looking at him; his expression told me it was okay that I saw him.

"I felt an incredible peace. This was my first taste of what I would call grace. Prior to this time, I hadn't the faintest notion of what grace meant and certainly had no prior experience with angels!

"Yet here was this being, visiting the bed of every patient—touching each of them as if giving a blessing. But he wasn't touching them in the order they would be called in for surgery, and I became concerned that someone might be called in before this being could bless them. Just then, the nurse came in and told several people their surgery had been delayed for various reasons—it turned out that the angel had touched each person in the exact order they were now scheduled for surgery."

Carol's surgery went well—she was free of cancer—but her liver was much worse than her surgeon had anticipated. He kept her in the hospital for three days, hoping a liver would become available. When none appeared, she finally went home. Soon, she had deteriorated to near the point in liver failure where most people just go to sleep, sink into a coma, and never reawaken.

During this twilight time, Carol began spending more time on "the other side." There, she met a new group of beings who seemed to be preparing her to cross over. They came to her in the daytime and at night she went to the other side to be with them in the dream state. She experienced a continuity between the worlds before and after death. (Carol, an extremely down-to-earth person, relates all of this matter-of-factly.)

"I felt so cared for by these beings," she reports. "They felt like friends with whom I had shared a hundred lifetimes. When I saw them, it was like I was going home. And I felt a joyous remembrance that they had always been there—but that somehow I'd forgotten this wonderful truth. It was as if I'd had amnesia all these years.

"I gave myself up completely to whatever was to be," she recalls. "I told them, 'If I'm needed to serve, then I trust you'll keep me alive; if I'm not needed to serve, then I'll go.' Then, the Saturday night before my transplant, David came to me in my dreams and said in his English accent, 'Hang on, luv—just a little longer—it's not your time.'"

To this day, Carol is certain that David's visit kept her going.

One evening two days later, as she lay on her sofa watching the film *Resurrection*, the phone rang. Too exhausted to rise,

Carol heard the voice of the transplant nurse on her answering machine: "I hope you're there and hear this soon, because we have a liver for you." That got her to the phone.

The doctors needed her there in two hours. Carol called a taxi, then her sister, Marla, in Ohio, who was at that moment also watching *Resurrection*. Carol headed for the hospital as Marla headed for the airport. In the taxi, Carol gazed through the window at the star-filled sky, knowing it might be her last night.

Carol's transplant, although successful, was marred by complications that triggered a severe illness. At her lowest point, as she lay ill and exhausted, she heard a voice say, "Remember the music." She knew exactly what it meant—through the dark days, to strengthen her immune system, Carol had visualized herself as a warrior while she played *The Planets*, a stirring symphonic piece by Gustavus Holst. At times, she had burst into tears, moved by an overwhelming sense of grace.

Now, remembering the music—with the support of her dear David and her otherworldly friends, the sense of grace, and her warrior's energy—Carol made an inner decision to live. "I'd had so much help, but now it was my turn, up to me, to my will, to do the fighting. It was like someone had lit a Bunsen burner under me. I was absolutely committed. I felt an energy that was unbelievable."

Carol Benjamin had returned to life.

With her return came a profound commitment to service. "I knew that you don't just get all this help and then do your own thing. It doesn't make sense at any level. I felt an overall sense of being connected to everything, everyone—to life itself. You can't pretend there's a separation between you and other people anymore. It just doesn't work. This experience of grace taught me that extending a helping hand to others, the way it was given to me, is what life is for."

She adds, "It's great to be alive, but I have no sense of fear of death. It's impossible to fear death now, because I know those beings are there. But for now, till the time comes to go home, it's a constant call to serve—I can't see my life in any other way. This light has come on. While I live, I'm here to serve. The rest of my life is about finding out what that means."

Carol Benjamin lives a full and active life of service as a physical therapist and dog-training teacher in Boulder, Colorado. Although her story is by nature personal and private, she explained, "If it can help bring hope to others, then I'll share it."

God's Shoemaker

From Dogmatic Child to Spiritual Genius

Jakob Böhme was born on a farm in 1575 in Old Seidenberg, a devout Protestant village in Upper Lusatia (later known as Germany). His education was limited to reading, writing, and religion. An unusually pious youth, even for those times, he applied himself to the diligent study of his Lutheran Bible.

His weak constitution made a life of arduous farmwork unthinkable. So when he was 14, his father apprenticed him to a shoemaker in the nearby city of Görlitz. There Jakob learned his life's trade while making his own life difficult—he was good-natured and honest but also a nuisance, due to his self-righteous and prudish habit of chastising anyone—both customers and his employer—who took the Lord's name in vain or transgressed in any way against his strict religious codes.

One day, early in his apprenticeship, as he worked alone in the shop, a stranger entered and approached him—Jakob was struck by the man's deep, luminous eyes. The man bought a pair of shoes and left, but a moment later he called from the street, "Jakob! Come out!" Jakob obeyed him, surprised, for he had not told this stranger his name. The man spoke to him as if they were intimates, saying, "Jakob, you are little as yet, but you will become great . . . a man so uncommon that the world will marvel. Be dutiful to God . . . read the Holy Scriptures. There you will find instruction and consolation for the poverty and trials you will endure and for the persecution you will suffer. Be brave, be persevering. God . . . will be gracious to you." The incident made a strong impression on Jakob and increased his already extreme piety and judgmental behavior.

At last, his infuriated employer dismissed him, saying that he had hired an apprentice, not a missionary. For the next three years, Jakob wandered as an itinerant shoemaker across Germany, amid the terrible suffering, poverty, and devastation caused by the civil and religious wars unleashed by the Reformation. Jakob witnessed the religious hypocrisy of his age—the corruption and greed of churches and their hierarchies; exploiting starving peasants; and the power struggles and the fanatical holy wars between Catholics and Protestants, often waged by mercenary armies.

Those bitter years devastated Jakob's idealism and shattered his faith in the Church. Traumatized, he returned to Görlitz and sought solace in prayer and the reading of Scripture, seeking a more personal relationship with God. His experience awakened in him a spiritual impulse that can only be described as desperate. "I resolved to unceasingly ask for God's love and mercy until His blessing should descend upon me," he later wrote.

In 1595, his prayers were answered by a vision that would change the course of his life. As he described, in the language of his time, "The illumination of Spirit was shed upon me. . . . I stood in the Presence, apprehending the very essence of Divine Being, . . . enfolded with love. . . . I cannot find words to express the exaltation. It was like resurrection from the dead. . . . By a miraculous light I saw God. The interior of all was illumined. Thenceforward I was able to recognize God in each separate thing, in the creatures, and in plants and grasses."

The internal change in Jakob Böhme was not yet ready to manifest in the world. He would spend years living an ordinary life as a cobbler in Görlitz—he would marry a butcher's daughter and have six children. There would be years of preparation, study, and contemplation—of coming to a deeper understanding of his vision.

On a summer afternoon in 1600, Jakob experienced his second illumination. A casual glance at the sun's brilliant reflection on a pewter dish somehow catapulted him into a transcendent state in which the presence of God was revealed to him "everywhere and in everything."

For the next 12 years, Jakob breathed not a word to anyone of his experiences. But his spiritual sight continued to expand, revealing to him divine truths beyond any that he had read or heard. Eventually, he began to feel a growing inner call to write down all that had been revealed to him.

Jakob knew well the dangers of such a course, foretold in his youth by the mysterious man in the shoe shop. The laws of heresy in his day could bring swift and severe retribution. So he prayed and waited for a clear sign before he dared write a word of what had been shown to him.

At last, the sign came from within, "with commanding power." And Jakob Böhme—who had read little more than his

Bible and written little more than his name—now began to commit his divine revelations to paper.

His first work, *The Aurora*, is one of the most staggering undertakings in all of mystical literature. In that work, he summarized its scope and conception and the vision that inspired it, as follows: "Within myself I perceived creation entire, in its order and movement; I saw first the divine world of the angels and of paradise; second, the darkened world, the fiery realm; and third, this world around us, visible and tangible, as an issue and expression of the two inner, eternal, hidden worlds. Moreover, I comprehended the whole being and reason of Good and Evil. . . . "

Though lacking the formal education and style of his contemporaries, he possessed the clarity and depth of vision that come only to the divinely inspired. In *Men Who Have Walked with God*, Sheldon Cheney writes, "In those matters that render literary art excellent and inspiring, in the basic clarity, pungency and vividness of his words, Böhme outran in innumerable passages most of the writers of his age."

Yet Jakob Böhme, who was to become one of the most profound and prolific mystical writers of any age, never sought recognition. Of his voluminous writings, only one book was published in his lifetime, and that without his knowledge or permission. Jakob wrote not for his own glory but only to record the divine truths revealed to him, knowing that to take them to his grave unuttered was to steal them from the world, like the poor servant in Christ's parable burying his single talent in the earth.

One day, Karl von Endern, a nobleman and student of philosophy and mysticism, found and perused *The Aurora* while in

Jakob's shoe shop. Awed by the text's profundity, von Endern borrowed it, made copies, and circulated them among his friends. Jakob soon found himself revered among this group of well-educated noblemen. But as he had feared, his work fell into the hands of unsympathetic readers. One Sunday in church, Jakob was attacked and reviled from the pulpit as a heretic by his own Pastor Gregory Richter, who held a grudge against the cobbler over a trivial misunderstanding. Richter began a one-man crusade against Jakob, whom he called an anti-Christ. As a result, Jakob was officially forbidden to ever write another word on spiritual matters.

But Jakob Böhme's persecution, and his fame, had only begun.

Many brilliant philosophers and great lords of his day came to speak with this humble cobbler about his divine revelations. Though Jakob's conversations and continuing visions clarified his understanding, he wrote nothing more for six years. But eventually, Pastor Richter, infuriated by the stream of exalted visitors to Jakob's shoe shop, renewed his campaign of persecution and extended it to Jakob's wife and children.

This unwarranted persecution released Jakob from his vow of silence, and he began writing again. In the six years that followed—his final years before his death at the age of 50—Jakob wrote his greatest works, achieved his greatest fame, and attained his deepest spiritual peace despite the bitter persecution he encountered.

Anonymous individuals who do little in life rarely reap criticism or praise. In contrast, Jakob Böhme was both assailed and admired in proportion to his selfless service, inspired creativity, and theological impact on our world. He was separated from his family and harassed and assaulted by hostile citizens, yet also revered as a saint and prophet by the great noblemen and scholars of his time. Shortly after being exonerated of all charges and allowed to return home, Jakob fell deathly ill and took to his bed. Before dying in peace in his own home, in the company of his family, he forgave everyone who had ever harmed him.

In the four centuries since his death, Jakob Böhme's writings have inspired and influenced generations of theologians and mystics, including such luminaries as William Blake and Emmanuel Swedenborg. "My whole work on earth is nothing else but an instruction how man may create a Kingdom of Light within himself," he wrote. "But open your eyes, and the world is full of God."

Shamanic Initiation

Awakening to Service in Copper Canyon

By the time Mexico's rain-swollen Urique River swept Don Jacobs underwater into a narrow stone corridor in Copper Canyon in February 1983, his life had reached an impasse.

Born in 1946, Don was raised in a family plagued by alcoholism, which eventually killed his father and imprisoned his mother. Don's way of coping was to be the strong one—he largely raised his two younger sisters and vented his quick temper in athletics. When he grew older, he joined the marines and became a pilot during the Vietnam War. He often sought his adventure in dangerous pastimes—flying missions, racing wild horses, and riding rapids.

But his strength could sometimes be a liability when it took the form of an aggressive, self-righteous temperament—the very temperament that had threatened his marriage, jeopardized his firefighting job, complicated his life, and driven him to seek a transforming adventure in the isolated canyon in Central Mexico. Don somehow needed to risk these notorious rapids that ranked among the most treacherous on the continent.

Copper Canyon, in some places four times wider and 2,000 feet deeper than the Grand Canyon, is inhabited by the Rarámuri Indians, a tribe renowned for their endurance, running 100-mile races along the canyon's steep, rocky trails. An endurance runner himself, as well as an avid kayaker, Don had come to the canyon with his friend Dave, hoping to ride the Urique and observe these legendary Rarámuri runners firsthand. His interest in Indians came partly from his own native ancestry—his great grandfather was a full-blooded Cherokee.

A short, stocky Rarámuri named Luis had guided them down into the canyon. Barefoot and carrying a heavy pack, Luis led them on a 10-hour hike along steep trails of jagged rocks, "through a maze of immense chasms," to the Urique River.

The next morning, Don and Dave mounted their inflatable kayaks and started down the river. That first day was exhilarating—the river coursed along at a manageable 1,200 cubic feet per second. But on the second afternoon, heavy rains began to fall; within an hour, the river had swelled to a churning deluge. Don, with Dave following behind, rode the muddy white-water rapids through an obstacle course of massive boulders jutting out of the river, testing their skills to the limit.

Then, unexpectedly, Don entered what appeared to be a quiet pool exiting through a narrow channel just ahead, between two immense boulders. Lulled by the deep pool's apparent calm, he realized too late the water's deception, as the full surging might of the rain-swollen river forced him into the bottleneck of a channel too narrow for his kayak to pass through. At the mouth of the channel, he saw a boiling maelstrom of sticks and leaves being sucked down and swallowed with tons of water.

Paddling furiously in a futile effort to avoid being swallowed as well, Don found himself lodged in the stone chasm, clinging desperately to his kayak with one hand while pressing the other against the stone as the water rushed over and beneath him, until finally, his strength gave out.

As he later reported, "Suddenly, a mysterious calm overcame me. A heightened sense of awareness propelled me into a state of consciousness where fear became a vibratory sensation. I continued searching for a way to survive, but something told me that what was about to happen was important and that I should not fear it.

"As these feelings pulsed through me like a current of electricity, a violent wave suddenly flipped my kayak. I disappeared into the cold, wet darkness of the hole. When I went under, all my experience informed me that I would certainly drown; even so, a remarkable feeling of calm and peace came over me again. I relaxed completely and surrendered to the river.

"In the next few moments, my entire life passed before me in a series of snapshots. With each image, I sent out loving thoughts to the characters and experiences they depicted. I embraced my family and friends. I prayed for Dave's survival and safe return home. . . .

"I sensed a radiant white glow of energy swirling about me. Just as I ran out of air and was about to drink the river into my lungs, the tunnel spit me out into the hazy daylight."

Dave, who had seen Don struggling in the chasm and paddled quickly to shore, now made his way downstream. To his amazement and relief, he found Don alive on the bank. The rain poured down in torrents as they climbed into a cave in the rocks, where they remained for three days until the rain stopped.

Don felt an immediate difference in himself but was not yet aware of the depth of the changes that would occur in him over time. For one thing, he had always enjoyed a good rapport with horses, but in the weeks after his return from Copper Canyon, an unusual ability to communicate with horses awakened in him. He first noticed it with Corazón, his formerly wild mustang—a horse so difficult and unruly that Don had decided to release it in the wild after his return from the canyon. Now Don found he was able to ride Corazón with ease. Where before he had needed reins and muscular force to direct Corazón, Don could now ride him bareback and direct him with mental commands—with nothing more than his thoughts.

"I discovered in myself, apparently from nowhere, an ability to 'talk' to wild horses—so remarkable," Don writes in his book *Primal Awareness*, "that it was eventually covered on national television and in almost every equestrian magazine in the country."

By closely observing his unusual new ability, Don discovered that it had something to do with the intense concentration often associated with fear. This "fear effect" appeared to create a heightened state of awareness that made telepathic communication possible. (Don would later use this same understanding to communicate with troubled youth—to put them in a state in which they could more quickly make positive shifts in attitude and behavior.) Don also began to understand how this same state of fear had led to his life-transforming near-death awakening in the Urique River.

Intrigued, Don continued to observe himself, noting the

sometimes subtle changes in his character: "I found myself to be more forgiving and more patient—reflection replaced reaction. . . . I no longer thought of truth as definite and unyielding but rather as something woven into both sides of an issue . . . a new energy and a new direction took hold of me."

Even more remarkable, Don started noticing psychic, clairvoyant powers he had not possessed before his near-death event in Copper Canyon.

Only later was he to learn that the same stone chasm in the river where he had nearly drowned was an ancient traditional initiation site of the Rarámuri shamans. There, aspirants were tossed into the watery vortex of that bottleneck passage; those who relaxed—who surrendered to the river's power—were, like Don, swept into the channel, from which they would be delivered reborn. Those who tensed and struggled found themselves in a bottleneck crack with no escape. Failing the initiation meant death by drowning.

Having survived that passage himself, Don now understood at a much deeper level the nature of fear and its potential as a window to heightened states of awareness in which latent abilities could be awakened and lessons learned. By incorporating the use of spontaneous hypnosis, he began to apply his insights in his work as an emergency medical technician (EMT) with the fire department.

Don first applied his new understanding to a man named Joe who had been accidentally electrocuted. Shortly after Don and his partner, Frank, arrived on the scene, Joe went into convulsions and his heart stopped. They put an oxygen mask on him and began CPR. Don, an EMT for years, had participated in numerous life-and-death situations. This time, something felt different: "I was no longer merely a technician, grasping at words that seemed appropriate," he says. "I felt empowered to move energy in an invisible world I shared with Joe, and I discerned a connection with a spiritual aspect of him. I knew this part was as important as his physical body."

In the presence of Joe's wife, Don spoke to Joe, then clinically dead, instructing him in how to start his heart again. Minutes later, as the paramedics arrived, Joe's heart started beating again. Later, these paramedics called Don's supervisor and asked "what the deal" was with Don Jacobs telling dead people to start their own hearts again—Joe's wife told them that Don had talked her husband back to life.

Don was reprimanded, but that same day, Joe himself called from the hospital to thank Don for his instructions and support. Joe, *while clinically dead*, had apparently heard and could remember everything Don had said to him. He also credited Don's instructions with his return to life.

This was the first in a series of remarkable successes. "Using these new methods with my emergency patients," Don writes, "I was able to speak directly to a deeper part of their psyches, and through my directives, people were taking amazing control of their autonomic nervous systems—coming out of shock, stopping their bleeding, and controlling their blood pressure in response to my suggestions. Later, using the same methodology on myself, I underwent deep abdominal surgery without anesthesia."

At first, Don's unusual but highly effective methods became standard procedure where he worked. But even though they raised Don's sector's CPR survival rate well above the national average, they proved too controversial within the organization and their use was eventually forbidden.

Then, in 1997, while surfing the Internet, Don happened

upon an article describing the current plight of the Rarámuri Indians of Copper Canyon and the native peoples of the surrounding area of the Sierra Madre: Due to the pernicious influence of drug traffickers and illegal loggers aided by corrupt police and military personnel, native timberlands were being ravaged and the Rarámuri Indians chased off their land or forced by threat of violence to grow marijuana and opium instead of the corn by which they lived. These Indians were also routinely beaten and tortured, and frequently murdered.

Don decided to return to the canyon where his life had been transformed, to see if he could somehow help. On this second trip to Copper Canyon, Don met a 100-year-old shaman named Augustin Ramos. In Augustin, Don witnessed extrasensory abilities like those that had spontaneously awakened in himself after his visit 14 years earlier. By working with Augustin and serving the Rarámuri Indians of Copper Canyon, Don reconnected to his own lost Indian heritage.

Today, Don Trent Jacobs serves as a professor in the education department of South Dakota's Oglala Lakota College on the Pine Ridge Indian Reservation. In *Primal Awareness*, Don calls for public awareness and support of the endangered Rarámuri Indians of Copper Canyon. He also encourages others to explore the shamanic consciousness within their own psyches—the same awareness awakened in him by his brush with death on the Urique River, a gift which even today continues to illuminate his life.

The Cokeville Miracle

A Terrorist Threat and Angelic Intervention

On May 16, 1986, the little town of Cokeville, Wyoming, became the site of a potentially devastating tragedy. At 1:00 that afternoon, white supremacist David Young and his wife, Doris, rolled a shopping cart loaded with powerful gasoline bombs, rifles, and handguns into the Cokeville Elementary School. Young was the town's former marshal, fired for incompetence and reckless behavior.

"This is a revolution, and I'm taking your school hostage," he told the startled school secretary. "Don't set off any alarms or make any calls, or you and all the children will die." With that, Young and his wife herded 150 children and several teachers—nearly a third of the town's population—into a large classroom.

Their demand: Within 10 days, they must receive $300 million from the U.S. government and a personal phone call from President Ronald Reagan. If their demands weren't met, they would detonate the incendiary bombs. There would be no negotiations.

Young's diaries later revealed his real plan—get the money, then blow up himself, his wife, and the children. The town of Cokeville would pay and Young would have his revenge. A severely disturbed man, he believed they would all reincarnate "in a more evolved dimension." He had more than enough explosives to carry out his threat. Two weeks before, he had gone to an isolated range and set off a test bomb, producing an enormous fireball more than sufficient to incinerate a schoolroom full of children.

For nearly 2½ hours, crowds of anxious parents and friends as well as news media and other onlookers waited behind the police lines in a tense vigil, hoping and praying for a safe resolution—even a miracle.

Then, the siege ended with a cataclysmic explosion. Minutes before that, Young had handed his wife, Doris, the bomb trigger and gone to the bathroom. According to evidence gathered at the scene, Doris detonated the bomb, apparently by accident—only yards away from the 50 children huddled in the back of the classroom.

Immediately after the explosion, Doris Young, now engulfed in flames, staggered out the door and met David in the hall. He shot her once in the head—a mercy killing—shot and wounded a teacher running down the hall, then returned to the bathroom and shot himself.

According to eyewitnesses in front of the school, bright orange fire engulfed the classroom—the whole town, by then gathered outside, watched in horror as black smoke poured out the windows. As they rushed toward the classroom, now a burned-out shell, the ammunition stockpiled in the bottom of Young's cart went off in the blast, and bullets streaked through the room.

The police chief's daughter, Barbara Frederickson, described the scene as it appeared just after the blast had gutted the room where the children were held hostage. "We heard a big boom and then children came out screaming. The teachers were crawling around on the floor and throwing children out the windows. The entire room was on fire." In the inferno after the blast, 32 people received second-degree burns to their faces and one child was hit by a stray bullet. But none of their injuries was life threatening. Incredibly, all the hostages survived.

But the miracle that happened in the town of Cokeville, Wyoming, wasn't fully revealed until later, when children separately began to describe to their parents, rescue workers, and police "beings of light" who had come "down through the ceiling." First-grader Nathan Hartley saw them and knew right away they were angels. Rachel and Katie Walker said that the beings they saw were "bright like light bulbs" and that one hovered over each of the hostages.

The angel hovering over Nathan told him she was his great grandmother and warned him, "The bomb is going to explode and the two bad people are going to die." She then told him, "Go stand near the window."

Another angel told Katie the same thing. Katie's brother Travis heard a clear voice tell him to take his sisters to the window and keep them there and that they would be all right. Still another six-year-old child said, "A lady told me that a bomb was going to go off soon; she said go to the window and hurry out."

Other children also saw, heard, or felt the presence of these beings.

"I can't begin to tell you how lucky they were," testified bomb expert Richard Haskell of the Sweetwater County sheriff's department. "When you look in that classroom—when you see all that charred furniture and burnt walls—it's amazing that there weren't 150 kids lying in there dead. To call it a miracle would be the understatement of the century."

Scientist of Sacred Energy

An Ordeal of Spiritual Evolution

Controversies have raged for decades between the creationist beliefs of religious fundamentalists and the evolutionary theories of scientific materialists. But according to Gopi Krishna—who applied the scientific method to understand mystical phenomena—there exists a direct but hidden link connecting God and evolution. He reached this conclusion after an ordeal that transformed his life after very nearly ending it.

Gopi was born in a village outside Srinagar, India, in 1903. In his youth, his devout father renounced the world, retreating into a meditative silence from which he never emerged, leaving Gopi's mother to raise the family. Her strength and sacrifice deeply impressed Gopi, her eldest son.

After graduating from high school at 17, Gopi entered college. There, he spent more time reading for pleasure than preparing for his college examinations, which he failed. Sobered and guilt-stricken after his mother's years of sacrifice on his behalf, he vowed to remedy the character flaws—a weak will and lack of mental clarity—leading to his failure. To improve himself, Gopi rose early each morning to practice meditation and yoga before going to school. What began as a preparation for his academic pursuits became a way of life. But as his character and spiritual nature deepened through these practices, his worldly ambitions faded.

Feeling obligated to support his parents and wishing to avoid the troubling extremes of his father, Gopi devised a compromise—he fulfilled his worldly duties by day and devoted himself to his spiritual practices by night. After his college graduation at 22, Gopi moved to Kashmir to become a civil servant, taking his parents with him. When he was 23, his mother arranged a marriage for him in the traditional manner, to a 16-year-old bride.

For the next 12 years, Gopi supported his family, playing the roles of husband, father, and civil servant, while continuing his spiritual practices. Then one morning in December 1937, as he was meditating before work, he noticed an odd sensation stirring and rising at the base of his spine. It ceased, then occurred again—the third time he ignored it and continued meditating. But it would not be ignored: "The sensation again extended upwards, growing in intensity," he wrote. "Suddenly with a roar like that of a waterfall, I felt a stream of liquid light entering my brain. . . . The illumination grew brighter and brighter, the roaring louder, I experienced a rocking sensation and then felt myself slipping out of my body, entirely enveloped in a halo of light, . . . the point of consciousness that was myself growing wider, surrounded by waves of light. . . . I was now All Consciousness, . . . immersed in a sea of light, simultaneously aware of every point, spread out, as it were, in all directions."

This experience left Gopi exhausted, nervous, and strangely depressed. The next morning, the experience repeated itself with equal intensity. He didn't yet know his life had forever changed or that a 12-year ordeal had begun—one in which he would teeter precariously between life and death, madness and sanity.

Gopi interpreted the event as the awakening of kundalini, the spiritual energy that resides, according to Hindu scripture, at the base of the spine. This event, sought by many in the East as the goal of spiritual practice, triggered a bewildering process in Gopi, who now found himself assaulted from within by a torrent of disturbing and extraordinary phenomena: Day and night, his mind became a theater of heavenly and demonic visions, of visible patterns of light, of force and sounds entering his brain in a continuous stream. He could not concentrate, sleep, or eat. He soon lost weight and grew ill.

"I seemed to have accidentally touched the lever of an unknown mechanism hidden in the extremely intricate yet unexplored nervous structure of the body; . . . the luminous appearances became wilder and more fantastic and the noises louder and more uncanny. . . . The dreadful thought began to take hold of my mind that I was irretrievably heading towards a disaster from which I was powerless to save myself."

Weeks passed into months as his mind swung erratically between torment and exaltation. His body burned, on fire from within. In the worst period, he lay down in bed each night wondering if he would still be sane—or even alive—in the morning. A growing terror began to alienate him from other people, even his beloved family.

In a desperate search for help, Gopi found a yogi who told him that in rare cases, the kundalini rose through the wrong spinal channel, producing hellish and destructive effects—but the yogi did not know how to undo these effects. Gopi's life-shattering process seemed headed toward a fatal conclusion.

One night, he realized he could hold out no longer—he felt madness approaching and death not far behind. Wasted to a skeleton, sleep-deprived, his nerves fried, he lay writhing and moaning in agony on his bed, burning up and drenched in sweat. Then, turning his head, he saw his three-year-old daughter watching him, wide-eyed with terror.

In despair, concerned for his daughter and the family he would leave behind, he recalled the yogi's words—and an idea came to him, "as if by divine inspiration," how he might raise the kundalini through the proper spinal channel and save his life. With his own and his family's future at stake, he made the attempt by mentally visualizing this process: "There was a sound like a nerve thread snapping and instantaneously a silvery streak passed zigzag through the spinal cord, exactly like the sinuous movement of a white serpent in rapid flight, pouring an effulgent, cascading shower of brilliant vital energy into my brain, filling my head with a blissful luster in place of the flame that had been tormenting me."

Now, he noticed a tongue of golden flame moving through his body with healing force. "I lay awake, dumb with wonder, watching this living radiance moving from place to place through the whole digestive tract, caressing the intestines and the liver, while another stream poured into the kidneys and the heart. . . . I watched with boundless gratitude to the Unseen."

The process had radically shifted—the chaotic, destructive force now flowed through him, bathing his cells with a benevolent energy of the highest order. Made sober and cautious by his prior ordeal, Gopi closely studied these new phenomena, more with the wary, objective fascination of a scientist than with the exalted hopes of a mystic. "I was in an extraordinary state: a lustrous medium intensely alive and acutely sentient, shining day and night, permeated my whole system, racing through every part of my body, . . . sure of its path."

This living, organizing, intelligent force seemed to inhabit his body-mind, commanding his dietary, sleep, and work habits. In exchange for Gopi's full cooperation, it rewarded him with astonishing gifts—not the least of which became the biblical "peace that passeth understanding."

Now when he closed his eyes, waking, sleeping, or dreaming, Gopi saw himself enfolded in a mantle of light, felt himself charged with the exquisite current of a divine life force. His dreams became ecstatic visionary voyages to fantastic realms of indescribable splendor. He began to intuit, then perceive, the universe as an infinitely conscious Being. Formerly mundane scenes of the physical world were now imbued with a silvery luster and charged with an ethereal glory that filled Gopi's eyes with tearful emotion. Ecstatic awe became his normal, moment-to-moment state.

Then one day as he walked across a bridge, a new phenomena occurred: "Near me, in a blaze of brilliant light, I felt what seemed to be a conscious Presence . . . encompassing me and overshadowing all the objects around, from which two lines of a beautiful verse in Kashmiri poured out to float before my vision, like luminous writing in the air, disappearing as suddenly as they had come."

Such visions became frequent occurrences—verses appearing before his open eyes, hovering in the air in luminous script in various languages. "The lines occurred one after the other as if dropped into the three-dimensional field of my consciousness . . . in fully formed couplets, like falling snowflakes, . . . complete with language, rhyme, and metre. . . . "

Gopi began writing them down. This poetry appeared first in Kashmiri, then in English, Urdu, Punjabi, Persian, German, French, Italian, Sanskrit, and Arabic. *He had not the slightest exposure to four of these languages—he simply wrote them down as visual symbols. Yet when translated, they proved to be not only grammatically correct but also poetically beautiful, full of profound spiritual insights and at times precognitive or prophetic in nature.* By the grace of this divine kundalini force, Gopi Krishna, who had never written a line of verse, became an accomplished and published poet in 10 languages, most of which he did not speak.

Despite the phenomena triggered by his kundalini awakening, Gopi never revealed his experiences or insights until he had observed this process for *a full 20 years.* By then, he had developed remarkable expertise on what he called "the evolutionary energy in man." Rather than seeing his experience as isolated, Gopi claimed that the entire human species is divinely programmed to awaken at a certain evolutionary stage. He conceived of kundalini as the sacred energy of God in man, a key to spiritual awakening—and believed that kundalini had inspired the great prophets and sages of history.

Over the next three decades, Gopi Krishna wrote nearly 20 books on the phenomena and significance of kundalini. He tirelessly urged science to investigate this evolutionary power somehow encoded in the human species and operating according to hidden laws. Once we understood it, he believed, both from a scientific and a mystical perspective, we would hold the key to understanding genius, creativity, and even forms of madness. As he wrote, "Kundalini is a natural but uncommon biological phenomenon . . . that leads to the emergence of a conscious personality . . . possessing such astounding attributes as to make the phenomenon appear to be the performance of a supernatural agency rather than the outcome of natural but as yet unknown biological laws."

Gopi Krishna saw this superhuman state as one "towards which mankind is evolving irresistibly." His own life supported this assertion—a poor civil servant catapulted from the common state of man to that visionary paradise of endless creativity and spiritual rapture in which he spent his final years. If Gopi Krishna is correct, both science and religion may need to revise their assessment of our spiritual and evolutionary origins.

From Sword to Spirit

A Warrior's Awakening

His sinewy body wielded the power of death, until he awakened and discovered a new way of living. This is how one of the greatest warriors in history began to teach the invincible power of love.

Morihei was not always a man of peace. Born in Japan in 1883, he fought as an infantryman in the Russo-Japanese war and later battled pirates and bandit clans in Mongolia. A seasoned soldier and martial arts master tested in life-and-death battles, Morihei became a martial arts instructor in Japan's elite military academies.

Morihei, steeped in the warriors' code, practiced and taught a variety of fighting systems. In order to temper the spirits of his students, he often trained them under adverse conditions, such as outdoors in the winter snow. According to *Sensei* Robert Nadean, one of Master Ueshiba's students in Japan, they practiced for a time on wooden floors from which loose nails protruded. Yet he had a sensitive and religious side, and the human folly he had seen firsthand—violence, greed, corruption, starvation, and war—troubled him. Fate had drawn him into the heart of the world's brutality, but his spirit moved him to seek a solution to this parade of human suffering that passed daily before his eyes.

Morihei Ueshiba became a warrior on a spiritual quest.

A major turning point occurred in the spring of 1925 when, at the age of 42, he was attacked by a high-ranking swordsman expertly wielding a razor-sharp sword, or *katana*. Morihei, himself unarmed, defeated his opponent not by injuring him but by skillfully evading all his cuts, slashes, and thrusts. Elated by this unconventional victory, he walked, in an inspired state, into his garden.

He related the event that followed: "Suddenly the earth trembled. Golden vapor welled up from the ground and engulfed me. I felt transformed into a golden image, and my body seemed as light as a feather. All at once I understood the nature of creation: the Way of a Warrior is to manifest Divine Love, a spirit that embraces and nurtures all things. Tears of gratitude and joy streamed down my cheeks. I saw the entire earth as my home, and the sun, moon and stars as my intimate friends. All attachment to material things vanished."

Morihei Ueshiba went on to develop the flowing martial art of aikido, translated as "way of blending with spirit" or simply "art of peace," whose key principles are harmony and love in action.

Morihei later had other visions, insights, and illuminations, and various supernormal abilities were awakened in him. One particular incident reveals not only his uncanny speed but also his extraordinary perceptual abilities. Morihei was confronted by a jealous suitor of the woman to whom he, Morihei, was engaged. The man, a military officer, aimed and fired a single-shot pistol directly toward the center of Morihei's chest at nearly point-blank range, intent on killing his rival. Morihei later reported that at the instant the would-be assassin's finger pulled the trigger, he "felt a pellet of light" strike his chest. In that moment—at precisely the same instant the bullet exploded from the gun barrel—he turned his body, moving just millimeters out of its path, eluding the bullet. After this, Morihei Ueshiba was regarded as one who could "dodge bullets."

Into his eighties, *O-Sensei* (Great Teacher) Morihei could move at impossible speeds and "see" opponents behind his back; he has been recorded on film moving a distance of three feet, from inside to outside a circle of attackers, in the space of *a single frame of film* (or 1/24 second)—in the film, he seems to disappear and reappear. Able to direct his powerful energy through and beyond his body, Morihei could effortlessly throw trained martial artists, even those with weapons, and pin them to the mat *without touching them, even from several feet away*, a feat witnessed by many and also documented on film.

One of Morihei Ueshiba's most powerful and accomplished disciples was aikido master Koichi Tohei, who was the author of several books on applying *ki*, or spiritual energy, in daily life. Yet Morihei, in his later years a wisp of a man, wielded a power transcending the limits of his slight frame. As one instructor observed, "Trying to push over Tohei is like trying to push over a mountain; but trying to push over *O-Sensei* was like trying to push over a feather—and not being able to do it." This was the grace of Master Ueshiba, who declared, "The Art of Aikido is invincible, because it contends with nothing."

Morihei Ueshiba, master of the arts of war, evolved into a spiritual sage, a peaceful warrior who lived and taught a way of life based in harmony and devoted to reconciliation. His art of aikido, whose principles were divinely revealed to him in a moment of illumination, has benefited the lives of many thousands of people worldwide.

"The Way of the Warrior," he wrote, "has been misunderstood. . . . Those who seek competition are making a grave mistake; . . . the real way of a warrior is the way of peace, the power of love."

Passion and Prayers

A Jewish Mystic Heals Bodies and Souls

Born in late-seventeenth-century Poland, where Jews were being slaughtered by the tens of thousands, Israel ben Eliezer grew up amid the poverty afflicting his devastated people. Orphaned as a youth, he set out wandering across Poland, working at odd jobs wherever he could find them. Traveling in a harsh land hostile to his race, surviving by wit and will, Israel grew into a hardy, determined, and independent spirit. Drawn to solitude, he began to question the assumptions of the culture in which he lived.

After his marriage to a strong and loyal woman, Israel wandered with his wife for a time before settling in a tiny village by the Carpathian Mountains. The Jewish community there consisted of ordinary Jewish villagers—they were mostly uneducated, poverty-stricken people cut off from participation in a meaningful spiritual life. They hungered for the true light of Judaism—a light that had grown dim during a century of persecution. Meanwhile, their religious leaders, a small educated elite, seemed absorbed in doctrinal abstractions and remained oblivious to the physical hardships and needs of their community.

Israel, himself a part of this uneducated peasant class, had little knowledge of the Torah or interest in scholarly religious debate. But he had gained a depth and wisdom during his years wandering in solitude, and the suffering he had seen and experienced awakened in him a yearning to know God. This yearning at last drove him into the wilderness to take up the life of a religious hermit.

His wife, lonely yet devoted, sensed something special in her husband. Several times a week, she drove their wagon to his campsite in the mountains, where Israel would fill the wagon with raw clay, which she then sold to the village potters. In this way, they were able to make their living.

The passing years allowed Israel to spend most of his time in prayer and contemplation.

Then one day, Israel began having visions—the prophets Elijah and Shijah the Shilonite appeared to him, revealing that the power of prayer lay in inner devotion rather than in hallowed formulas or visible acts of piety. This and other mystical truths appeared in a kind of illumination resonant with those of Jesus, Muhammad, Buddha, and other great spiritual teachers—self-evident truths forgotten or ignored in the orthodox temples of his day.

Unconcerned by the opinions of the villagers, who viewed him as an eccentric or madman, Israel remained an unknown mystic while growing in spiritual power and wisdom. Then, in the turning of his 40th year, while meditating in his cave, Israel heard a resounding voice speak to him, saying, "The time has come for you to reveal yourself."

Israel ben Eliezer, recognizing this as the voice of God, came out of his cave and his seclusion and began to share with others the gifts and revelations that God had shared with him. One of Israel's gifts was the power to heal, and he spent his fifth decade traveling from village to village—this time with a clear purpose—healing the afflicted, apparently by miraculous means. Barren women were enabled to conceive, the sick were restored to health, the crippled were made whole, the mad were made sane, and tortured souls were given peace. Israel's fame quickly spread.

In an era plagued by "evil spirits," when group hysteria swept over whole villages with devastating consequences, Israel restored calm to entire villages gripped by fear and superstition. He became renowned for his power to foresee the future, and on occasions his precognitive warnings helped others avoid tragedy. He also claimed to see the Angel of Death following those about to die, and he helped turn many souls to God in the time they had left to live.

More a mystic than a magician, Israel ben Eliezer is re-membered today as much for his teachings on passionate worship as for his healing powers or precognitive abilities. As time passed, the people to whom Israel ministered came to recognize his deeper mission—not merely healing bodies but saving lost souls through the practice of ecstatic prayer. His joyous devotion was infectious, as with divine authority he taught the mystical truth that *God is everywhere, in every-thing, and in everyone*—that anyone could know God if they prayed with true passion. "Wooden prayers cannot fly to heaven," he said. "Only passionate faith awakens the human heart and touches the heart of God." And he reminded many that sorrowful brooding upon our sins blinds us to God's joyous presence.

Israel's path of ecstatic prayer, which would be called *the Way of the Hasidim*, bloomed like a fresh flower on the ancient tree of Judaism. Disciples came from far and wide to learn from him this path to God, unique in his time and place. Israel ben Eliezer grew famous throughout Poland as *Bal Shem Tov* (Master of Names).

The very teachings so beloved among the poor made Bal Shem Tov infamous among the orthodox elite. Just as the Pharisees criticized Jesus, viewing him as a threat to their power and position, many Jewish leaders branded Bal Shem Tov a heretic and warned people to shun him. Even so, some of his enemies later became his disciples. And so many people flocked to him that he eventually had to move to the larger town of Medzhibozh.

During Bal Shem Tov's later years, many claimed to see light emanating from his body. But such mystical perceptions pale beside the tales of his joyous humor and passion for God. His spirituality was more earthy than ascetic, more akin to Zorba the Greek than Saint Francis of Assisi. Like devout practitioners of tantra yoga, Bal Shem Tov saw sex as a divine activity in which God participated if one performed the act of love as prayer. He even told his son that he was a holy child because "the heavens shook" during his conception. The passionate prayer and life of Bal Shem Tov bridged flesh and spirit.

The Hasidic movement, this ecstatic, mystical branch of Judaism, survived against all odds, despite resistance by orthodox leaders. And the remarkable man known as Bal Shem Tov might have remained a hermit sitting in caves and wandering in the wilderness but for a defining moment when the voice of God called him into the world.

By heeding his call and entering the world as a servant, Bal Shem Tov left a legacy that has lasted for centuries. His teachings on ecstatic prayer and his example of a joyous life of devoted service remain as relevant today as they were in his own time.

Lighter Than Air

The Extraordinary Feats of a Flying Friar

On the subject of levitation, like that of religion, most of us take one of three positions: believer, nonbeliever, or agnostic. We've all seen people "fly," of course—in popular films, on stage, and in our dreams. But few, if any, of us have personally seen a mortal being truly rise up from the earth to float or fly. For the empirically minded, it isn't enough to read about it in books—we must see to believe. Yet the fact that we've never seen electricity or atoms (much less quarks or neutrinos) or our late Great Aunt Ethel or God doesn't seem to faze us.

But when it comes to levitation, devotees of gravity may smirk. After all, the laws of physics are the laws of physics—aren't they? Well, according to the gospel of quantum, we are simultaneously energy, light, and matter—and two of these three, as anyone will tell you, are lighter than air.

So the real question may not be how is it that others levitate but rather *how is it that we do not?*

Consider the case of Joseph of Copertino, famed in his own lifetime as "the Flying Friar." Of all the reported cases of levitation, the flights of Joseph were by far the most extensively witnessed and documented. Born in 1603, the son of a carpenter, Joseph displayed a religious nature and inclination early in his life. By age 8, he experienced and described states of mystical rapture. By 16, he had entered the Capuchin order as a monk. For many years, Joseph took food only two days a week—on Thursdays and Sundays—saying that he otherwise fed on the "Bread of Angels."

But even in the monastery, Joseph's otherworldly and impractical nature soon caused him to be sent away. After a brief sojourn, he entered another monastery near the town of Copertino, where, at age 25, after years of practicing severe austerities, he became a priest.

Soon after his ordination, Joseph's legendary career as the Flying Friar began with a round-trip inaugural flight in a church in Naples, where he had been sent to defend himself against a charge of heresy before a Church tribunal. There, while saying mass in the presence of a fellow friar and several nuns, Joseph suddenly rose into the air, floated across the church, briefly landed, then rose again and flew back to land at his original point of departure. The charge of heresy against Joseph was dropped; whether this was due to the levitation incident or to other factors was not reported.

On the same journey, soon after this first reported flight, Joseph went to Rome to pay his respects to Pope Urban VIII. As he knelt to kiss the papal feet, he was again wafted into the air, where he literally hovered above the astonished pope and his retinue.

Joseph's next stop was a monastery in Assisi; there he levitated 15 feet in the air and then floated over the heads of dozens of astonished worshippers in order to kiss the feet on the painting of the Virgin Mary placed high on one wall of the chapel.

Without a doubt, such lighthearted reports of a human being flying read like fiction—with more levity than levitation—reminiscent of *Peter Pan* or the television series *The Flying Nun*, most likely inspired by Joseph's life.

Yet in the years that followed Joseph's first displays of his divine aerial abilities, hundreds of people, including some of the most respected men and women of the day, personally witnessed and testified to his miraculous and ecstatic flights. Among them were Juan Alfonso Henriquez de Cabrera, Spain's ambassador to Rome; Johan Friedrich, Duke of Brunswick; the son of Cosimo II of Austria, future cardinal under Pope Clement IX; and of course, Pope Urban VIII and his exalted retinue.

On more than one occasion, those present who tried to hold Joseph down were lifted into the air with him.

Johan Friedrich, the Duke of Brunswick, was a non-Catholic who traveled to Assisi in 1651 specifically to witness one of Joseph's then-legendary levitations. After witnessing two of Joseph's spontaneous flights, one of which lasted a full 15 minutes, Friedrich was so overcome with awe that he converted from Lutheranism to Catholicism, which was then tantamount to converting to an enemy faith.

Joseph's most spectacular feat occurred in his monastery garden while he walked with a fellow priest, Friar Antonio Chiarello. Friar Antonio thoughtlessly triggered the episode with a remark to Joseph on the beauty of the Heaven God had made. At that point, Joseph gave a shriek, went into a rapture, rose into the air, and came to rest kneeling on a fragile branch atop an olive tree, where he remained lost in ecstasy for half an hour. The slender branch, Friar Antonio reported, barely quivered beneath Joseph. When at last the Flying Friar recovered his senses, he could not get down from the tree—Friar Antonio had to fetch a ladder and help him down.

In 1653, due to Joseph's widespread fame and the passion aroused in the public over his numerous miraculous flights and healings, Pope Innocent X ordered that he be transferred to an isolated monastery on Mount Carpegna and allowed to come into contact only with his brother monks.

The 1,000-page Vatican report compiled on Joseph cited more than 70 levitations witnessed by others in Copertino, not counting the frequent levitations that occurred during daily mass in the presence of his brother monks or the numerous levitations, witnessed by many others, that occurred in his various travels over the years.

D. Scott Rogo, in his book *Miracles*, writes, "The evidence authenticating St. Joseph's levitations is awesome. (They were) publicly observed by both his friends and total strangers; we have numerous firsthand accounts of them; they were not secret events but often occurred in public places; and they do not rest merely on St. Joseph's own word. In short, the testimony pertinent to St. Joseph's levitations is a perfect rebuttal to the types of criticism to which St. Teresa's levitations are prone."

Based on this abundant testimony to his miraculous powers, Joseph of Copertino was declared blessed in 1753 by Pope Benedict XIV.

Adversity's Teacher

Prison-Camp Hardship to Heroic Service

Young Laurens's relationships with the Bushmen of the
African veldt deeply influenced his values, character, and
destiny. These people of the bush nursed him, taught him, and
befriended him—he marveled at their intimate embrace of nature and their affinity with the world of spirits. He loved their
tales of wonder and magic and hungrily absorbed their perception of the world as a mythic realm where humans, confronted
by mysterious powers, found stories that gave life meaning. He
took to heart the importance of finding a defining "story" for
himself and resolved that he, too, would create his life out of
his dreams.

Every childhood contains elements of magic and mystery;
Laurens lived it. A Bushman hunter once explained to young
Laurens, "You see, it is very difficult and unpredictable because
there is a dream dreaming us." Raised in the presence of such
people and infused with their enchanting view of reality, it is no

surprise that Laurens's character blended realism and idealism, with a large dash of the heroic thrown in.

A farm boy later drawn to war, Laurens became a soldier for 10 years and led commando guerrilla units behind enemy lines in Abyssinia (Ethiopia), North Africa, and the Far East. At one point, he and his men were captured by the Japanese and put in a concentration camp. There, they entered into those extreme twilight depths the Bushman call the Time of the Hyena: "a state of madness," Laurens wrote, "of unbearable tragedy, . . . when not only the light of the mind was invaded by darkness, but life itself was overcast with the approach of . . . death."

They were starved and tortured—forced to watch their comrades executed for minor infractions. Yet in the midst of this madness, Laurens also encountered that power that the Bushmen embraced as "the source of existence," and he confronted the mystery that, even as a child, he had sensed in their way of being. "Taken out to what we thought could be our own execution," Laurens wrote, "we were made by the Japanese to watch the most brutal execution of others. During this forced spectacle, an officer standing between me and a friend called Nick—fainted on thin and trembling legs. Nick and I supported him as he stood there; in the process we all touched hands. I was startled by this, because throughout my physical being there was an inrush of what I can only describe as electricity, which was not just a thing of energy, but was charged with a sense of hope, certainty, belonging, and life everlasting.

"I knew then—and the knowledge has since grown and not dimmed—that this is what flesh and blood is about and is meant to be. But for this illumination I do not know how I could have steered my course in the years that have followed. . . . The post-war human world appears stubbornly determined to deny and destroy that oneness of life we are meant to share."

That sudden Promethean flash of spirit, ignited in the face of death, had far-reaching effects. Filmmaker Mickey Lemle tells how Laurens spent his remaining years in the camp: "Laurens created a make-shift university . . . that at one point offered 144 courses a week. The prisoners wrote out textbooks on toilet paper, and after three and a half years, men matriculated and received diplomas, also written out on toilet paper."

"After the war," Laurens told Lemle, "six people armed with their toilet paper diplomas got jobs in the British foreign service." Billy Griffiths, a fellow prisoner who had lost both hands and both eyes, credited Laurens with keeping him alive "when I no longer wanted to live. He would say to me, *'Hang on Billy. Hang on. There is more to life than hands and eyes.'* He was right."

They remained friends for nearly 50 years.

Like others before him, Sir Laurens van der Post survived adversity and inhuman atrocity by finding light in the darkness and meaning in the madness. More than that, he found a way to share that meaning with his fellow prisoners and with others in the world at large. Laurens's prison experience and awakening turned his life into an urgent quest for meaning, an inquiry into fundamental questions—a "continuous search after self-knowledge," he wrote.

After the war, his life came full circle, back to his childhood roots. Laurens was one of the first to recognize that the Bushmen he loved, among whom he was born and raised, faced extinction under European colonialism. He was also among the first to act: He began exploring hidden Africa, determined, he said, "to make one last effort to preserve the Bushman and his culture in the heart of what I called the lost world of the Kalahari, and try to arrest there, this age-old story of persecution and annihilation." Laurens persuaded the British government to help him in his task. "All I wanted was recognition of (the Bushman's) humanity and his values that were at their best precious qualities that we had neglected in ourselves and at our peril; and his right to native land wherein his security was guaranteed so as to give him time enough to find a way of his own into the world of the future."

To this cause Laurens devoted much of his writings and remaining years. His expeditions to the Kalahari Desert and his prolonged heroic effort to save the Bushmen from extinction produced numerous books and several documentaries, most famous among them *The Lost World of the Kalahari.*

Shortly before his death at the age of 90, Sir Laurens van der Post shared the following insight with his friend Mickey Lemle: *"Meaning transfigures all. . . . Once what you are living and what you are doing has meaning for you, it is irrelevant whether you are happy or unhappy. You're content. You're not alone in your spirit. You belong."*

Immaculate Apparition

A Visionary Life—From Childhood to Sainthood

Bernadette Soubirous and her family lived in Lourdes, France, in a single room in a former jail called *le Cachot*—the Dungeon. Despite her family's poverty, Bernadette was like many other children of her time and place. But everything changed one winter's day in 1858—February 11, to be precise—when 14-year-old Bernadette, her sister, and a friend went gathering driftwood by the river Gave.

She had sat down to remove her shoes and socks at the millstream when she heard "a noise like the sound of a storm." Leaping up, she looked across the stream at a niche above a cave in the great rock called Massabielle and saw a rosebush swaying in the wind.

"All else was still," Bernadette recalled. "A golden cloud came out of the cave and flooded the niche with radiance. Then a lady, young and beautiful, . . . the like of whom I had never seen, stood on the edge of the niche, . . . beckoning me to come closer as though she were my mother."

The luminous lady, dressed in white, had a veil on her head, a blue sash about her waist, a rosary of white beads on a golden chain draped over one arm, and a golden rose on each bare foot. Bernadette fell to her knees and prayed. She looked up to see the lady smiling as she silently passed her white beads through her fingers; then she bowed, vanishing into the niche as the golden cloud faded away.

When Bernadette's parents learned of this apparition, they forbade her to return to the rock of Massabielle, afraid that the specter might not be of God. But that Sunday, she asked her father's permission to return. "A lady with a rosary can't be evil," he reasoned. According to reports, Bernadette returned, armed with holy water and accompanied by a small group of curious and hopeful friends. They were not disappointed. As Bernadette began to pray, her fingers on her rosary, the lady appeared again in the niche and smiled.

Bernadette later wrote, "I sprinkled some Holy Water and said, 'If you come from God, please stay. If you don't, go away!' The more I sprinkled, the more she smiled. I knelt and gazed at her lovingly."

Abruptly, Bernadette fell into a trance, frightening her friends. They ran back and found a Madame Nicolau, who took her son Antoine to carry Bernadette, still in her divine swoon, to their home. But Bernadette was fully conscious in another realm. "Along the way," she reported, "the Lady kept in front of me and slightly above me. Only when Antoine carried me into his home did the Lady disappear, whereupon I returned to Earth."

Bernadette called the lady *Aquero,* which means "reverence in the presence of a sacred reality." She described her next encounter with Aquero, which occurred on a Thursday morning:

"The Lady appeared, surrounded with light. I went into the grotto and the Lady came down from the niche and stood beside me. 'If you are from God,' I said, 'please tell me what you want; else go away.' At 'are from God,' she smiled. At 'else go away,' she shook her head."

Then she spoke: "Would you have the graciousness to come here for 15 days?" she asked Bernadette, then added, "I do not promise to make you happy in this life, but in the next. Go and tell the priests that a chapel must be built here."

Word of Bernadette and her vision spread. By the sixth visit, hundreds of onlookers were kneeling with Bernadette by the grotto. "I scarcely noticed them," she reported. "The light around the Lady was brighter, yet softer than the sun. The roses on her feet were brighter than gold—she was surrounded by light as she disappeared, the glow faded, but its warmth lingered in my soul."

These incidents soon came to the attention of police commissioner Dominique Jacomet, who, suspecting fraud, reportedly grabbed Bernadette by her cloak and took her to his office to question her about her visions. He wrote down her story and read it back to her. She called his version "twisted, untruthful, incorrect." When she protested, he shouted angrily at her.

"The next day at catechism class," she says, "the girls shunned me as a criminal and the Sister Superior thanked God I had been arrested for my misbehavior. One woman called me a brat; another slapped my face."

This abuse pained Bernadette. Yet when she communicated with Aquero, she was visibly transfigured. In one of many documented incidents, a local doctor held a burning candle under her hand for a full 15 minutes as she prayed. She felt no pain, and her hand was not burned or injured in the slightest.

On February 25, Aquero appeared and told Bernadette to drink and wash in a spring, while pointing to a muddy spot beneath the rock. Bernadette obediently scraped the earth on that spot and tried to wash her face, smearing it with mud. The crowd jeered, thinking her mad, and her aunt slapped her face and sent her home. When she returned that afternoon, however, water bubbled from the hollow she had dug in the mud. When stirred with a stick, the water began to flow, minutes later turning into a crystal-clear spring that would become world famous.

Those who had jeered before now began to drink and wash in the spring—the next day, a dramatic healing occurred. Louis Bouriette, nearly blind in one eye, had his sight fully restored after water from the spring was poured into his eyes. Next, a dying two-year-old was restored to health after being immersed in the spring.

That same evening, the imperial prosecutor interrogated Bernadette and her mother and threatened to throw them into prison.

On March 4, 8,000 people followed Bernadette to the grotto. "We started the rosary," Bernadette wrote, "and at the second decade of the beads *the Lady came and lifted me into a world where the language is prayer, and the environment is Heaven.*" Not for the first time, Aquero pleaded with Bernadette to have the priest, Father Peyramale, build a chapel by the grotto. Bernadette had asked Peyramale before.

His response was always the same: "She must tell her name. If I knew it was the Blessed Virgin, I would do all she desires."

Three weeks passed without a visit from Aquero. "Meanwhile," wrote Bernadette, "the people pestered me, the police watched me and the public prosecutor almost crushed me. What my parents suffered from the town officials, only Eternity will reveal; . . . plottings and intrigues, . . . the Mayor and the police accused me, . . . threatened me with jail; . . . they seemed incapable of realizing I had knelt in the presence of a Lady who could only be of Heaven."

On March 25, Bernadette was awakened and drawn once again to the grotto. "It was still dark when I reached Massabielle. The Lady was there. . . . I knelt down, we said the rosary together. . . . I told her how I loved her."

Then, four times, Bernadette asked Aquero her true name. "The Lady extended her hands towards the ground, swept them upwards to join them on her heart, raised her eyes, but not her head to Heaven, leaned tenderly towards me and said, 'Que soy era Immaculada Conceptiou,' 'I am the Immaculate Conception.' Then, she smiled at me and disappeared."

Bernadette rushed straight to Father Peyramale and told him, "Aquero said, 'I am the Immaculate Conception.'"

"The good Priest stood there stunned. Suddenly he stammered, 'Do you know what that means?'"

She shook her head.

Deathly pale, Father Peyramale said, "Go home now, child."

The harassment of Bernadette by the local authorities increased after that and the grotto was shut down and barricaded, with a note that read, "Entrance to this property forbidden."

The last visitation occurred on the day of the feast of Our Lady of Mount Carmel. Bernadette, again called by the Lady at night, went and knelt in the grotto by candlelight. Aquero appeared. "She looked more beautiful than I had ever seen her. This would be the last time I would see her on this earth, . . . I knew, because of the way she held her head as she said good-bye. She left heaven in my heart, and it has remained there ever since."

Yet somehow the tide had turned. All of France, from the lowest peasant to Emperor Napoleon III and his wife (who personally intervened), knew of the miraculous events at the grotto called Lourdes and of the young visionary, like Joan of Arc, chosen by Mary as a vehicle of divine grace.

Twelve days later, a commission was formed to investigate the apparitions. The presiding bishop wrote, "To deny the possibility of supernatural happenings would be to plod along in the rut worn by the skepticism of the last century."

On October 5, the mayor of Lourdes reopened the grotto. Bernadette, shy of all the publicity, moved into a convent. At 22, she took her vows and became a nun. She lived in relative seclusion for another 16 years, loved by all who knew her and beloved by all of France.

Bernadette died on April 16, 1879, at the age of 35. The local villagers, grief stricken at the news of her death, rushed towards the convent wailing, "The saint is dead! The saint is dead!" She was buried in her convent in a sealed casket by the chapel of Saint Joseph. In 1908, her sealed casket was exhumed from Saint Joseph's chapel by a commission formed to examine her body, her life, and her character. She was found perfectly intact—uncorrupted from her outer flesh to her internal organs. In June 1925, she was formally beatified (declared blessed). And on December 8, 1933, Bernadette Soubirous was canonized as a saint.

For more than a century, Lourdes has been the site of many thousands of miraculous healings.

From Hack to Genius

The Mysterious Transformation of Walt Whitman

On Long Island, New York, on May 31, 1819, a child was born who would grow from an ordinary seedling into a literary giant. Yet for the first half of his life, Walt's greatness, and even his potential for it, were nowhere in evidence. And this is the mystery at the heart of our story.

Walt, an adventurous boy, was raised in a farmhouse built by his father's hand, on a farm populated by chickens, pigs, and apple orchards, with herds of sheep and cattle nearby. Walt survived the cholera epidemic of the early 1830s that killed millions. At age 12, by chance, he entered the trade of journalism, working as a typesetter's apprentice at a local newspaper.

In time, Walt's experience in the newspaper trade, as well as his physical size and strength, gave him a natural authority and self-confidence—and an explosive temper. From ages 20 to 30, Walt worked as a journalist, printer, and editor in the rough-and-tumble early-American newspaper trade. In an era when editors of competing papers fought verbal brawls in print, Walt flung himself into the fray, making friends and enemies aplenty. He slandered, maligned, and baited his enemies and trumpeted his opinions from the public soapbox of his editorial columns. According to Justin Kaplan in *Walt Whitman: A Life*, the young journalist "could be seen kicking a politician downstairs, manhandling a church attendant, and grappling with a carpetbag senator who had insulted him."

Although journalism had much to recommend it, Walt aspired to success at poetry and fiction. But the fruits of his first 15 years of creative writing were an utterly mediocre and deservedly forgotten body of work consisting largely of bombastic, third-rate poetry, syrupy short stories, clumsy romantic morality tales, and hack adventure novels—the overripe harvest of a profoundly unoriginal, uninspired mind. Biographer Kaplan described them as "full of shabby melodrama, false sentiment and gothic dodges; . . . derivative and imitative, preachy and didactic, dripping with false sentiment, cliché, and melodramatic contrivance."

His appraisal of Whitman's work to that time garners universal agreement among scholars.

No one could have predicted the genius and originality that would burst forth out of nowhere, suddenly in full bloom, in his epic *Leaves of Grass*, written at age 35 after an almost five-year literary silence.

Although Whitman's poetry, both earthy and transcendent, speaks of his illuminations and furnishes abundant clues that point to divine inspiration, Walt never directly explained what happened to him over time or overnight during that five-year period. We only know that an entirely new energy flooded into his work—a poetic voice rendering profound insights into life, death, sex, humanity, love, the body, and eternity, from the intimate perspective of an illumined mystic.

Richard Bucke, Whitman's personal physician and disciple and author of *Cosmic Consciousness*, commented on Whitman's mysterious transformation from mediocre hack to illumined genius: "The line of demarcation between the two Whitmans is perfectly drawn; . . . writings of absolutely no value were *immediately* followed by pages across each of which, in letters of ethereal fire, are written . . . such vital sentences as have not been written 10 times in the history of the race."

His poetry now expressed eternal truths with a stunning vitality, originality, and power unmatched by any Western writer before him, except perhaps Shakespeare—a revelation of the Divine alive in all of earthly life, in everything and everyone.

Unlike many mystics, Walt's visions did not separate him from the world; instead, he awakened into the world, his body, his earthly desires, and to his full humanity. In the following poem, Whitman describes a moment of divine and fleshy grace, when his immortal soul took possession of his mortal being, lifting him from mediocrity to genius and catapulting him into life with an impassioned sensuality and sublime eroticism that, while shocking to the Victorian era, was to him nothing less than sacred.

> *I believe in you, my Soul. . . .*
> *I mind how once we lay,*
> *such a transparent summer morning;*
> *How you settled your head athwart my hips*
> *and gently turn'd over upon me,*
> *And parted the shirt from my bosom-bone,*
> *and plunged your tongue to my bare stript heart; . . .*

> Swiftly arose and spread around me the peace
> and joy and knowledge that pass all the art
> and argument of the earth;
> And I know that the hand of God
> is the promise of my own,
> And I know that the spirit of God
> is the brother of my own;
> And that all the men ever born are also my
> brothers, and the women my sisters and lovers. . . .

Singing ecstatic hymns in a tone and tempo never heard before, in a voice universal yet uniquely American, Whitman leaped in a single bound into the rarefied company of literary immortals. His mysterious illumination transformed not only his work but also his identity and character—a change visible even in photographs. In his 50s, during the Civil War, Walt volunteered as a nurse in the camps along the battlefields and devoted himself for the duration of that hellish war to relieving the suffering of combatants on *both* sides of the conflict. His biographer estimated that Walt made over 600 hospital visits and in one form or another had ministered to nearly 100,000 sick and wounded soldiers.

He was deeply loved by the young, often tragically wounded soldiers whose lives he touched and changed. Most of them remembered him for the rest of their lives and many corresponded with him for years after the war ended.

We can only speculate as to the precise nature and time of Whitman's illumination, but his words testify to its reality—for even in the terrible carnage of the war, he could say, "I see something of God in each hour of the 24, and in each moment then. In the faces of men and women I see God, and in my own face in the glass. I find letters from God dropped in the street, and every one is signed by God's name."

Whitman's transformed character and presence turned people toward him like flowers to sunlight. In his old age, he was surrounded by many who regarded him as a beloved teacher. In describing this literary genius, Richard Bucke wrote that "his outward life, his inward spiritual existence and his poetry were all one; . . . indeed, no man who ever lived liked so many things and disliked so few. . . . For young and old his touch had a charm that cannot be described. This charm, if understood would explain the whole mystery of the man, and how he produced such effects not only upon the well, but among the sick and wounded." Bucke went on to describe Whitman's brief meeting with one of those who sought his company: "Whitman only spoke to him about a hundred words altogether, and these quite ordinary and commonplace; but shortly after leaving (Whitman) a state of mental exaltation set in that lasted six weeks. . . . I may add that this person's whole life has been changed by that contact, . . . in an extraordinary degree."

Even now, on the edge of a slow-moving stream somewhere or in a grassy mountain meadow, lovers may be reading aloud the words of Walt Whitman, America's saintly blue-collar rogue, whose inspired gospel of earthy-divine love still sounds "over the rooftops of the world."

Young Joan's Call

The Divine Destiny of Heaven's Heroine

In 1425, the Hundred Years' War was 88 years old. The English armies occupied much of France. The dauphin Charles, driven from Paris and his rightful throne by Henry V, had fled to Borges in the south. All French hopes for freedom seemed lost.

No one yet knew of a 13-year-old farm girl living outside the village of Domrémy, whose name, by the time she was 18, would become legend. Until that year, Joan was like most village girls raised in a time of war—devoutly religious and accustomed to great hardship and poverty.

Then one summer afternoon in her father's garden, the divine entered young Joan's life—she began hearing the voices of angels and saints and seeing an otherworldly light. "Rarely do I hear it without the brightness," she said, "usually a great light. . . . I knew it was the voice of an angel. This voice told me, twice or thrice a week, that I, Joan, must go away, . . . that I should raise the siege laid to the city of Orléans, . . . also that I should make my way to Robert de Baudricourt in the fortress of Vaucouleurs, the Captain of that place. . . . I answered that I was a poor girl who knew not how to ride nor lead in war." A poignant response to a disembodied voice by an illiterate peasant girl ordered to save a great city under English siege—as if she were a general to command the armies of France. Yet for three years, the voices of Saint Michael, Saint Margaret, and Saint Catherine commanded Joan to do exactly that.

At the age of 16, Joan relented to her voices and set out under pretext for Vaucouleurs to fulfill her divine mission. When she arrived, she told her mother's cousin Durand Laxart why she had come. Convinced of her sanity by the passion of her faith, Laxart took her to Baudricourt, captain of the dauphin's army.

The captain listened to her tale, skeptical and unmoved, then sent her away, advising Laxart to thrash the audacious young girl. Two more times Joan went to Baudricourt; each time he refused to see her. But her voices would not let her give up. When Baudricourt refused her a third time in early 1429, she began to plead her case to the citizens of Vaucouleurs.

Joan's purity and passionate urgency convinced many that if she was mad, it was divine madness. She gained a devoted following, including two local noblemen who supported her cause. Finally, Baudricourt relented. After having her exorcised, he met with her, then sent her to Chinon to meet the dauphin Charles.

There, court ladies first examined Joan to verify her virginity; then a committee of clergymen questioned her to determine her faith. Found satisfactory on both counts, she was taken to a large hall where the dauphin had hidden himself in a crowd to test her powers. Joan went directly to him; they then retired to talk in secret.

When they returned, it was clear that something extraordinary had occurred. "After having heard her," said one court eyewitness, "the King appeared radiant." Sixteen-year-old Joan had convinced the dauphin of her God-inspired mission—that she would lead his armies into battle, drive the English out of France, then make him king.

But the dauphin, lacking Joan's moral courage and certainty, wavered for weeks while his ecclesiastics interrogated her. Meanwhile, France's armies lost battle after battle, until England's final victory seemed near. In her frustration, Joan dictated on her own an ultimatum to England's King Henry VI. It read in part, "Jesus-Maria, King of England, . . . who call yourself regent of the Kingdom of France, . . . acknowledge the summons of the King of Heaven. Render to the Maid, sent here by God the King of Heaven, the keys of all the good towns which you have taken and violated in France. She is here, come by God's will to reclaim the blood royal."

This farm girl with the heart of a lion further warned King Henry that if his soldiers did not flee, she would "have them all slain," as their power could not match that which God would give to her.

King Henry presumedly found this letter amusing.

After delaying for six more weeks, the dauphin of France finally gave Joan her army.

Joan's angelic voices now told her to send a messenger to the chapel of Saint Catherine in Ferbois to dig beneath the altar and take up a sword put there for her by God, which she must carry into battle. The messenger was sent; the sword was found exactly in that spot. So, on April 27, 1429, Joan donned soldier's armor, buckled her sacred sword at her side, and led her troops to break the siege of Orléans.

Orléans commanded the key bridge across the Loire river. If Orléans fell, so would France, as England could then move her armies unhindered into southern France. When Joan and her soldiers reached the Loire, Dunois, commander of the dauphin's troops, told her she could not cross by the bridge that the English held, nor could she cross by boat, as the wind was blowing in the wrong direction—he counseled caution for the sake of her safety.

"The counsel of . . . God is wiser and safer than yours," Joan answered.

"In the same moment," Commander Dunois would later testify, "the wind which prevented the boats from moving upstream changed and became favorable." He added, "it seems to me that Joan—and also what she did in warfare and in battle— was rather of God than of men."

That very day, Joan delivered crucial supplies to Orléans. That evening, with Dunois beside her, she rode her white charger into the liberated city. Yet for days afterward, the fearful French command still refused to fight.

Then one afternoon, Joan lay down for a nap and received her call. She promptly rose, put on her armor, and declaring that the time for battle had come, led her army to an English stronghold. Their arrival precipitated a full-scale battle. Boldly, Joan charged the English, calling out encouragement, leading her men into the thick of the fight. Inspired by her presence and courage, her soldiers fought like men divinely possessed. At last, the English abandoned their fort and fled, broken at their greatest strength.

Two days later, Joan's army took another key English fort. Afterward, Joan told her confessor, Jean Pasquerel, "Tomorrow the blood will flow out of my body above my breast." The next day, she led her troops into another great battle and was wounded in the shoulder. But she quickly bandaged her wound and returned to the battle, which lasted far into the night.

The next morning, she assembled her army at sunrise facing the English, outside the walls of Orléans. It being the Sabbath, she ordered her troops not to charge but only to defend themselves if attacked. The two armies faced each other in battle formation. Then, suddenly and unexpectedly, the English turned and fled. Orléans was free at last.

In little more than a week, Joan had turned the tide of the Hundred Years' War and resurrected the spirit of a demoralized France. The invincible English were beaten, humiliated, and put to flight.

Joan, the Maid of Orléans and God's avenging angel, became the heroine of France.

More triumphs followed. Yet the dauphin wavered, reluctant to seize the victory Joan had delivered into his hands. On July 17, the dauphin Charles was anointed king in the Cathedral of Rhiems. Still, he called off battles, made truces and needless compromises, and ignored Joan's angelic counsel. Joan pressed on, hoping to liberate Paris, England's final stronghold, and was wounded again. She had been told "by the voices of Saint Catherine and Saint Margaret" that she would soon be captured. And she was—in May of 1430, after a two-day battle.

Now 19 years old, she was sent to Paris to face an inquisition by the English Church. Denied representation, Joan, an illiterate peasant girl shackled in irons, confronted a group of English church scholars schooled in the arts of theological debate—and performed brilliantly. Her responses to their strategic questions are reminiscent of Christ's table-turning replies to the crafty Pharisees. To put her on the spot, her chief examiner, Bishop Pierre Cauchon, asked her to recite the Paternoster and Ave Marie. "I will say them willingly, provided you hear my confession," said Joan, putting Cauchon on the spot. For if he heard her confession, he lost the right to judge her; and if he refused to hear it, he violated his sacred duty as a priest. He immediately withdrew his request. Next, he asked Joan if Saint Michael had appeared to her naked, a crude attempt to impugn her purity that failed to ruffle her.

"Do you think that God cannot afford to clothe him?" she calmly replied.

When one clever judge asked Joan if she believed herself in God's good grace, she responded, "If I am not, may God bring me to it; if I am, may God keep me in it."

The courage, grace, and maturity Joan showed throughout her more than three-month interrogation were worthy of the Gospels. She was often ill from abuse by her captors, who sought to confuse her, to break her will, to make her doubt her voices and herself. The clerics hounded her relentlessly, assuring her she was a deluded heretic and that her voices were demonic. They urged her to renounce her "errors and scandals."

On May 23, she responded: "The way that I have always spoken and held to in this trial, that will I still maintain. And if I was brought to judgment and saw the fire lit and the kindling ready, and the executioner ready to stoke the fire and that I be within the fire, yet should I not say otherwise and should maintain what I have said in the trial, even unto death."

The following morning, they took Joan to Saint-Ouen cemetery. The executioner led her onto a scaffold, where the wood was indeed stacked and ready for burning. A long and terrible sermon was then preached against her.

Until finally, she broke.

"I abide by God and our Holy Father the Pope," she said. Priests swarmed around her. A secret conversation took place. Joan signed a statement of abjuration and was returned to prison in irons with a life sentence. Part of her agreement was to never again wear men's clothes—an act her accusers equated with blasphemy. Yet three days later, on May 27, she put them on again. Bishop Couchon went and asked her why.

"I have resumed it," Joan replied in part, "because what had been promised me has not been observed, to wit that I should go to Mass and should receive the Body of Christ and should be taken out of irons." Then she bitterly renounced her own abjuration as an act of moral cowardice. "My voices told me, when I was on the scaffold and the tribune before the people that I should reply boldly, . . . it is true that God sent me. My voices have since told me that I did a great injury in confessing. . . . All that I said and revoked . . . I did only because of fear of the fire."

Joan knew that by these words she had lit the fire herself.

On the morning of May 30, 1431, declared a "relapsed heretic and excommunicate," Joan was taken to a public scaffold in Rouen and tied to the stake. She asked French officer Jean Massieu for a cross. He gave her two sticks tied together. She kissed and pressed them to her heart, then asked Jean

Massieu to get a cross from the church and hold it before her eyes until she was dead.

"Being in the flames," Massieu later testified, "she ceased not until the end to proclaim and confess aloud the holy name of Jesus." Witnesses saw the name of Jesus written in the flames. And as Joan died, many saw a white dove fly out of her burning pyre. Immediately after her death, her ashes were thrown into the Seine River.

In 1920—five centuries after Joan rode into battle—three miracles attributed to Joan were finally authenticated. Joan of Arc was formally declared a saint.

Giving Up to God

The Healing Mission of an Alcoholic

With the possible exception of Jack Daniels and Jim Beam, no man's name is more closely associated with alcohol than that of Bill Wilson. His story began, ironically, in a room behind a bar, where he was born on November 26, 1895, in East Orson, Vermont.

Bill adored his father, the manager of a marble quarry who played ball with Bill after work. But one day when Bill was 10, his mother took him and his sister out for a picnic and informed them that their father had left for good. Bill never even got to say good-bye.

He wouldn't see his father again for nine years. Although devastated, Bill never spoke of the incident. To manage his turbulent emotions, he vigorously applied himself to sports and music, excelling in both. In the process, he cultivated a highly competitive nature.

At 16, Bill fell deeply in love with Bertha, a local minister's daughter. This was the happiest year of his life—until the eve of his 17th birthday, when the school principal announced to the assembled students that Bertha had died unexpectedly during a minor operation. Bill fell into a deep depression. Formerly a top student, he now failed his classes and was unable to graduate.

Two years later, he met a young woman named Lois, who would, in her way, help shape Bill's destiny. She believed in him and helped him once again to believe in himself. As his depression lifted, he began to recover the drive he had lost with his first love's death.

By 1915, Bill was back on his feet. After attending college, he joined a military program in Virginia, and at 21 was commissioned as a second lieutenant. Now an officer, Bill was sent to Fort Rodman in Massachusetts, where he attended dinner parties in the homes of the good people of the town. At one of these gatherings, Bill took his first drink.

Socially awkward and self-conscious, he soon discovered that alcohol transformed his character—it seemed to put him at ease, loosen his tongue, imbue him with energy and charm, and make him feel connected to others. This seemingly magical potion made Bill the life of every party. But he drank to excess, often passing out by the end of the night.

In 1918, Bill married his sweetheart Lois before shipping off to England to fight in World War I. But by the time he got to France, the war was winding down. Having never made it to the front, Bill returned home determined to succeed at something. He studied law for the next three years, but his drinking continued. Foolishly, he showed up for his bar exam drunk, and he failed. Landing on his feet, Bill began dabbling in Wall Street, and by luck or intuition, his investments brought him considerable profits. Finding himself a well-to-do young man, he seriously studied the market, and the profits kept rolling in. Bill had found his niche—in 1926, a prestigious Wall Street investment firm hired him at a handsome salary, with an expense account and a $1,000 credit for buying stocks. His drinking increased with his fortunes, shaking the foundation of his marriage. In the height of the Roaring Twenties, alcohol seemed a symbol of liberation, and Bill appeared to many to be celebrating his success. Only he and Lois knew he had a problem.

Bill was a successful drunk—his money and charm made his liability seem to be only a quirk. While he was on top of the world, his company viewed him as a wonder boy, worth his weight in gold. To his friends he was a live wire, a good-time Charlie.

But by 1927, Bill and Lois both realized he was in a fight for his life; he wrote vows of abstinence in the family Bible, but never kept them for long. Bill was living out the pattern of an alcoholic—vows of abstinence followed by drunken binges and bouts of crushing remorse. As countless lost battles with the bottle destroyed his confidence, Bill's desperation deepened, and his employers and associates began raising eyebrows.

Then the market crashed in 1929. Now financially ruined, Bill Wilson appeared as he really was: a desperate man in the grip of a terrible disease. He who had once fancied himself a future J. P. Morgan destined to rule a financial empire was $60,000 in debt—a pauper who could not stop drinking to save his life.

He now entered the demonic phase of alcoholism, terrifying friends and strangers with his insane behavior: He flew into drunken rages, hurled a sewing machine across a room at Lois, roared through his house kicking out door panels, and, with his utterly predictable binges, he sabotaged his few potential business comebacks.

During his bouts of drunken insanity, Lois feared him. But in his sober moments, when she saw him overwhelmed by remorse and grief at what he had become, she pitied and loved him. She knew that deep inside, Bill was a good person, an honest and hardworking man who cared about people. Neither of them understood his problem—alcoholism had not yet been identified as a medical condition.

By late 1933, they had both lost hope. The self-destructive ordeal that Bill's life had become seemed fated to end in his early death. By 1934, he was suicidal, and his binges left him mentally deranged for days. When doctors diagnosed early signs of brain damage, the prospect of madness terrified him into several months of sobriety. For a time, his willpower seemed resurrected.

His fall came on Armistice Day, triggered by a celebratory drink "on the house" offered by a patriotic bartender. Lois found him passed out in the street at five in the morning, bleeding from a wound to his head.

It was the last straw for Bill. He had had enough of life.

He spent the following months on a nonstop binge aimed at the grave, settling into his last bout as into a comfortable, well-worn armchair, holed up in his room. That is where Ebbie T. found him. Ebbie, an old school friend and drinking buddy, had kicked the bottle.

When Bill asked him why he was not drinking, Ebbie replied, "I've gotten religion." Bill would not ordinarily have given this statement much weight—he saw religion as a mere social convention. But Ebbie's sobriety impressed him. Bill knew that Ebbie's drinking problem had been on a par with his own. Ebbie told Bill about a group of down-and-out men, some of them drunks, uniting with each other to overcome their problems—with God's help.

The group's founder, a minister named Rowling, was a former drunk who had been personally treated by the great psychologist Carl Jung. When Rowling relapsed, Jung had told him the only thing that could save him was a spiritual awakening. Rowling protested that he already believed in God. But Jung said only the direct experience of God could transform him, and he advised Rowling to find a religious group that could support this quest.

Jung's advice proved to be prophetic—Rowling was cured after a mystical experience of God. Afterward, he founded the Oxford Group, based in early Christian teachings of purity, mystical prayers, and surrender to God. There Ebbie T. was released from his own slavery to the bottle and given peace of mind and happiness such as he had never known. Ebbie's words reawakened a desire in Bill to be sober again, and his example provided a ray of hope. Now all Bill needed to do was pray and surrender his life to God.

There was only one problem—Bill didn't believe in God. He continued drinking while contemplating his inevitable death— until one day, alone in his room, he cried out in desperation, with no faith at all: "If there be a God, let Him show Himself!"

"Suddenly," he later recalled, "my room blazed with an indescribably white light. I was seized with an ecstasy beyond description. Every joy I had known was pale by comparison . . . was conscious of nothing else for a time. Then . . . there was a mountain. I stood upon its summit where a great wind blew. A wind not of air, but of spirit. In great, clean strength, it blew right through me. Then came the blazing thought, 'You are a free man.' I became acutely conscious of a Presence, a veritable sea of living spirit. I lay on the shores of a new world; I seemed possessed by the absolute, and the curious conviction that no matter how wrong things seemed to be, there could be no question of the ultimate rightness of God's universe. . . . For the first time, I felt that I really belonged. I knew that I was loved and could love in return."

Bill Wilson would never touch alcohol again. When Lois came home and saw him, she reports, "I knew something overwhelming had happened. His eyes were filled with light. His whole being expressed hope and joy. From that moment on, I shared his confidence in the future."

Bill's illumination left him with a deep gratitude for the life given him and an urge to help others—to share the grace he had been given. He began to formulate the idea of a movement of alcoholics who would help one another, a movement that would spread out to "reach every alcoholic in the world capable of being honest enough to admit his own defeat," he said.

Bill Wilson had found his life purpose.

He soon realized that alcoholics could not tolerate preaching. He needed an approach uniquely suited to the alcoholic temperament—one that would penetrate their denial, awaken self-understanding, and make them available to God's grace. The Twelve Steps began evolving in Bill's mind.

Then, his fateful meeting with another alcoholic, Dr. Robert Smith, known as Dr. Bob, catalyzed the birth of Alcoholics Anonymous. Their lasting spiritual partnership would contribute to saving millions of alcoholics from addiction and death, as did the book, *Alcoholics Anonymous.*

A first edition of 300,000 copies was published in 1939. Today, the book is read by millions, and Alcoholics Anonymous groups meet each day in cities and towns all over the world. Bill Wilson's Twelve Step program, conceived after his illumination, based in principles of self-understanding, divine will, and service, has helped countless souls to treat many forms of addictive behavior.

In 1971, on his and Lois's 53rd anniversary, after years of love and service, Bill Wilson passed away, leaving behind a loving wife and a legacy that will live forever.

A Sleeping Gift Awakens

The Revelations of a Modest Prophet

Edgar was born in 1877 on a Kentucky farm to devout but uneducated parents. He himself would not pass beyond the ninth grade. A quiet, deeply religious boy, he was also a bit otherworldly; until he was nine years old, "little folk" that only he and his friend Anna could see came out of the woods to play with them. One little fellow once told them, "We live in the flowers and the music."

"What music?" Anna had asked.

"The music of everything," the little fellow replied.

Anna died that winter. In the spring, a lonely Edgar looked for her in the flowers with the little folk. But he never found her.

At age 10, Edgar made a vow to read the Bible once through for every year of his life. Over the next three years, he read his Bible 13 times. One day, while studying his Bible in a secret place in the woods, he felt a presence near him. He looked up and saw standing over him a beautiful woman with shadowy appendages shaped like wings on her back. Her voice, when she spoke, was soft and musical: "Your prayers have been heard," she told Edgar. "Tell me what you would like most of all so that I may give it to you."

After hesitating, he mustered his courage and said, "Most of all I would like to be helpful to others, and especially to children when they are sick."

As suddenly as she had come, the woman vanished.

All the next day, Edgar's mind was dull. His teacher reported his poor school performance to his father, a stern man everyone called Squire. Disgraced, Squire tested Edgar on his schoolbooks that night, and in frustration at his son's seeming stupidity, he slapped Edgar and knocked him to the floor. That's when Edgar heard her voice: "If you sleep a little, we can help you," the angel said.

Edgar pleaded with his father for a chance to rest. He promised he would know the lesson when he woke. After his father went into the kitchen, Edgar curled up on his chair, with his schoolbook under his head, and fell fast asleep.

When the Squire woke Edgar minutes later to test him, he was astonished to find that *Edgar could now answer any question on any page of the book, much of which he hadn't even read.* After that, Edgar slept with his schoolbooks under his pillow and, in the morning, knew their entire contents—he saw the pages in his mind. He was soon moved a grade ahead in school.

Two years later, after a baseball struck Edgar on the spine, he came home delirious and acting strangely. When his worried parents put him to bed, he fell asleep and began to speak. *In a calm, clear voice he told his parents of his spinal injury and described in detail the making of a poultice that would cure him. They followed his instructions and by morning his symptoms were gone and his spine healed. Edgar had no memory of the previous day or of his sleeping diagnosis.*

Years passed. Edgar grew up, left the farm, and moved to a nearby town. He worked in a bookstore where he met Gertrude, his future wife. They would eventually have three sons. Edgar became a photographer and a respected member of his church and community. He seemed in all ways ordinary, except for his secret talents, which manifested periodically.

A turning point came when Edgar healed himself of a serious throat condition using self-hypnosis, with the help of an amateur hypnotist named Lane. Lane began experimenting on Edgar, whom he found was able, in trance, to diagnose others, even people far away, with uncanny accuracy. Edgar had no medical background. Yet in his trances, he used precise medical terminology unknown to him while awake and prescribed wide-ranging remedies that proved remarkably effective.

This young man was apparently a gifted doctor in his sleep.

Edgar was leery of his odd ability, and only after much persuasion by Lane and soul-searching on his own did he agree to use it. When he saw that the people who came to him were cured, he couldn't refuse. But he wouldn't accept any money. If it was God's gift, and he prayed that it was, he could not in good conscience profit by it.

Edgar's medical advice was often vigorously opposed by doctors—they insisted his unorthodox treatments would prove disastrous and perhaps fatal to patients they themselves had been unable to help. At times, fearing the worst, Edgar suffered agonies of doubt. He knew that if one patient died, it would ruin him. But seeing so many people healed gave him faith in his gift and the courage to use it.

Some of the doctors who first accused him of quackery

were won over by his remarkable cures and offered to team up with him, hoping to make their careers and fortunes. Edgar always declined. To one such adversary-turned-entrepreneur he said, "You, like all the other doctors who investigated me, found that I'm not a fake. Now if you fellas could convince me that *you* all are not all fakes, maybe I'd join up with you."

When a nationally syndicated newspaper article appeared about this country boy with a miraculous gift, a flood of people came: believers seeking magical healing, hucksters seeking to exploit him for a buck, and skeptics seeking to expose him as a fraud. And thousands of desperate letters began pouring in, requesting help. Often, in trance, he gave detailed readings in answer to *letters that had not yet arrived.*

Edgar Cayce would become known as the Sleeping Prophet. Arrested more than once, charged with fraud, fortune-telling, and practicing medicine without a license, he was always exonerated in the end. Not one person he diagnosed ever complained, and no one who followed his treatments ever died as a result. Cayce's percentage of documented cures was higher than those of the physicians of his time, or for that matter, ours.

One day, a man whose passion was metaphysics came to Edgar for a reading. When Edgar went into his trance, the man asked a wide range of metaphysical questions, and the readings took off into new territory. Edgar now spoke of reincarnation, karma, and of the "akashic records"—a library in another dimension where all knowledge and information was stored. These records, the reading said, were the source of the material given in Edgar's trances.

When Edgar woke and learned what he had said while asleep, he was unnerved, even frightened. These things, which he'd never read in his Bible, now turned his world upside down. He questioned his gift all over again. Did it come from God or from the Devil? Was he possessed by demons? How could he tell? He suffered a crisis of conscience, fearing a threat to his most cherished religious beliefs. After much thought and prayer, he decided to apply biblical wisdom to the matter of his gift. By its fruits he would know it—he would examine the results of his readings in people's lives. If they were truly helped, then it must be God's gift. In that case, to withhold his readings would be the real sin.

One day, his son Hugh lit a pile of flash powder on the floor and it blew up in his face, burning both his eyes. Doctors told Edgar one eye would have to be removed to save his son's life. The other eye would likely remain blind. But young Hugh told the doctors his father could heal him. "When my daddy goes to sleep, he's the best doctor in the world," he said. Then he asked his father to help him. In a trance, Edgar prescribed a poultice using tannic acid to be placed on Hugh's burned eyes. The doctors opposed it. But as Hugh was already blind, the matter was academic. So the poultice was applied—and Hugh regained his sight.

Over the years, Edgar's readings helped thousands of people, healing their bodies and renewing their faith. The readings always turned people to the purpose of existence: relationship with others and with God. Edgar was leery of metaphysical enthusiasts who dabbled in psychic phenomena for the sake of thrills or the aggrandizement of their egos. He feared such people would turn his work into a cult, and he wanted no part of it.

Edgar's mind was tuned to the cosmos, but his feet were

planted firmly on Earth. He knew his knowledge must help people in tangible ways or it was of little value. Fascinating information was never the point. As the readings often said, "To know, and not to do, becomes sin." Truth, to be of value, had to be lived, not merely believed.

Over the years, a vast body of medical and metaphysical wisdom came through Edgar's trances, emerging from the depths of some Universal Mind to which he seemed to be a doorway. He accurately prophesied many future events, including the Civil Rights movement, and the assassinations of the Kennedy brothers and Martin Luther King. He foretold a spiritual renaissance in the last quarter of the twentieth century. Meanwhile he read his Bible daily, each year completing one cycle, keeping his childhood vow.

In 1943, Edgar Cayce's biography, *There Is a River*, by Thomas Sugrue, was published. It resulted in an avalanche of letters from people requesting help. To meet the demand, Cayce tripled his daily readings. But the strain of it was too much, and his health began a rapid decline. His friends and family warned him to cut back and take it easy. But moved by the suffering of those who wrote to him for help, he could not turn away. In a trance state, Cayce even warned himself to rest immediately. When asked, "How long shall Edgar rest?" the Sleeping Prophet answered in the third person: "Until he is well or dead." A prophet to the end.

Edgar Cayce died on January 3, 1945. His last words were, "How much the world needs God today." Three months later, on Easter Sunday, his wife, Gertrude, followed him. An extraordinary life had run its course after enriching many others. In his lifetime, Edgar directly helped more than 30,000 people.

His readings, all recorded, now reside in the Association for Research and Enlightenment in Virginia Beach, Virginia.

The life of Edgar Cayce points to a fairy-tale reality where winged angels grant prayers in lonely woods to humble youths; where little people teach children about "the music of everything;" and where simple souls grow up to help heal the world with their magical gifts. But, more important, Edgar's life and work remind us that the world in which we live is more mysterious than we know, and the spiritual powers that he demonstrated may also lie dormant within each of us, waiting to be awakened and used in the service of others.

The Rebirth of a Madwoman

The Resurrection of Byron Katie

The sudden transformation of Byron Katie serves as a remarkable testimony to the powers of spiritual resurrection that live in each of us.

Born Byron Kathleen Reid in Breckenridge, Texas, in 1942, she was raised in the small town of Needles, California, in the years following World War II. Her mother, a homemaker, and her father, a railroad worker, saw Byron grow from a quiet, thoughtful little girl into an aggressive, competitive teenager who sought to be the best in everything she did. A top student, she played piano and sang in a regional choir. Beautiful, energetic, and fun, Byron was voted first runner-up for queen of her high school prom.

At 19, she married Robert, her high school sweetheart. They moved to Fresno—two sons and a daughter were soon born. Robert and Byron formed their own company as equal partners. When her marriage, like many, met with difficulties, Byron, a perfectionist and high achiever, suffered the belief that who she was was not enough. She began striving for the usual symbols of happiness and security—money, beauty, talent, and success.

She invested their mutual earnings in real estate. Within a few years, she and Robert owned shares of numerous buildings in Needles's business district. They bought a grand riverfront house and threw lavish parties attended by an elite and influential local crowd. In the 1970s, Byron became a millionaire.

She now had her long-sought success. She was doing big business, raising a family, living high. But it wasn't enough; nothing pleased or satisfied her. In her increasingly frustrated and ultimately futile search for happiness through money and power, Byron had "bullied, intimidated, and badgered" anyone, even her husband and children, to get her way. But in the midst of having everything and seeking more, her passion had turned to desperation. Her marriage with Robert became a battle of wills, her family life a series of skirmishes. They were all casualties, especially the children. "If I didn't get my way," Byron says, "I would leave the house and take the children with me."

The third time she did this, Robert found himself another woman.

This was a time of darkness for Byron and for her children, but the seeds had been sown long before. For years, she had held back the darkness and emptiness with food, alcohol, tobacco, and constant striving. But her strategy took its toll—her progressive disintegration led to rages, alcohol abuse, and paranoia. At one point, she bought a gun and kept it loaded under her bed. Finally, even her children feared her. When her marriage ended in 1976, she and the children wound up penniless in Barstow, California.

Then, in 1979, Byron married Paul, an old friend, 15 years

her senior. When Paul was 19 and Byron 4, he had paved the street on which she lived. She still recalled being captivated by his laughter; she had loved him even then. Byron and Paul began buying, fixing up, and reselling old houses and were soon quite wealthy—Byron still had the knack. Once again, she had money, friends, a thriving career, and a family she loved. But the meaning had drained out of her existence. She felt herself dying inside.

Paul, a good man, had married Byron on her way down. He had seen a couple of friends have nervous breakdowns. But he'd never witnessed anything like Byron's terrifying descent.

She had once taken on the world, charmed people, closed deals, made money. Now, afraid to leave the house, Byron went weeks without bathing, changing her clothes, or brushing her teeth. She spent days in bed—drinking, smoking, raging, popping codeine, and eating ice cream by the gallon. Her weight shot up to over 200 pounds. Her torment, and her rage, were unrelieved.

"Nothing felt good, nothing made me happy, nothing brought me peace. In the end, I was obese and starving. . . . I was in so much pain and the pills weren't working. I was insane, a dead woman still breathing. . . . "

Her children spun off in their own mad directions, fleeing their cyclone mother raging on her bed. Paul became Byron's primary caretaker—her buffer to a world she now feared. During the first seven years of their marriage, Paul suffered four heart attacks—the strain of caring for her was literally killing him. Byron spent the last two of those years lying on the bed, her unchanged clothing often plastered to her body and her unwashed hair matted to her head.

In 1986, after his fourth heart attack, Paul took Byron,

now 43, to a halfway house. She lived in the attic, sleeping on the floor. All she wanted was to die.

Then one morning, for no apparent reason, Byron Katie woke up reborn.

The bare facts of this event cannot begin to convey its impact or explain its occurrence. Morning dawned, Byron stirred, lying on the floor. She opened her eyes and saw a cockroach crawling across a human foot. She did not, in that moment, know what a foot, or for that matter, what anything, was. All was a mystery.

Yet the sight of the insect, the foot, the leg, the room, filled Byron with delight and awe. She was a newborn, gazing in wonder at life. "It was the most amazing thing," she recalls. "I looked at the foot and the leg and I had never seen anything so beautiful and marvelous. It was the same with the floor, with the cockroach, and with the light, seeing it for the first time; . . . and the unfolding of it was so incredible . . . total, total joy. . . . "

The world was new. She had awakened from "an ancient dream." Whatever had previously obscured her view of life's inherent perfection was gone. Now, from moment to moment, she saw and joyously embraced reality exactly as it was. Everything she gazed upon, within and without, glowed with radiant life.

No one will ever know what catalyzed this simple yet absolute turnaround in perception and consciousness. But one thing was certain: Overnight, Byron Katie had moved from suicidal despair to ecstatic freedom. The madwoman had vanished. In her place appeared a beautiful changeling, an innocent child.

No one, least of all Byron, understood what had happened. Her daughter, Roxann, at first believed that her mother was playing a trick. Yet she saw a different person come home. "Her face was changed completely," Roxann reports. "Her eyes were cleared. She was not the same person."

Understandably, Roxann feared the return of the mad-woman she had known. But what had happened to Byron Katie persisted and only deepened over time. Her past behind her, her future yet to unfold, she now lived in the eternal present. Her contact with everyday reality—with people, objects, and situations—though at times bewildering, continued to fill her with joy.

For a time, Roxann led her mother, still absorbed in a childlike state of awe, around by the hand. Byron would spon-taneously hug people on the street—friends, strangers, the homeless—with equal delight. Surprisingly, many let her, per-haps sensing her unconditional love and acceptance.

For seven years after the awakening, inner revelations came to her, which she tried to put into words and share with others: "There is only love; . . . there is no time; . . . unlearning is every-thing. . . . " But she had leaped across a chasm of consciousness, and no words could build a bridge for those who could not see to the other side. She says of that time, "I was wild with love, mad with love." But words could not convey it. She had to live her realization to sustain it.

She stopped trying to tell people what they had not asked to hear and began to simply love—those she had known, those she had harmed, and those she now met—no longer expecting them to understand, to be good, to love her back, *or to be any-thing other than who they were.* Living the truth had nothing to do with changing other people. Who they were and what they did was their business, God's business. Her only business was to love them unconditionally. By living in this way, Byron Katie gradually regained the trust of—and helped to heal—the family she had nearly destroyed.

One night six months after her awakening, Byron experienced a kind of spiritual agony from the tension of trying to live and love in a world that did not yet understand or accept who she was. An old woman appeared to her, sitting in a chair beside the bed, "a wonderful, voluptuous old lady with her hair tied in a bun." Byron merged into this lady and found herself looking out through ancient eyes. In this altered state, she saw herself and Paul, lying on the bed, as two primal beings who did not yet realize that *they did not have to suffer*. Life itself was unfolding perfectly.

For the next seven years, the marvelous old woman appeared to guide Byron Katie. "What I've come to know," Byron now says, "is that I projected the lady . . . like a movie . . . as a result of painful limitations I was experiencing in this dimension. We give ourselves exactly what we need. We supply our own medicine. . . . Today, I don't wait for angels. I am always the angel I have been awaiting, and so are you. It's not out there, it's in here. . . . Some people would project Christ, others Krishna. . . . I projected a fat lady with a bun on her head wearing a paisley dress—that's who I could trust. Now I trust All. I woke up knowing that God is everything. . . . There is no exception in my experience."

The stream of thoughts eventually returned, of course, as thoughts do—and with them, judgments, fears, and expectations. At such times, she felt herself slipping from the freedom of her awakening into the mind of suffering. But whenever this happened, she worked her way back by a compassionate vigilance, inspecting the thoughts, beliefs, and false assumptions that separated her from others and set her against life. Doing this work returned her gracefully to the pristine awareness of her original awakening. This work became her constant practice.

Through this process and her unconditional acceptance of life, Byron Katie made peace with each moment—every event, past or present. "All that I went through—every breath," she says, "was what it took for me to finally wake up. All teaches love in the long run. All needs are supplied. . . . Every experience of life is for this."

Today, Byron travels widely, freely teaching the Work—the fruit of her past struggles and spontaneous awakening.

Modern Man of Miracles

The Healing Powers of Padre Pio

After Saint Therese Neumann, Padre Pio is perhaps the most widely observed Western saint to demonstrate divine powers of healing and regeneration. The first signs of his extraordinary qualities occurred unexpectedly on September 20, 1918. Then a 31-year-old Capuchin monk, Padre Pio was sitting alone in the monastery chapel, praying after mass. Outside, Padre Leone heard a scream within the chapel and ran in to find Padre Pio lying unconscious on the floor, bleeding profusely from the five wounds of the stigmata.

Several monks carried him to his room, where he begged them to keep his condition a secret. But word spread. The Church quickly put a ban of silence on Padre Pio, concerned that this untested monk might be manifesting symptoms of hysteria. He was forbidden to write or speak in public—*yet over the next five decades, Padre Pio would prove to be one of the most remarkable Western saints in history.*

Like Saint Therese Neumann, Padre Pio bore for his entire life wounds of the stigmata that never healed. And thousands of individuals—from ordinary Italian peasants and fellow clerics to high public officials and pilgrims from around the world—witnessed and testified to his powers of telepathy, prophecy, bilocation, levitation, and healing.

Although Padre Pio never left the city of San Giovanni Rotondo, Italy, in his last 50 years, he often appeared to those in need far from his physical body—to teach, admonish, comfort, and heal. Numerous testimonies, by telegram, letter, telephone transcript, and personal declaration, document Padre Pio's long-distance appearances in places he never physically visited—throughout Italy, Austria, Uruguay, and even in Milwaukee, where Padre Pio admitted appearing on June 25, 1950, to attend the death of a fellow monk's father. When asked about his ability to appear in two places, Padre Pio replied, "If Christ multiplied the loaves and fishes, why cannot he multiply me?"

And the fragrance of violets that often emanated from him also often manifested to those who prayed to him and was noticed by witnesses in those places where he had miraculously appeared.

His miraculous healing powers were demonstrated beyond any doubts—he cured many illnesses deemed incurable and, on more than one occasion, restored sight to the blind. His most well-documented, and astonishing, case of healing involved a little blind girl named Gemma Di Giorgi, from Ribera, Sicily, born with no pupils in her eyes. In 1947, her grandmother took her on a long journey to see Padre Pio. Gemma's grandmother, ardently devoted to Padre Pio, believed the saint could give sight to her granddaughter, even though her doctors declared it physically impossible for a human being to ever see without pupils.

That morning, Gemma and her grandmother arrived in Padre Pio's village to wait in the enormous crowds that always attended Padre Pio's masses. Afterward, in the silence following mass, all heard a voice shout, "Gemma, come here!" Gemma's grandmother led her through the crowd, up to Padre Pio, where they knelt at his feet. Padre Pio, after hearing Gemma's confession, sweetly administered her first Communion, then gently stroked her eyes. Before they left, Padre Pio bid them farewell, saying, "May the Madonna bless you, Gemma. Be a good girl."

At that very moment, before the crowd of witnesses, Gemma uttered a shriek as the power of sight was given to her for the first time—a miracle that would last for the rest of her long life. Numerous doctors who examined Gemma later admitted their bewilderment. *By all known science, she should not have been able to see without the apparatus required for sight.*

The astonishing testimonies of miraculous cures and the demonstrations of Padre Pio's supernatural abilities fill volumes. And the volumes written about this great contemporary saint are increasing each year.

Padre Pio cast off his body on September 23, 1968. On September 26, more than 100,000 people came from around the world to San Giovanni Rotondo to attend his funeral. Many thousands wept at his passing, for the awe with which he was regarded for his miraculous powers was less than the love that his kindness and sanctity had awakened in the hearts of his people.

Love on the Line

Saving Souls on the Streets

Before Christ spoke to Bill Tomes from a painting on the altar of Saint Joseph's Church in Chicago, he'd lived a relatively ordinary, if somewhat adventurous, life. A middle-class boy from Evanston, Illinois, a talented painter with a love of football, he attended Notre Dame University, and earned a bachelor's degree in English and philosophy and a master's degree in counseling and guidance. He lived fully, pursued his art, dated, and drank with his friends. He traveled throughout Europe on nine trips, visiting 28 nations, collecting antiques, and interviewing various psychiatrists as preparation for his doctoral dissertation.

Then, in 1980, a simple dilemma took him to the altar of Saint Joseph's Church. He'd been offered two very different, well-paying jobs: as a hospital therapist, and a promising position with a major airline.

"When I knelt down, hoping for guidance," Bill relates,

"everything turned dark and fuzzy except the face of Christ on a painting near the altar."

Then a voice, which Bill believes was that of Christ, commanded him:

"Love," it said. "You are forbidden to do anything other than that."

Bill, not a particularly religious man, was astonished—the life he'd led the past 45 years had not prepared him for such an event. Next, his prayer over which job to take was answered—the same voice said three times, "I'll lead, you follow." And then, "Never be afraid." And five times in a row, "All your trust."

Bewildered, yet struck to the core, Bill revisited the altar and the painting numerous times over the next few months. Later, in another location, Christ continued to utter direct commandments, instructing him with the following words: "You must forgive everyone everything." And "Judge not, and you will not be judged."

Several months passed. Bill struggled to understand the meaning of his experiences as well as these commandments—to know how to carry them out. He started reading the Bible and other religious books—at one point, he encountered the line "Take nothing with you for the journey" seven times in a row in three books, until it became personally significant. After prolonged resistance to its apparent implications, and with the intervention of a priest, Bill gave in—and gave away nearly every possession he had. Keeping only his clothes, he moved into a friend's basement, where he slept on cardboard, and began working manual labor for food only—not accepting money.

Bill had worked until 1978 as a counselor for Catholic

Charities, a community service organization. Then, after going into art and other work, in 1983 he was offered and accepted a position as a youth minister working with street gangs in the Chicago projects. His first visit there was greeted with everything from indifference to hurled objects. He viewed the challenge of these youths as a test of his commitment. After Bill's next visit, he later learned, one local gang met to consider whether or not he should be killed. They decided he was a good guy and that he should be allowed to do what he thought he should, and that he would be "protected," which meant killing anyone who would hurt him. Bill spoke against this kind of protection.

Little by little, Bill got to know these troubled gang members, and their territory became his own. At Cardinal Bernardin's request, Bill's ministry grew in time to include other gang-infested projects. Others joined Bill, and he found himself with a large troubled flock of at-risk youth, outsiders and outcasts living on the edge of death, many fated to be casualties of the code of violence that lay at the center of their lives.

Brother Bill, as he came to be called, has personally encountered that violence, often in tragic forms—like the time he found a young gang leader dying in a stairwell with four bullets in his chest. All a grief-stricken Brother Bill could think to do was to hold the 21-year-old man and whisper in his ear, "God made you. He loves you. He wants you to be with him forever." Perhaps it was enough.

This incident is one of many that demonstrate the earnestness and commitment that Bill Tomes has lived for the last 15 years in carrying out Christ's personal commandment to "love without judgment."

Bill may not always feel loving, but he shows love in tangible ways, in action. He treats all he meets with all the kindness and compassion he can bring to bear. He shows love to seemingly unlovable souls by spending time with them, playing basketball, taking them to football games, helping them find work if they want it—by countless simple acts of kindness and generosity offered with no strings attached. Brother Bill understands that these young men find deeds more powerful than words and that acting with simple kindness is more potent than preaching. So he doesn't preach; his is a ministry of love, support, and the faith that a divine power that many call God will somehow penetrate the hearts and minds of the souls in his care.

Ron Stodghill wrote of Bill in a *Time* magazine article, "He believes that gangsters will not change their ways simply through fear of prison or even the carrot of education or employment . . . but only by viewing themselves as under the light of a divine presence. . . . His vulnerability, his willingness to put his life on the line, his unconditional offering of acceptance and forgiveness, and yes, love, are a constant source of astonishment for men and boys weaned on hate and rejection.

"'I think he's an angel,' says a twenty-two-year-old Vice Lord. 'I really think God sent him here.'"

But Bill has shown his love and proven the courage of his convictions by following another of Christ's injunctions: "No greater love can a man show, than that he be willing to lay down his life for his friends."

Fifty-three times in the last 15 years, Bill Tomes has walked into the line of fire and stood between two warring gangs until they stopped shooting. They do stop, sometimes reluctantly. He is often secretly told by gang members what's "coming down." His sources probably range from a reluctant tough ordered to make a hit on an opposing gang member to a boy who doesn't want to engage in a shooting skirmish but can't back out in front of his friends. Whatever the reason, they call Bill. And he goes—often after the shooting has already begun. He walks out and stands in the midst of the flying bullets. When they shout at him to get out of the way, he tells them he will not, because he loves them. They can see it in his eyes, in his posture, and in his commitment to being there. Is there greater proof of love than this? Maybe that's why they stop shooting.

Over 150 of his "parishioners" have died in the last 15 years—from drugs, beatings, knives, and bullets—some of them innocent bystanders who, by living in these neighborhoods, also live in the line of fire. One woman criticized Brother Bill for giving too much of himself to those who bring so much pain and trouble to the neighborhoods. While he understood her point of view, he explained that he must follow higher instructions. Gang leaders say that 500 lives have been saved—saved through the divine intervention of Bill Tomes, working tirelessly for peace on the streets.

Jesus Christ, who also lived among outcasts and who said, "I have come to call not the saved, but the sinners, to righteousness," is Bill Tome's role model and inspiration—his commander on a spiritual battlefield where real lives are on the line, real bullets are fired, and real blood is spilled. Brother Bill's is a flock of prodigal sons. And he is calling them home through love.

Hidden Blessings

When Bad Luck Becomes Good Fortune

B orn in the late 1940s in southern California, Danny was raised in blissful ignorance in a middle-class home of hard-working parents, with an older sister, a dog, and two cats. He grew up in the seeming fantasy world of the 1950s—a world of school yards, friends, games, sports, and double-feature movies on weekends. He did all the things he was supposed to do: he worked hard, behaved himself, and lived up to his parents' expectations.

Small and wiry, Danny inherited his mom's smarts and his dad's strength. He loved climbing trees, swinging like Tarzan, and jumping off everything in sight. When his junior high school homeroom teacher started a trampoline and tumbling club, he loved bouncing on the trampoline. Danny came alive in a new way—he had found his passion.

By the age of 14, he had won a state trampoline championship. While still in high school, he won the U.S. Championship and performed in Europe. Then, in his freshman year at Berkeley, he won the first World Trampoline Championship in London and began training toward a spot on the U.S. Olympic Gymnastics Team.

Life had taught Danny that he could control his own destiny, as long as he did the right thing and worked hard. Now life had other lessons to teach.

Near summer's end, before a senior year filled with promises of glory, he packed for an upcoming trip to Yugoslavia, where he was being sent by the U.S. Gymnastics Federation as an elite gymnast and potential Olympian, to train with the best gymnasts on the planet at the World Championships—a final stepping-stone to the Olympic Trials and Games beyond. It seemed as if his whole life had directed him toward this goal.

Danny spent his last evening in Los Angeles visiting with his sister before catching his flight. He was on his Triumph motorcycle, heading home, when his life was abruptly transformed by an intervention that seemed far less than divine. There were no visions, no blissful revelations, no angelic voices—only the thud of metal against metal, the sound of shattering glass, and a terrible crunch of bones. And then, unbelievable pain.

In his book, *Way of the Peaceful Warrior*, author Dan Millman tells what happened: "I was driving into a future even brighter than the headlights of the oncoming cars. I observed the speed limit, wore a helmet, and exercised caution. But I soon learned that being good and doing the right thing sometimes makes no difference at all."

The older-model white Cadillac facing him in the intersection, waiting to make a left turn, knew nothing of his future plans. As Dan entered the intersection, the driver, who didn't see him, gunned his accelerator and turned directly in front of him.

Dan had a half-second to choose what he would do—should he swerve right and hit the car head-on? Or swerve left into oncoming traffic he couldn't see? Or should he lay the bike down, slide, and maybe get crushed beneath the car's wheels? Instead, he made a decision he was to replay over and over in the coming days—he jammed on his brakes, hoping to slow down enough to avoid serious injury on impact. It wasn't enough.

Dan slammed into the right bumper, shattering his femur into nearly 40 pieces. According to one eyewitness, his body did a one-and-one-half somersault over the top of the Cadillac before crashing to the concrete. When Dan regained consciousness, he looked up to see a huddle of faces standing over him. In those first moments of awareness, he confirmed that he was alive, that he could move, and that he had all his limbs. Then he heard the wail of a siren approaching. He saw something white sticking out of his torn sneaker—all the toes of his left foot were dislocated and fractured. In shock, he asked the ambulance driver, "Is that white thing sticking through my shoe one of my bones?"

"Yeah," said the ambulance driver, unsympathetic to motorcycle riders. Then, taking a look at Dan's right leg, he added, "But that's the least of your worries." That's when Dan suddenly became aware of the searing pain. The rest was a blur of constant, throbbing agony—the emergency room; a tired doctor who hand-drilled a bolt through Dan's right knee with only a shot of local anesthetic; his ashen-faced parents. Still in shock, he asked the doctor if his leg would be healed soon because he had to be ready to train in Yugoslavia in a few days. The doctor didn't even answer.

All the while, a part of him was thinking, "This can't be happening."

The next morning, Dan awoke in traction in his hospital room with the realization dawning that he was not going to the World Championships, not enrolling for classes this semester, not likely going to the Olympics, and maybe never walking normally again. His gymnastics career, the passion of his life and part of the foundation of his identity, had apparently come to an end.

No one, least of all Dan Millman, would have ever predicted that the divine would enter his life in the shape of a white Cadillac—or that shattered bones and broken dreams would open doors to a new future that young Danny had never even glimpsed.

Three weeks later, after major surgery and a bone transplant—after treading water in a sea of pain between morphine shots—a different Dan Millman, now quieter, more reflective, more compassionate, and 20 pounds lighter, left the hospital. He crutched slowly toward the car of a waiting friend who had invited Dan to stay with his family near the beach in Santa Monica so he could begin a long process of physical rehabilitation.

Dan had entered the hospital a voracious meat-eater; he left the hospital a lifelong vegetarian. He had always been a cocky, fast-talking kid; now he observed more and listened thoughtfully. He finally returned to college, to intensive rehabilitation, and to his training—first on crutches, then using a cane, and finally, walking with a limp.

Inch by painful inch, as he fought his way back—through physical setbacks, self-doubt, and dark depression—Dan saw clearly how he had been racing down a single path his whole life, with concentration, but also with tunnel vision, never looking up to question where he was going or what life was about. Now he began to ask some of life's larger questions—"Who am I?" "What is life for?"—questions that had not occurred to him before, at least not with the same impact. Dan began to wonder about death, which had brushed against him that night months before when he had felt nearly invincible. He also wondered about God and spirituality.

"It was during this painful period of soul-searching," Dan says, "that I limped, late one night, into a Texaco station near campus and stumbled upon an old man I called Socrates. I sometimes wonder—would I have met him, or awakened to my current life as a writer and teacher, if I hadn't broken my leg? All I can know is that it served as a catalyst and carried me to this present moment—to my wife, my children, and my calling."

Remarkably, little more than a year later, Dan helped lead his team to win the 1968 National Collegiate Championship and was chosen Senior Athlete of the Year. As the years passed, he was appointed head gymnastics coach at Stanford University, later joined the faculty at Oberlin College, and was eventually named to the Berkeley Athletic Hall of Fame and U.S. Gymnastics Hall of Fame.

But long before, Dan had come to see all such accomplishments only as preparation for another path of teaching, writing, and service.

The pain of that accident, and the ordeal of recovery, somehow purified and opened him to another dimension of reality hidden behind the familiar world he had known. "Sometimes you fall into a dark hole and have a difficult struggle climbing out of it. Then, when you finally get up out of that hole, you appear to be the same place you were before you fell in. But you're not in the same place, because you're no longer the same person; you've changed in the process. You're stronger, wiser, and more compassionate—you've learned something about yourself and about life.

"That accident," Dan adds, "gave me new perspective I might not have seen any other way. It revealed a bigger picture and divine reality behind the scenes of my life. I've had other spiritual experiences—joyous revelations and mystical openings in my life—but that 'accident' turned out to be one of the most transformative events of my life. I certainly don't recommend fractures as a method of spiritual awakening. But when adversity visits, with all of its pain, grief, or disappointment, it's good to also notice the hidden gifts and surprising grace that it may bring—depending on how we respond.

"I recently came across words that spoke directly to my accident and its evolutionary aftermath: Max Cleland wrote, '*I had not always believed that strength could come from brokenness, or that the thread of a divine purpose could be seen in tragedy. But I do now.*'"

As one dream dies, another is born: Dan Millman began writing during his recovery and in the years that followed. Now a best-selling author published in more than 20 languages worldwide, the former athlete has become a respected international teacher of practical spirituality, combining the lessons of athletic training with the laws of spirit to form the "way of the peaceful warrior"—a universal path to greater awareness, meaning, and spirit in everyday life.

Final Words

Take courage;
the human race is divine.

~Pythagoras

Stories of divine intervention remind us that every saint has a past and every sinner has a future. And on our spiritual journey, we travel different paths toward the same goal.

By turning within, to the silent depths of our own divine nature, we find the answers we seek, and we reap a harvest of wonders. By turning without, into relationship with each moment arising, we may serve a higher good in our world.

Thomas Merton wrote, "We are living in a transparent world, and God shines through in every moment . . . everywhere, in everything. We cannot be without God. It's impossible . . . simply impossible.

Maybe God invented men and women because God loves stories.

Every human life is a spiritual epic, every story is divine, and you were born into this world to live *your* story, as only you can live it. We ourselves are the doorway between worlds. And when angels come to visit, they come home to visit their own kind.

One cannot help but be in awe,
contemplating the marvelous structure of reality.
It is enough if one tries merely to comprehend
a little of this mystery every day.

~Albert Einstein

The Most Important Story of All

An Invitation to the Reader

Having completed our tour through a sampling of divine interventions, we now invite you to reflect upon an extraordinary turning point in your own life or in the life of someone close to you. What happened? How did it shape or change the course of your life or theirs?

Use these final pages as your journal. *The last and most important story in our book is your own.*

_____

_____

_____

_____

_____

_____

_____

Would You Like to Be Part of Our Next Book?

Whether or not you've just written a story of your own on the preceding pages, we cordially invite you to contribute your personal story to a forthcoming book, currently titled *Divine Interventions in Everyday Life*. You need not have encountered angels or passed through a tunnel of light or experienced a miraculous healing. You don't even have to be a skilled writer.

We will consider any true and factual story that describes, like the stories in this book, who you were (and what you were like) before your turning point; what occurred to transform your life; and finally, how you were changed—what you're doing today as a result of your experience. We want to get a sense of why and how you might consider your experience a divine intervention. If your story is selected to be included in the book, we will send an edited version of your story for your corrections and approval, along with a $100 honorarium. You will, of course, later receive your own personally signed advance copy of the book.

All you need in order to begin is a story to tell about yourself—or about someone close to you. Please submit your typewritten, double-spaced, 3- to 10-page story in one of two ways (in order of preference): (1) via e-mail to dc@dougchilders.com or (2) via mail to Divine Interventions, PMB 336, 448 Ignacio Boulevard, Nuvato, CA 94949.

Acknowledgments

Our gratitude to all those who helped, directly or indirectly, in the creation of this book. Our first editor, Karen Kelly, showed the faith and good sense to acquire our book for Daybreak and offered invaluable editorial suggestions; then editor-Renaissance man Ken Winston Caine, who inherited the project, went the distance for us. Heartfelt thanks to our literary agent, Candice Fuhrman, for her instincts, integrity, objectivity, and support in ways both numerous and ongoing; to freelance editor Nancy Grimley Carleton for her help with the introduction; and to Elsa Dixon for her stellar administrative support throughout the process

We are also indebted to researchers, biographers, and others whose germinal work formed a foundation and starting point for our inquiries into the realm of divine interventions—people such as Jacques Vallee, Ph.D., astrophysicist, researcher, and author, viewed by many as the real-life model for the

French scientist in *Close Encounters of the Third Kind*; Mario and Hedy Baldassarrini, who provided research related to the incorruptibles; and Ervin Jindrich, M.D., Marin County coroner, who offered empirical insights based upon 30-years' experience as a pathologist.

Many thanks, too, to each and every contributor who personally submitted, related, or gave permission for us to use their stories: Carol Benjamin, Jaia-Sun Childers, Si Tai Gong, Chris Griscom, Don Trent Jacobs, Allison James, Sean Kilcoyne, Andy Lakey, Jean Munzer, Irene Opdyke, Ann and John Rush, Richard Sabinski, Jack and Lois Schwarz, Nancy Siscoe, Malidoma Patrice Some, Ed Spielman, Brother Bill Tomes, and Valerie Vener.

Special appreciation to the following manuscript readers willing to sample our cake before it was fully baked and to offer their recipe suggestions: Reneé Brewer, Brenda Brown, Holly Demé, Elsa Dixon, Barry Elkin, Candice Fuhrman, Dawn Michelle Glanzman, Karen Pierce Gonzalez, Isa Howard-Cohen, Allison James, Dave Kraft, Chuck Marco, Julia Marrero, Christine McDermott, Joy Millman, David Moyer, Sandra Nadalin, Dwight and Celeste Parcel, Terry Patton, Heather (and Madeleine) Picard, Sharon Root, and Beth Wilson.

Finally, our enduring gratitude to Joy Millman and Jaia-Sun Childers, who serve as divine interventions in our lives.

Literary Sources and Resources

The stories you have read emerged from a global heritage of divine interventions and from a variety of cultures and epochs. The authors of this book could rarely speak personally with the principals involved in the stories. Thus, we were limited to searching and researching well-documented literary sources. Most often, we found two or more sources to serve as cross-references and background for historical accuracy. We are grateful to the authors of the following primary literary sources, who provided the background—shoulders on which we stood to present, in our own words, these stories of mystery and miracles that change lives.

Alcoholics Anonymous. New York: Alcoholics Anonymous World Services, 1976.

Basham, A. L. *The Wonder That Was India*. New York: Taplinger Publishing Company, 1967.

Carrel, Alexis. *The Voyage to Lourdes*. New York: Harper Brothers, 1950.

Carty, Reverend Charles Mortimer. *Padre Pio: The Stigmatist*. Rockford, Illinois: Tan Books, 1989.

Chaney, Sheldon. *Men Who Have Walked with God*. United States/Canada: The Ryerson Press, 1945.

Cruz, Joan Carroll. *The Incorruptibles*. Rockford, Illinois: Tan Books, 1974.

Cunneen, Sally. *In Search of Mary*. New York: Balantine, 1976.

Dana, Barbara. *Young Joan*. New York: HarperTrophy, 1991.

David-Neel, Alexandra. *Magic and Mystery in Tibet*. New York: Claude Kendall, 1932.

Durham, Michael S. *Miracles of Mary*. San Francisco: HarperCollins, 1995.

Green, Arthur, and Barry Holtz. *Your Word Is Fire: The Hasidic Masters on Contemplative Prayer*. Woodstock, Vermont: Jewish Lights Publishing, 1993.

Hatch, Alden. *Buckminster Fuller: At Home in the Universe*. New York: Crown Publishers, 1974.

Jacobs, Don Trent. *Primal Awareness*. Rochester, New York: Inner Traditions, 1998.

James, William. *The Varieties of Religious Experience*. New York: Collier-Macmillan Publishing Company, 1961.

Johnson, Francis. *Our Lady of Guadalupe*. Rockford, Illinois: Tan Books, 1981.

Jung, Carl. *Memories, Dreams, Reflections*. New York: Vintage Books, 1965.

Kaplan, Justin. *Walt Whitman: A Life*. New York: Simon & Schuster, 1980.

Kapleau, Philip. *The Three Pillars of Zen*. Boston: Beacon Press, 1965.

Kasich, John. *Courage Is Contagious*. New York: Doubleday, 1998.

Long, Haniel. *The Marvelous Adventures of Cabeza De Vaca*. Clearlake, California: Dawn Horse Press, 1992.

Lowenkopf, Anne N. *The Hasidim: Mystical Adventurers and Ecstatics*. Los Angeles: Sherbourne Press, 1973.

Melton, J. Gordon. *New Age Encyclopedia*. New York: Gale Research, 1990.

Monroe, Robert A. *Journeys out of the Body*. New York: Anchor Doubleday, 1977.

———. *Far Journeys*. New York: Doubleday Books, 1985.

Morse, Melvin, and Paul Perry. *Transformed by the Light*. New York: Villard Books, 1997.

"New Century," *October Magazine*. Beijing, China, 1991.

Opdyke, Irene Gut, with Jennifer Armstrong. *In My Hands: Memories of a Holocaust Rescuer*. New York: Alfred A. Knopf, 1999.

Pass It On: The Story of Bill Wilson and How the A. A. Message Reached the World. New York: Alcoholics Anonymous World Services, 1984.

Pastrovicchi, Father Angelo, O.M.C. *Joseph of Copertino*. Rockford, Illinois: Tan Books, 1980.

Pilgrim, Peace. *Peace Pilgrim: Her Life and Work in Her Own Words*. Santa Fe, New Mexico: Ocean Tree Books, 1994.

Praeger, David Daiches. *Moses: The Man and His Vision*. New York: Praeger Publishers, 1973.

Ronner, John. *The Angels of Cokeville and Other True Stories of Heavenly Intervention*. Murfreesboro, Tennessee: Mamre Press, 1995.

Rossman, Doreen Mary. *A Light Shone in the Darkness: The Story of Stigmatist and Mystic Therese Neumann*. Santa Barbara: Queenship Publishing Company, 1997.

Schulberg, Lucille. *Historic India: Great Ages of Man*. New York: Time-Life Books, 1968.

Spear, Percival. *India*. Michigan: University of Michigan Press, 1961.

Spielman, Ed. *The Spiritual Journey of Joseph L. Greenstein: The Mighty Atom*. New York: 1st Glance Books, 1998.

Steiger, Brad. *Revelation: The Divine Fire*. New Jersey: Prentice Hall, 1973.

Sugrue, Thomas. *There Is a River: The Story of Edgar Cayce*. New York: Dell Books, 1967.

Terrell, John Upton. *Journey into Darkness: A True Account of Cabeza De Vaca's Remarkable Expedition across the North American Continent*. New York: William Morrow and Company, 1962.

Underhill, Evelyn. *Mysticism*. New York: Dutton Books, 1961.

Vallee, Jacques. *Passport to Magonia*. Chicago: Contemporary Books, 1969.

van der Post, Laurens. *About Blady*. New York: William Morrow and Company, 1991.

Van Dusen, Wilson. *The Presence of Other Worlds*. New York: Swedenborg Foundation, 1974.

Wakefield, Dan. *Expect a Miracle*. San Francisco: HarperCollins, 1995.

Walsh, William Thomas. *Our Lady of Fatima*. New York: Image Books, Doubleday, 1990.

Weber, Christin Lore. *A Cry in the Desert: The Awakening of Byron Katie*. Barstow, California: The Work Foundation, 1996.

Wiesel, Eli. *Messengers of God: Biblical Portraits and Legends*. New York: Random House, 1976.

Yogananda, Paramahansa. *Autobiography of a Yogi*. Los Angeles: Self-Realization Fellowship, 1990.

Biographical Sketches

A number of stories in this book describe individuals living today. Those who provided us with biographical sketches are included here. If readers wish to contact them, please do so directly if they have provided contact information. If a story had particular relevance to your life, you may wish to familiarize yourself with their books, services, or source material.

Carol Benjamin (Remember the Music): Carol can be contacted by mail c/o Alta Physical Therapy, 1790 30th Street, Suite 314, Boulder, CO 80301.

Joseph L. Greenstein (Mind over Matter): Joe passed away in the 1980s. His friend and biographer, Ed Spielman, chronicled Joe's amazing life in his book, *The Spiritual Journey of Joseph L. Greenstein.* Those who would like to order this stirring biography can do so through their local bookstore, online, or by writing Mr. Spielman c/o Eastwind One Corporation, 17411 Lahey Street, Granada Hills, CA 91344.

Chris Griscom (How Death Teaches Life): Chris is a healer, humanitarian, speaker, author, and founder of the Light Institute of Galisteo, New

Mexico, and Nizhoni School for Global Consciousness. A devoted mother of six children, she focuses much of her healing talents in the field of birthing. She developed an internationally recognized acupuncture technique, "Windows to the Sky," the basis for her work at the Light Institute. Chris presents seminars internationally. For informatiion about her work, contact the Light Institute at HC 75, Box 50, Galisteo, NM 87540 or www.lightinstitute.com.

Don Trent Jacobs, Ph.D. (Shamanic Initiation): Don holds doctorates in both health psychology and education. He is the author of nine books on wellness, management, persuasion, clinical hypnosis, education, horse training, and co-psychology, including *Primal Awareness*—insights into the nature of learning and change based upon his near-death initiation on the Urique River in central Mexico. Don has been a Marine Corps pilot, rodeo cowboy, firefighter/emergency medical technician, piano player, and sports psychologist. In 1996, he and his mustang Brio made the U.S. Equestrian Endurance Team. Don currently directs the education department at Oglala Lakota College on the Pine Ridge Indian Reservation in South Dakota. You can write to him at Route 1, Box 1261, Fairfield, ID 83327.

Byron Katie (The Rebirth of a Madwoman): The core of Byron's work involves a compassionate inquiry into belief systems to help people discover what is true and bring an end to suffering. The Work, as she describes it, allows individuals to observe how their thinking shapes their experience in order to find greater freedom and inner peace. Many people report relief from chronic physical, psychological, and spiritual suffering. Byron shares The Work worldwide in schools, churches, corporations, prisons, hospitals, and households. Her workshops and intensives are offered by donation. Books, tapes, and videos are also available. The Center for the Work of Byron Katie is in Barstow, California. Certification trainings are also available. For information, write to The Work Foundation, P. O. Box 667, Manhattan Beach, CA 90267, or visit the Web site at www.thework.org.

Andy Lakey (Addict to Artist): Andy is now the most famous living painter of angels in the world. His tactile acrylic designs, fusing painting and sculpture, can be "seen" by the blind via touch, as they depict the forces and structures of inner and outer space. For some years, he has donated up to 30 percent of his earnings from sales of his paintings to charities for the blind. For information, write to 30141 Antelope Road, Suite D-335, Manifee Lakes, CA 92584, or visit www.lakeyart.com.

Robert Monroe (Unexpected Journeys): The Monroe Institute has conducted hundreds of thousands of documented experiments over the years, mapping various brain-wave states and training thousands of individuals to alter their own states of consciousness at will. The technology created by the Institute is used in such varied fields as out-of-body research, deep relaxation, rapid learning, enhanced healing, and recovery from illness, injury, and surgery. It also enables people from all walks of life, including the terminally ill, to prepare for and come to terms with the death process before it occurs at the end of physical life. You can contact the institute at 62 Roberts Mountain Road, Faber, VA 22938.

Jean Munzer (Grandmother's Guidance): Jean Munzer, who contributed this wonderful story about her mother and grandmother, has, since 1978, served as director of the Metaphysical Center of New Jersey, a non-profit, all-volunteer, educational organization dedicated to teaching esoteric studies and related modern research. Jean offers intuitive readings and has a personal hypnotherapy practice in Oakland, New Jersey. For information about the center and about Jean's work, write 10 Pequot Path, Oakland, NJ 07436.

Irene Gut Opdyke (The Price of Freedom): For many years, Irene tried to forget her experiences during the war. She married, she raised a daughter, she lived happily. But in the late 1970s, Irene began hearing neo-Nazi groups say that the Holocaust was a hoax or propaganda. This she could not bear, so she began to speak, to tell her story, to share her story so that others would not forget. She recently completed a book on her life titled *In My Hands: Memories of a Holocaust Rescuer*, published by Alfred A. Knopf in 1999.

Peace Pilgrim (An Unlikely Pilgrim): Peace Pilgrim (Mildred Norman) passed away on July 7, 1981, while on her seventh cross-country trek. Her writings have been translated into 26 languages. Although donations are welcome, books and tapes are distributed free of charge by the Friends of Peace Pilgrim, a nonprofit, all-volunteer organization. To receive a free book, audio and videotapes, newsletter, and a 32-page booklet, *Steps to Inner Peace*, contact Friends of Peace Pilgrim at 43480 Cedar Avenue, Hemet, CA 92544, or send e-mail to peacepilgrim@znet.com.

Jack Schwarz (The Power of Love): An educator, philosopher, author, and humanitarian, Jack has distinguished himself as an internationally recognized authority on self-regulation and human energy systems. He has participated in many research, lecture, and publication activities in these fields throughout the world. Mr. Schwarz achieved his extraordinary abilities through a program of self-experimentation and self-training. He is the author of seven books and is president of the Aletheia Institute.Write to the institute at the Stanford Inn by the Sea, 44850 Comptche-Ukiah Road, P.O. Box 2400, Mendocino, CA 95460, or send e-mail to Aletheia@mcn.org.

Bill Tomes (Love on the Line): After growing up in Cleveland, Philadelphia, and Evanston, Brother Bill attended Loyola Academy and Notre Dame University. He has worked as a social worker in Catholic Charities and as a counselor for the Illinois Department of Corrections and Catholic Charities of Chicago, has created portraits of 13 head coaches at Notre Dame, has sold lithographs of scenes in Europe, and has worked in Saint Joseph's Ukranian Catholic Church in Chicago. Bill has received numerous honors and much recognition, plus media attention on French television and the BBC as well as in *Reader's Digest, Time, Der Speigel*, and other magazines. Film rights have been acquired by Quincy Jones. Meanwhile, Brother Bill continues his work in the streets. In 1985, he founded Brothers and Sisters of Love, a not-for-profit organization—money goes directly to service and is tax-deductible. If you would like to contact Bill or make a donation, contact Brothers and Sisters of Love, P. O. Box 430, Evanston, IL 60204.

Valerie Vener (Surrender in the Flames): Valerie serves as a spiritual teacher, counselor, choreographer, performer, and founder/director of Body and Sound: A Moving Spectrum of the Arts. Applying her experience in the healing and performing arts, Valerie teaches others, in her words, to "embrace self and life even in the midst of fears and limited self-perceptions." Her work is designed to facilitate the reorganization of the nervous system to allow for greater physical, emotional, and spiritual freedom. She regards her experience in the fire as an intimately personal, yet archetypal lesson. Valerie offers seminars, workshops, and couple and individual sessions; she can be reached at 632 Jean Street, Oakland, CA 94610 or by e-mail at vrvener@aol.com.

Index of Topics

Index of People

Stories of Well-Known, Historic, or Public Figures

About the Authors

Dan Millman, a former world champion athlete, coach, and college professor, is the author of 10 books, including *Way of the Peaceful Warrior*, *The Life You Were Born to Live*, *The Laws of Spirit*, and *Everyday Enlightenment*. His writings and seminars have inspired millions of people in more than 20 languages and influenced men and women from all walks of life, including leaders in the fields of health, psychology, education, business, politics, entertainment, sports, and the arts.

Dan and his family reside in northern California.

For information about Dan Millman's books and seminars, you are invited to visit his Web site at www.danmillman.com.

Doug Childers is co-author of the critically acclaimed book *The White-Haired Girl*, an alternate selection of the Book-of-the-Month Club. A professional ghostwriter, freelance editor, and "book doctor," Doug has edited or collaborated on numerous book projects in the fields of popular psychology/spirituality, memoirs, and fiction. A writer of both nonfiction and fiction, he is currently working on a trilogy.

He is also an authorized teacher of Shaolin Temple Boxing, a Buddhist martial art and meditation path.

Doug lives with his life-collaborator and best friend, author Jaia-Sun Childers, in northern California.

For information about Doug Childers's literary works and editorial/collaborative services, you are invited to visit his Web site at www.dougchilders.com.